THE
SURVIVAL
OF THE
PRINCES
IN THE
TOWER

MURDER, MYSTERY AND MYTH

THE
SURVIVAL
OF THE
PRINCES
IN THE
TOWER

MURDER, MYSTERY AND MYTH

MATTHEW LEWIS

The
History
Press

First published 2017

The History Press
The Mill, Brimscombe Port
Stroud, Gloucestershire, GL5 2QG
www.thehistorypress.co.uk

British Library Cataloguing in Publication Data.
A catalogue record for this book is available from the British Library.

ISBN 978 0 7509 7056 3

Typesetting and origination by The History Press
Printed in Europe

Contents

Introduction

The antiquity and general acceptance of an opinion is not assurance of its truth.

Pierre Bayle, Philosopher

For over 500 years, one unsolved murder mystery has exerted an unrelenting and undiminishing grip on the imaginations of people around the world. It is as hotly debated on social media today as it might have been in the bawdy, rush-strewn taverns of England at the end of the fifteenth century. In the fragile, superheated politics of the early Tudor years, it was a hot coal that might burn down the new regime. Foreign rulers at least feigned a deep interest and concern, though each had their own priorities at heart and motives that cannot be ignored behind their words and actions.

This book does not seek to solve a mystery that has evaded any definitive resolution for five centuries. No smoking gun has yet been unearthed and what evidence is available is, almost without exception, circumstantial and open to the broadest interpretations. Work continues in various quarters, not least in private family libraries in England and on the Continent, to uncover something more substantial. The purpose of this book is not to provide a definitive answer to a question that still defies answering, but to look beyond the traditional argument centred around who killed the Princes in the Tower in the summer of 1483 to ask a different question and to see where that inquiry leads.

Rumours and reports sprang up early in the reign of their uncle, King Richard III, that the Princes in the Tower, King Edward V and his younger brother Richard of Shrewsbury, Duke of York, had been put to death, though even in the very eye of the storm, the method and the perpetrator were not clearly known. Men of power in England and abroad did not know what had happened and that is telling and worthy of note. King Richard lay dead on the field of the Battle of Bosworth just two years later, yet his sudden, probably unexpected departure from the pinnacle of government did not allow the truth to become known. If men were afraid to let slip what they knew in 1483, by the end of 1485 it would have been valuable information that would help sure up the burgeoning Tudor government. Henry Tudor, Earl of Richmond, by then King Henry VII, had promised to marry a sister of the Princes, Elizabeth of York, but to do so he had to reverse the Act of Parliament that had made all the siblings illegitimate, thereby handing a far better, and probably more popular, right to the throne to Edward V. It is striking that this information was not forthcoming; no definite proof was provided as the new king took up the reins of government, or at least none that was made public, and the matter was left open, gaping and just asking for trouble, which was not slow to come.

During the sixteenth century, the story of their murders began to solidify, but remained amazingly variable until Shakespeare's masterpiece *The Tragedie of Richard the Third*, written in the early 1590s. The play is a brilliant study of the anti-hero but the greatest tragedy of all is that for centuries it became accepted as the true history of King Richard III so that an overwhelming majority believe that they know Richard was an evil monster who murdered the Duke of Somerset, Edward of Westminster, son of Henry VI, Henry VI himself, Richard's brother George and his own wife Anne, with his nephews the Princes in the Tower being the worst of a raft of dastardly deeds. Even though Richard was 2½ years old when Somerset was killed at the First Battle of St Albans in 1455, reports place him away from the fighting chasing another section of the army at Tewkesbury when Edward of Westminster was slain, Edward IV ordered the death of their brother George for a string of offences and Anne died of what is believed to have been tuberculosis, these charges have stuck fast. The death of Henry VI is less clear and Richard may well have been involved as Constable of England, but it would not have been without the instruction of Edward IV. The death of his nephews will be explored in the pages that follow, but the popular consciousness finds Richard guilty of all these crimes despite the flaws in the charges, just as he is found guilty of cowardice at the Battle of Bosworth for calling 'A horse! A horse! My kingdom for a horse.' That last charge still has traction despite being diametrically opposed to the text of the play, in which Richard demands a fresh horse to return to the fighting to look for Henry Tudor and despite every hostile source crediting him with the brave death of a warrior.

King Richard III found defenders almost as quickly as he was condemned, with Sir George Buck completing his sympathetic *The History of the Life and Reigne of Richard the Third* in 1619. In 1791, Jane Austen wrote in her *The History of England From the Reign of Henry the 4th to the Death of Charles the 1st* that 'I am rather inclined to suppose him a very respectable Man'. Today, the Richard III Society promotes the study of this contentious king's era to better understand the issues swirling around him and a simple tweet on the subject is almost guaranteed to draw passionate responses at both extremes of any argument about him. The deaths of the Princes in the Tower have long been the heaviest millstone around the neck of Richard's reputation. It is hard to pinpoint precisely why it remains so high in the public consciousness. There are perhaps two reasons. The first is that it is a case of murdered children, innocents given in sacrifice to a political end that causes revulsion in people now as it would have in 1483. The second is simply that it is a mystery and a mystery, particularly a murder mystery, as fiction book sales will attest, appeals to something deep within human beings.

The prevailing belief has always been that Richard III ordered the murder of his nephews, whether as part of a long and devious plot to take the crown or as a panicked reaction to the chaotic events of the spring of 1483. There have always been theories that it was done at the instigation of someone else, from Henry Stafford, Duke of Buckingham to Henry VII or his mother. Few subscribe to the theory that they survived. This book will seek to explore that possibility more fully. The early Tudor government was perilously insecure, suffered pretenders who challenged its authority in various guises and under the second Tudor king, the famous Henry VIII, became intensely paranoid, lashing out in all directions in fear for its future. The actions of foreign powers might be written off as political machinations aimed at destabilising the Tudor family, but should not be ignored completely, particularly those documents that were never intended for public consumption. Ambassadors might guild the lily, kings, queens, dukes and duchesses might have their own agenda for making statements, but words written to be secret have no cause to lie.

Single stories of these pretenders might seek to suggest that they were or were not who they claimed to be depending on the writer's conclusion, but it is important at some point to stop looking at pieces of a jigsaw puzzle individually and try to see the whole picture. England was undergoing a period of radical upheaval that tried to disguise itself as sure-footed continuity. Events and relationships on the Continent evolved, sometimes bumping into English politics. It is time the jigsaw puzzle pieces were arranged to tell the whole story.

For years, the argument has been about who killed the Princes in the Tower. At the end of the fifteenth century and well into the sixteenth, a different question was asked to which this book seeks to return.

Were the Princes in the Tower murdered at all?

1

To Construct a Murder

And therefore since I cannot prove a lover
To entertain these fair well-spoken days,
I am determined to prove a villain
And hate the idle pleasures of these days.
> *The Tragedy of Richard III*, William Shakespeare, Act I, Scene 1

As Shakespeare's villain hobbles around the stage drawing his audience into his horrible conspiracies, we find ourselves liking this funny, irreverent man despite the evil he tells us he will do. There are strong reasons to believe that Shakespeare was writing about Robert Cecil, the son of William Cecil, Lord Burghley. Robert had kyphosis – in Shakespeare's unkind terminology a 'bunchback' – unlike Richard's scoliosis, a curvature of the spine believed to have been barely visible beneath clothing. When Shakespeare was writing, the Cecil father and son held the reins of Elizabeth I's government and, as staunch Protestants, were trying to organise a Stuart succession. Shakespeare had many Catholic patrons and it has been suggested that he himself remained a secret Catholic all his life. It seems entirely possible that Elizabethan audiences would have understood that they were looking at Robert Cecil, scheming and plotting and getting away with it. Taken out of context over following centuries, it somehow became accepted as a work of biography rather than drama, fact rather than fiction, a damning account of an historical figure rather than a sly modern political commentary.

Shakespeare accused King Richard III of a myriad of crimes, most of which it can be demonstrated were not perpetrated by him, if any crime was indeed committed. Edward of Westminster, Prince of Wales and heir to Henry VI, was killed on the battlefield at Tewkesbury on 4 May 1471, as was Edmund Beaufort, Duke of Somerset at St Albans on 22 May 1455, when Richard was just 2½ years old. George, Duke of Clarence, the older brother closest in age to Richard III, was executed for treason following a trial in Parliament which, though hardly impartial, was nevertheless legal and many will argue well deserved following a list of betrayals. There were reportedly rumours circulating that Richard meant to harm his wife, enough at least to cause two of his closest advisors to council him to publicly deny the stories along with the other rumour that he planned to marry his niece, Elizabeth of York. It is far more likely though that Anne Neville was taken by consumption, or tuberculosis as it is better known today, just as her sister Isabel, wife to George, had been. Henry VI was probably put to death when the Yorkists retook the throne in 1471 shortly after the Battle of Tewkesbury and although there is no real evidence of his involvement, it seems possible that, as Constable of England, Richard might have been involved, though the order would undoubtedly have come directly from King Edward IV. It was perhaps unpleasant, but nevertheless an execution ordered by the king like so many before and after. In none of these cases is there any evidence that a crime was committed, yet Richard stands in the court of public opinion convicted and condemned as Shakespeare's accidental villain.

The one act that would truly condemn Richard was the murder of two young children, his own nephews, who were in his care. Edward V was born on 2 November 1470 in sanctuary at Westminster Abbey, his father, King Edward IV, having briefly lost his throne and been forced into exile in Burgundy with his brother Richard, then Duke of Gloucester, amongst other loyal men. Edward won back his throne and made it to London after the Battle of Barnet in April 1471, before leaving again to finish the Lancastrian cause at the Battle of Tewkesbury in May. By the time the king met his first son and was reunited with his wife and three daughters as they emerged from sanctuary, the baby was already 6 months old. On 26 June 1471, the tiny boy was created Prince of Wales and Earl of Chester by his father, a grant that was confirmed in Parliament on 6 October 1472 when Prince Edward was established, as the *Parliament Rolls* record it, in 'the name, style, title, rank, dignity and honour of prince and earl of the same'. In 1473,

Edward IV established the Council of Wales and the Marches, based at Ludlow on the Welsh border and nominally headed by Prince Edward, who was approaching 3 years old. The care of the young prince was entrusted to Anthony Woodville, Earl Rivers, the queen's brother and a noted scholar who was an early Renaissance man before such a thing became fashionable. It was here, far from London, that little Edward was to spend the majority of the next decade, learning the craft of ruling in a miniature kingdom with a court of his own, building networks and cultivating the craft of using connections to rule effectively.

Richard of Shrewsbury, the second son born to Edward IV and Elizabeth Woodville, joined a burgeoning family of one brother, four sisters and two half-brothers on 17 August 1473. He was, as the toponym given to him suggests, born in Shrewsbury, Shropshire. Unlike his older brother, Richard was kept within the royal nursery and spent the following decade of almost unbroken peace in England in the various lavish royal palaces along the Thames in and around London. Richard was given the previously primary family title of his father, Duke of York, initiating the tradition that the second son of a monarch will usually hold this title. One of the few occasions when these two royal brothers came together was the marriage of Richard of Shrewsbury to Anne Mowbray on 15 January 1478 when the little prince was just 4 years old. Anne, who was 5 years old, was a ward of Edward IV and the pair were married because Anne brought into royal hands a vast inheritance. On their union, which was celebrated with full ceremonial, possibly to the bewilderment of the two infants at the centre of the event, Richard became Duke of Norfolk, Earl of Nottingham, Earl Warenne, Earl Marshal, Lord Mowbray, Lord Seagrave and Lord Gower as well as acquiring the rights to swathes of land in the east. Edward IV used Parliament to rather dubiously alter the laws of inheritance in this particular case so that if Anne died, Richard retained full rights to her lands and titles rather than them reverting to a Mowbray heir. In 1481, at the age of 8, Anne did pass away.

The differences in the upbringings enjoyed by these two boys until 1483 are stark and important. It is easy to characterise the Princes in the Tower as one unit, clinging together in fear for their lives as Victorian portraits present them. In fact, they would have been virtual strangers. Their prolonged separation would also have had another impact on this story. Richard of Shrewsbury would have been a very visible presence in London. Many of those working in the palaces as well as men of the government would have regularly encountered the young boy, watched him grow and change, perhaps even have spoken to him frequently. In short, Richard would have been well known to the men and women of Edward's court, to servants and to foreign dignitaries and ambassadors visiting England. In stark contrast, Prince Edward spent the vast majority of his time at Ludlow, visiting London only infrequently for major state occasions such as his little brother's wedding. As he approached his teens, few at court would have seen much of him and his appearance, personality and mannerisms would have been all but unknown to them. So, in 1483, we in fact see two boys who shared the royal blood in their veins and possibly a fear and lack of comprehension of what was happening, but who were virtual strangers to each other. They were thrust together and then lost from men's sight, their fates treated as one and tragic, but it is to be remembered that they were not the same. Their upbringings had been very different and at a long distance from each other. For the purposes of the events that followed, it is crucial that Richard was a recognisable boy in London and Edward a virtual stranger.

A detailed analysis of the spring and summer of 1483 is beyond the scope of this book, but an outline of the events leading up to the day when the two boys were placed in the Tower of London together may be helpful. King Edward IV died on 9 April 1483, a few weeks short of his forty-first birthday. His death was entirely unexpected. Edward remains the tallest monarch in English history, at 6ft 4in, and held a fearsome martial reputation in his younger years, never having been defeated on the field of battle. Although Edward's waistline may have spread and his interest in pursuits beyond those he found pleasurable may have diminished to the point that he had, just the previous year, despatched his younger brother Richard, Duke of Gloucester to lead a campaign against Scotland that Edward seems simply not to have been able to motivate himself to undertake, his death was still a shock. The traditional story is that Edward caught a chill whilst fishing and the infection quickly took hold and killed him, though there have been much later rumours that his wife, Elizabeth Woodville, had him poisoned. There is no evidence for this, and certainly if the queen did take this course, it backfired spectacularly.

More than the unexpected suddenness of the king's death, the age of his heir was a cause for concern. Prince Edward was 12, still a minor. The king would have been only too aware that minorities had ended in disaster for Richard II and Henry VI. He knew too that there would be a bitter struggle to fill the vacuum he was about to create. The king was an immensely likeable and affable man so that he, personally, was the glue that kept his court and the country together. Such adhesion to him was needed because there was bitter division within his walls. The main factions revolved around the Woodville family, led by Edward's stepson Thomas Grey, Marquis of Dorset, and around Lord Hastings, probably Edward's oldest and closest friend. Dorset and Hastings had conceived a deep hatred for each other that the king's presence kept a lid on, but which would threaten the fragile position of his minor heir should that lid be removed by the king's death. Edward reportedly added a late codicil to his will to resolve this perceived threat, falling back on provisions made for the minority of Henry VI by making his brother Richard, Duke of Gloucester, Lord Protector of the Realm, a position their father had held twice during Henry VI's periods of incapacity and which was a curiously English invention.

Richard was 30 years old, a decade younger than his brother, but had effectively ruled the north for over ten years. Like his nephew the prince, Richard was perhaps less well-known in the capital because of his long and distant separation, but he was nevertheless a truly national figure who had become a prominent bulwark of his brother's rule. The position of Lord Protector of the Realm formed part of a separation of power during a minority. This tripartite solution was created after the death of Henry V and was not quite what the warrior-king had himself instructed should happen. Nevertheless, the care of the person of the young king and provision for his education was to be given to one person. Government was carried out by the Council and the Lord Protector of the Realm was given full military authority to deal with both foreign and domestic threats to the kingdom, though the Lord Protector was usually to hold a senior position within the governing Council too. Thus, in 1422, the infant King Henry VI was placed under the care and tutelage of Thomas Beaufort, Duke of Exeter and Richard de Beauchamp, Earl of Warwick, amongst others. The king's uncle Humphrey, Duke of Gloucester was made Lord Protector of the Realm (though he was required to relinquish this position to his older brother John, Duke of Bedford whenever he returned to England from his position as Regent of France, which otherwise kept him out of England) and the Council governed in the king's name, with Humphrey as a senior member.

This situation was to be replicated in 1483. Earl Rivers, the queen's brother, already had responsibility for the care and education of Prince Edward, under instructions strictly laid down by the king, and there is no sign that this position was meant to change. Richard was appointed Lord Protector of the Realm, having proven himself capable in Scotland. It is important to note that the dying king saw a Lord Protector as a necessity, doubtless to provide a senior presence on the Council, but also because King Louis XI of France had recently reneged on the 1475 Treaty of Picquigny and was showing signs of aggression, coupled with the similar and linked threat from Scotland that had seen Richard dispatched there in 1482. Finally, the Council would govern. As the senior adult male of the blood royal as well as Lord Protector, Richard, Duke of Gloucester was the natural choice as a prominent figure within the Council.

There is no record that the queen informed her brother-in-law, then in his northern heartlands, that the king had died, Lord Hastings apparently writing to warn Richard that her Woodville family were planning a coup. The Marquis of Dorset, Hastings' bitter enemy, was reportedly bragging in Council that the Woodvilles could and would rule without Richard and the idea was mooted of having Prince Edward crowned swiftly and proclaimed of age to govern, bypassing a Protectorate and maintaining the Woodville family's influence at the centre of power which they clearly felt was coming under threat. Even before Richard left the north, battle lines were being drawn in London. Nevertheless, Richard ordered a funeral mass for his brother in York at which he caused all the northern nobility present to swear fealty to the new King Edward V. After this, he set out to meet his nephew on the road to London. Edward V did not leave Ludlow until 24 April, having celebrated St George's Day the previous day, and met his uncle Richard at Stony Stratford. The uncle and nephew would have been virtual strangers to each other and if Richard was suspicious of the Woodvilles, his concern was surely heightened when Earl Rivers overshot their agreed meeting place and installed the king before going back to meet Richard in Northampton. Richard's reaction was harsh and decisive. He took Earl Rivers and others of the new king's household into custody and sent them to his castle in the north before taking control of his nephew and continuing slowly to London.

The Woodville plan had been to crown Edward on 4 May 1483, but instead he only arrived in the capital on this date. Edward was installed at the Bishop of London's Palace and Richard again caused oaths of allegiance to be sworn to the new king. Preparations continued for the rule of Edward V, with the coronation planned for 22 June, coins minted and proclamations issued in the new king's name. Over the following weeks, the situation changed for reasons beyond the scope of this story and which remain deeply contentious. Edward V was moved to the Tower of London, then a royal palace yet to acquire its bloody reputation as a grim prison roughly equivalent to death row. Elizabeth Woodville had taken her other son Richard, along with her daughters and her oldest son the Marquis of Dorset, into sanctuary at Westminster Abbey. Richard applied pressure to the queen until the 9-year-old Duke of York was given into the care of the Archbishop of Canterbury and sent to join his 12-year-old brother at the Tower. There was little that caused much concern to this point. The Woodville family were generally unpopular and few were mourning their loss of power.

On 13 June, Richard had Lord Hastings summarily executed on a charge of treason during a Council meeting. Lord Stanley, Bishop Morton and Bishop Rotherham were also arrested. On 25 June, Anthony Woodville, Earl Rivers, the dowager queen's brother and the king's uncle who had effectively brought the boy up, was executed at Pontefract Castle along with Richard Grey, the younger brother of the Marquis of Dorset, and Thomas Vaughan, Edward V's Chamberlain. On 22 June, rather than seeing Edward V crowned, London heard a sermon preached declaring that the marriage of Edward IV and Elizabeth Woodville was bigamous and all the children of that union were therefore illegitimate and incapable of inheriting the throne. The story may have originated from Robert Stillington, Bishop of Bath and Wells and was not entirely new, having probably formed part of the downfall of George, Duke of Clarence in 1477–78. Those who had been summoned to London for the session of Parliament that had now been cancelled heard the evidence and subsequently petitioned Richard to take the crown as the only legitimate male heir of Richard, Duke of York. The petition was not presented by Parliament, which was not in session, but was later included in the business of Richard's only Parliament in 1484 as the Act of *Titulus Regius*. The text details the illegitimacy of Edward IV's children as well as heavily criticising the late king's reign, declares that the son of Richard's older brother George, Duke of Clarence, the 8-year-old Edward, Earl of Warwick, was excluded by his father's attainder and concludes that Richard is the rightful heir. Accepting the request, Richard III was crowned in Westminster Abbey alongside his wife Anne Neville on 6 July 1483.

Soon after Richard's coronation, the sons of Edward IV in the Tower became a focus of attention. They had been moved from the Royal Apartments, though there is nothing necessarily sinister in this since those apartments were traditionally required for a monarch's preparation for coronation, so Richard and Anne needed them. They were probably initially moved to the Garden Tower near the outer curtain wall. However, stories rapidly developed that the boys had been consigned to a dank cell in the Tower and as they were seen less and less, rumours sprang up about what had happened to them just as tabloids might speculate today. Just two years later, Richard III's reign ended with his defeat and death at the Battle of Bosworth. History has long remembered that Richard had his nephews killed and many historians reach the same conclusion. It is possible to chart the development of this conclusion through the contemporary, near contemporary and later sources.

The following chapter will examine the reliability of the materials that contribute to what is known of the suspected murder of the Princes in the Tower, so for now the story will simply be laid out and traced as far back as possible to contemporary accounts. William Shakespeare's story of the murder of the Princes in the Tower has become an accepted, authoritative piece of historiography. Shakespeare drew heavily on existing stories inspired by Sir Thomas More's almost equally famous account *The History of King Richard the Third*, which provides great dramatic detail of the events of 1483. Sir Thomas wrote of Richard's increasing distress at the threat his nephews posed to his reign and his decision whilst on progress to rid himself of them. Richard despatches a page to take an instruction to Sir Robert Brackenbury, Constable of the Tower of London, to have the deed done but Sir Robert refuses. The page returns with the news, which is broken to the king while he sits on the privy. Despairing of his servants, Richard laments 'Ah, whom shall a man trust?' before the page suggests Sir James Tyrell, who is just outside. Richard hands the task to Tyrell who sets out for London, where he engages two ruffians Miles Forest and John Dighton. The two men smother the princes with pillows before showing Sir James that the deed is done. Tyrell then rides back to the king to report his success. Richard asks where his nephews were buried and is told they lie beneath a staircase. A pang of guilt causes Richard to order them dug up and placed somewhere more fitting, a task duly undertaken by a priest who dies without revealing the final location of the bodies. Sir Thomas informs his reader that he has strong sources for his detail, writing 'Very truth is it, and well known, that at such time as Sir James Tyrell was in the Tower – for treason committed against the most famous prince, King Henry the Seventh – both Dighton and he were examined and confessed the murder in manner above written, but to where the bodies were removed, they could nothing tell.' Tyrell's involvement is given an air of authenticity by the fact that he was sent from York to London at the beginning of September 1483 to retrieve clothes and wall hangings for the investiture of Richard's son, Edward, as Prince of Wales on 8 September.

The account written by Polydore Vergil, an Italian engaged by Henry VII to prepare a history of England for the first Tudor king, bears a striking similarity to More's account. Begun a few years earlier, the two men probably had access to the same sources, materials and even people who had lived through the events of 1483. Vergil relates that Richard:

> took his journey to York, and first he went straight to Gloucester, where the while he tarried the heinous guilt of wicked conscience did so fright him every moment as that he lived in continual fear, for the expelling whereof by any kind of mean he determined by death to dispatch his nephews, because so long as they lived he could not be out of hazard; wherefore he sent warrant to Robert Brackenbury.

The similarity to More continues as Vergil recounts that:

> Richard understood the lieutenant to make delay of that which he had commanded, he anon committed the charge of hastening that slaughter unto another, that is to say James Tyrell, who, being forced to do the king's commandment, rode sorrowfully to London, and, to the worst example that hath been almost ever heard of, murdered those babes of the issue royal. This end had Prince Edward and Richard his brother; but with what kind of death these sely children were executed it is not certainly known.

Vergil does not provide as much detail on the murder as More, though he wrote after Tyrell's execution too.

These two accounts, built upon by Shakespeare, have become the pillars of the belief in the murder of the Princes in the Tower in 1483, though both

Vergil and More were writing decades after the events they described. There are, however, more contemporary sources that offer the same conclusion. During the early years of King Henry VII's reign the story of the death of the sons of Edward IV was being spread widely. On the Continent, Phillipe de Commynes wrote his *Memoires* between 1490 and 1498. A Burgundian who later transferred to the French court, de Commynes, had met several of the prominent protagonists of the Wars of the Roses, including Edward IV, though he had never travelled to England. His account of the matter perfunctorily notes that Richard III 'killed Edward's two sons, declared his daughters bastards, and had himself crowned king'. Casper Weinrich of Danzig, who wrote his chronicle before 1496, recorded of 1483 that 'later this summer Richard the king's brother seized power and had his brother's children killed'.

As early as March 1486 a Spanish ambassador to England, Diego de Valera, wrote to King Ferdinand and Queen Isabella that 'it is sufficiently well known to your royal majesty that this Richard killed two innocent nephews of his to whom the realm belonged after his brother's life', stating quite clearly that the murder had been committed, that it had been ordered by Richard and that the fact was well known. Even earlier than de Valera's despatch was a report by Guillaume de Rochefort to the French Estates General that King Edward's 'children, already big and courageous, have been slaughtered with impunity, and their murderer, with the support of the people, has received the crown'. So, it seems, both official accounts and those of private citizens on the Continent were fairly confident that both Princes were dead and that their uncle, King Richard III, had been behind their deaths.

There is damning contemporary evidence available from within England too. Early in the reign of Henry VII, the Warwickshire antiquarian and biographer of the Earls of Warwick John Rous wrote 'the usurper King Richard III ascended the throne of the slaughtered children'. Robert Ricart, the Recorder of Bristol, wrote in his entry for the year ending 15 September 1483 (though it is unclear precisely when it was written) 'in this year the two sons of King Edward were put to silence in the Tower of London', though the entry does not identify Richard III as the instigator of the murders. The uncertainty regarding the boys' killer is also reflected in a fragment amongst the Ashmolean Collection (MS Ashmole 1448.60) which states Richard killed the princes 'at the prompting of the Duke of

Buckingham as it is said'. This position is supported by a snippet in *Historical Notes of a London Citizen*, which records that the Princes 'wer put to deyth in the Tower of London be the vise of the duke of Buckingham', though the precise meaning of the word 'vise' is open to interpretation, possibly referring to the duke's *advice*, so that Richard was counselled to do the deed by Buckingham, or meaning the *device* of the duke, so that he was the prime mover in the affair. *The Great Chronicle of London* notes during the entry for the mayoral terms covering the end of 1483 and into 1484 that 'all the wyntyr season', 'the land was in good Quyet, but after Estryn [Easter] there was much whysperyng among the people that the King had put the childryn of Kyng Edward to deth', returning to a definitive statement that Richard III was behind the deaths.

One of the most important and most poorly interpreted sources for the events of the spring and early summer of 1483 is the account of Dominic Mancini, an Italian who visited London, leaving in July 1483 and writing his account at the request of his patron before the end of the year. Entitled *The Usurpation of Richard III*, it is an invaluable eyewitness account of the critical weeks of 1483, which will be more closely examined in the next chapter. Mancini recalled that after the execution of Lord Hastings on 13 June, 'all the attendants who had waited upon the King were debarred access to him. He and his brother were withdrawn into the inner apartments of the Tower proper, and day by day began to be seen more rarely behind the bars and windows, til at length they ceased to appear altogether'. The familiar attendants of Edward V were apparently dismissed and the boys were withdrawn into the 'Tower proper', which most likely refers to the White Tower. Added to the arrests at Stony Stratford, this isolated the child king and his brother from possible help. Amongst Mancini's sources was Dr John Argentine, a physician who attended Edward V and later the first Tudor Prince of Wales, Arthur. Mancini wrote that 'The physician Argentine, the last of his attendants whose services the king enjoyed, reported that the young king, like a victim prepared for sacrifice, sought remission of his sins by daily confession and penance, because he believed that death was facing him.' This testimony has been used to suggest that Edward feared his death was imminent at the hands of his uncle, who was taking his throne from him too. Mancini also recorded on the subject of Edward V that 'I have seen many men burst forth into tears and lamentations when mention was made of him after his removal from men's sight;

and already there was suspicion that he had been done away with. Whether, however, he has been done away with, and by what manner of death, so far I have not at all discovered.' Although Mancini could offer no means of their death and did not directly accuse Richard III, he nevertheless asserts that men were weeping for the fate of the boys even prior to Mancini's departure from England before the end of July and that there was a strong belief they had already been killed.

It is perhaps surprising how little firm evidence remains of the fate of the Princes in the Tower. There are a handful of snippets from England and from the Continent that appear to offer a clear indication of their fate, that they died in the summer of 1483, and that they were killed at the instruction of Richard III, perhaps in collusion with or at the suggestion of Henry Stafford, Duke of Buckingham. These snippets were the seeds from which the more detailed accounts of Vergil and More took root and began to grow. Shakespeare's play is the final blooming of the story and for centuries after, Richard has stood condemned of the murders of his two young nephews, convicted in the courts of public opinion and by the majority of historians. There are strong reasons to believe that it is true; the long-held belief is not simply based on a few flimsy pieces of evidence and a dramatic story.

A criminal investigation will always look for three key elements; motive, means and opportunity. Richard III ticks all three. The second two are easily established. As king, with the boys under his control, Richard had both means and opportunity aplenty. The boys were within walls that Richard controlled, surrounded by men that obeyed the new king having been stripped of those who might have been loyal to them. Assuming that Richard could find someone willing to carry out the deed, which many might do for the rewards such a service would surely bring, means and opportunity lay wide open to him. For traditionalists, motive is equally easily established. Richard could never be secure on his throne while his nephews lived. Although they had been declared legally illegitimate, an Act of Parliament could overturn that status as easily as it had marked them.

Amongst a set of *Historical Notes* compiled by a London citizen is a reference to 'a resistance made in the parlement tyme', which is presumed to mean during late June and early July 1483 when Parliament was not in session, but when members of the Three Estates gathered in London had offered Richard the crown. The frustratingly cryptic reference speaks of four servants of the king who were 'hangyd at The Towur Hill' but gives no detail of their crime. It is not even clear whether the king these four served was Edward IV, Edward V or Richard III, but it does make it clear that there was at least one small pocket of unrest in London that led to four executions. If these were servants of Edward V who resisted either his deposition or their removal from his service it might have caused Richard to assess whether he could permit such a threat to persist. On 29 July 1483, Richard wrote to his Chancellor Bishop John Russell regarding 'certaine personnes' implicated in an 'enterprise' now 'in warde'. It is unclear whether this is the same small group referred to by the *Historical Notes* or a different incident, but it confirms that all was not well, though the men were at least in custody. Russell was instructed to issue commissions 'to sitte upon thaym and to proceed to the due execucion of our lawes in that behalve'. The matter is made more intriguing by Richard's instruction that Russell should consult with 'our counsaill', suggesting that it was of enough import to require the Council's attention. The king was writing from Minster Lovell in Oxfordshire, the family seat of his close friend Francis, Lord Lovell. Following his coronation on 6 July, Richard and his queen, Anne, had set off on a royal progress, reaching Reading on 21 July, visiting Oxford for three days from 24 July, moving to Woodstock on 27 July and then to Minster Lovell on 29 July. Had an attempt been made to free the boys after Richard left the capital? Perhaps news of the death of the princes had arrived and Richard was either genuinely shocked or ordering an investigation to cover his own instruction to do away with them. This 'enterprise' may also have been completely unrelated to the king's nephews and the vagaries of both pieces of evidence only serve to highlight the problems of seeking the truth of the events of 1483.

With motive, means and opportunity established, in the eyes of many beyond a reasonable doubt, the jury of historical opinion has long returned a guilty verdict. Richard had the most to gain by their deaths because it was the only way to secure his crown. They vanished whilst under his protection without explanation. If Richard III had ruled longer, he might have been able to reveal the truth but he was killed on 22 August 1485 at the Battle of Bosworth. Whatever else history has painted Richard III as, even his harshest critics did not deny his bravery on the battlefield at the end. Polydore Vergil, writing for Henry VII, explained that 'kyng Richard alone, was killyd fyghting manfully in the thickkest presse of his enemyes'. The hostile account of John Rous conceded that 'he most valiantly defended himself as a noble knight to his last breath' whilst the Crowland Chronicler, no fan of the king, noted 'As for King Richard he received many mortal wounds and, like a spirited and most courageous prince, fell on the field and not in flight.' Richard had been beloved in the north and when news of his defeat arrived there the York Register recorded 'He was piteously slain and murdered, to the great heaviness of this city.'

Did Richard's secret die with him? He cannot have been the only one who knew what happened to the Princes in the Tower but Brackenbury, John Howard, Duke of Norfolk, Richard Ratcliffe and many of those closest to the king died with him on Bosworth Field. Sir William Catesby was executed in Leicester a few days after the battle. The core of Ricardian support was destroyed in one morning and anyone else who knew the regime's secrets might have been too frightened to share what they knew. It is easy to see how the story of Richard killing his nephews had taken hold. Shakespeare presented the deed as fact and it added the final pinnacle of drama to his play, but it built upon a story that had been growing throughout the century that was closing with Shakespeare's play. Sir Thomas More is perhaps the second most famous architect of Richard's evil reputation but Polydore Vergil presented a similar story and there is contemporary and near contemporary evidence that appears to support the charges. The guilt of Richard III is a construct that has endured for over five centuries and continues to defy revisionist attempts to topple it. It is closely guarded by a traditional interpretation of events that resists reassessment. Having examined the construction of this accepted truth, the remainder of this book relies on being able to at least breach the walls of the construct, if not tear it down.

So, how certain are we, really, that Richard III killed his nephews?

2

Deconstructing the Myth

some write that they were both secretly taken out of the Tower and both set afloat in a ship and conveyed together over the seas'

Sir George Buck, *The History of King Richard III*

The most striking thing about the solid edifice of the story of Richard III's guilt in the murder of his nephews is the shaky foundations on which it is built. William Shakespeare was writing a dramatic spectacle so had no desire to leave the matter ambiguous – he needed his audience to see Richard commit the ultimate evil act. However, one step back to the Tudor antiquaries and the foundations of Richard's reputation reveals a less certain attitude. The earlier account of Sir Thomas More, begun around 1513, is equally unequivocal in accusing Richard of ordering this heinous act, but accepting More's book at face value ignores several very important facts that should warn us against such blind reliance.

Just as it is possible to interpret Shakespeare's *Richard III* as a political commentary on the events in England at the end of sixteenth century, so Thomas More's writing should be read in a wider context than simple history as we may expect it to be written today. More's other great work, *Utopia*, is far from a literal piece. It is an allegory, a vehicle for the discussion of a perfect society, which appears to consist of a world without private property that promotes religious freedom, euthanasia, divorce and married clergy, concepts that More demonstrably did not believe in. Sir Thomas was born in London in 1478, the son of a successful lawyer. He spent the years between the ages of 8 and 14 years old in the household of John Morton, Archbishop of Canterbury and Chancellor to Henry VII. Morton had been the implacable enemy of Richard III and a key architect of Henry VII's propulsion to the throne and it seems likely that More gleaned much about the old king from his mentor. The first moment in which Thomas came to prominence was in 1504 as a 26-year-old Member of Parliament. Trained as a lawyer, More made so eloquent a speech in Parliament against a tax of three-fifteenths requested by King Henry VII that the grant was reduced by around two-thirds. The idealistic lawyer's victory saw his father imprisoned in the Tower and forced to pay a hefty fine for no obvious offence but his son's open opposition to the Tudor government. If Thomas learned a lesson from this episode it was surely that such flagrant criticism was to be avoided.

Allegory was a literary style popular in Ancient Rome and used by writers such as Plato and Livy. The Cambridge Dictionary defines allegory as 'a story, play, poem, picture, or other work in which the characters and events represent particular qualities or ideas that relate to morals, religion, or politics'. As a Renaissance man, Sir Thomas would have been interested in Roman classicism and allegory allowed a writer to direct criticism and comment at the establishment of the day in an indirect way that could always be denied. The device can be seen in More's *Utopia* and other famous works over following centuries such as Jonathan Swift's *Gulliver's Travels* and its use in other places by More should offer a note of caution when reading his account as literal history. It is important to also consider that More never completed his *History of King Richard III*. Just after detailing the murder of the Princes, More set down his pen and never returned to the work. When he started writing in 1513 he was serving as Undersheriff of London but was about to embark on a career in royal service as a close friend to Henry VIII that perhaps precluded even allegorical criticism of the government. Why snipe at it in writing when he could try to change the system from its very heart? That may, at least, have been the idealistic notion. We only know of More's version of the events of 1483 because his nephew, William Rastell, edited and completed the story, publishing it in 1557, over twenty years after More's execution. There was even a Continuation written by Richard Grafton, the Tudor antiquary, which continued More's story to Henry Tudor's victory at Bosworth. It is unclear how much Rastell changed More's manuscript and he is a man we shall return to shortly.

What if, rather than ceasing his account because he was embarking on a career in service to Henry VIII, More had other reasons for stopping his writing? It is entirely possible that the research More carried out, including interviewing those alive in 1483, quickly uncovered the gaping holes in the monstrous version of the old king handed him by Archbishop Morton. This may have mattered less when the work is read as allegory, since in that case Richard III becomes a vehicle for the lessons of the work concerned with the dangers of tyranny and perhaps aimed at the new, young King Henry VIII, amongst whose first acts was the executions of Richard Empson and Edmund Dudley essentially for doing as they had been told by his father, Henry VII. There are clues that we are not meant to take More's work literally. The very first line of the book is an error. 'King Edward of that name the Fourth, after he had lived fifty and three years, seven months, and six days, and thereof reigned two and twenty years, one month, and eight days, died at Westminster the ninth day of April'. Edward IV in fact died nineteen days short of his forty-first birthday. A traditional interpretation would suggest that this would have been fact-checked later and corrected, but this comes from the same readers who seek to rely utterly on More's account of the murder of the Princes. Would such a fastidious investigator really have guessed so precisely at an age? Might More not have added an 'about' to mitigate his possible error? One explanation is that More offered an immediate signpost to a knowledgeable reader that what followed was not a literal truth, but an allegorical, metaphorical exercise. It is perhaps interesting that Henry VII also died in April, in 1509 at the age of 52 after twenty-four years as king, coming far closer to More's description than Edward IV does.

It is not necessary to rely entirely on setting aside More's account as fiction with a hidden purpose in order to doubt the traditional story of the murder of the Princes in the Tower. One key feature of More's version is his assertion that:

> Very truth is it, and well known, that at such time as Sir James Tyrell was in the Tower – for treason committed against the most famous prince, King Henry the Seventh – both Dighton and he were examined and confessed the murder in manner above written, but to where the bodies were removed, they could nothing tell.

Sir James was indeed arrested in 1501 and executed in 1502 for treason as a result of assisting Edmund de la Pole, a nephew of Richard III, in his escape from England and through Calais to the Continent. Tyrell was not arrested for anything in relation the Princes in the Tower. There is no record of a confession nor even that he was questioned on the matter nearly twenty years after the event. It is interesting too that More also wrote that 'Miles Forest at Saint Martin's piecemeal rotted away; Dighton, indeed, walks on alive in good possibility to be hanged before he die; but Sir James Tyrell died at Tower Hill, beheaded for treason'. Yes, that's right. More claims that John Dighton confessed to the act of killing Edward V and Richard, Duke of York alongside Tyrell and that, although Tyrell was executed, Dighton walked free and was still at liberty a decade later when More began writing. The traditional approach requires us to believe in a confession of which More's assertion that it existed is the only evidence and that one of those who committed not only the double murder but a regicide too was allowed to walk free after his confession. It would be remarkable indeed if the Tudor government had mislaid such a critical document to their security after more than a decade of threats to it and more remarkable still if Henry VII had allowed a killer of a king and a duke to walk free. It is almost unthinkable that Henry's queen, Elizabeth of York, would not have wanted justice for the man who smothered her brothers to death.

The other key element of More's story is the burial of the bodies of the Princes. More wrote that following the murder by Forest and Dighton, 'they laid their bodies naked out upon the bed and fetched Sir James to see them. Who, upon the sight of them, caused those murderers to bury them at the stair-foot, meetly deep in the ground under a great heap of stones.' Crucially, More continues that when Tyrell reported what had been done to a grateful Richard, the king 'allowed not, as I have heard, the burying in so vile a corner, saying that he would have them buried in a better place because they were a King's sons' so that 'they say that a priest of Sir Robert Brackenbury took up the bodies again and secretly buried them in a place that only he knew and that, by the occasion of his death, could never since come to light.' More claims that his story comes directly from Tyrell and Dighton's confessions, which he says are 'well known', yet the details of the burial are couched in terms of 'as I have heard' and 'they say' which gives it an air of oral tradition, the reliability of which More cannot be certain of.

Nor is he willing to commit to his own story, yet the two positions appear mutually exclusive; either the detail came from a confession, or it is a story that More has heard from others. It surely cannot be both. This is not the only doubt cast by Tudor sources.

John Rastell, the father of William Rastell, More's nephew who published his uncle's work posthumously, published his own chronicle in 1529 entitled *The Pastymes of the People* in which he, in similar fashion to More, lays out the fate of the Princes in the Tower. Rastell's story is that:

... the lord protector by the council of the duke of Buckingham as it was said, caused this young king and his brother to be conveyed to ward, which were never after seen but there put to death.

But of the manner of the death of this young king and of his brother, there were divers opinions. But the most common opinion was that they were smothered between two feather beds and that in the doing the younger brother escaped from under the featherbeds and crept under the bedstead, and there lay naked a while, till that they had smothered the young king, so that he was surely dead. And after this one of them took his brother from under the bedstead and held his face down to the ground with his one hand, and with the other hand cut his throat ... with a dagger. It is a miracle that any man could have so hard a heart to do so cruel a deed, save only that necessity compelled them, for they were charged by the duke the protector, that if they showed not to him the bodies of both those children dead on the morrow after they were so commanded, that then they themselves should be put to death. Wherefore they that were so commanded to do it, were compelled to fulfil the protector's will.

And after that the bodies of these two children as the opinion ran, were both closed in a great heavy chest, and by the means of one that was secret with the protector, they were put in a ship going to Flanders, and when the ship was in the black deeps, this man threw both those dead bodies so closed in the chest over the hatches into the sea, and yet none of the mariners, no none in the ship, save one the said man knew what things it was that was there so enclosed. Which saying divers men conjectured to be true, because that the bones of the said children could never be found buried, neither in the Tower nor in no other place.

This version is perhaps not so distant from More's, yet it nevertheless differs, not least in the fate of the bodies of the dead princes. Rastell's *Pastymes* was published some fifteen years after More began his work, yet Rastell appears to have no knowledge of Tyrell's involvement, or his confession, or the details of the burial and removal of the bodies. Rastell instead had heard – rather than read in an official account or a confession – that the bodies were taken into the Channel and thrown overboard in a chest. Given that no one but the murderers and the single man on the ship knew these details, we are left to wonder how they reached Rastell. There is an important twist, though. Rastell continues his story by writing:

> Another opinion there is, that they which had the charge to put them to death, caused one to cry suddenly 'treason, treason'. Wherewith the children being afeared, wished to know what was best for them to do. And then they bad them hide themselves in a great chest that no man would find them, and if anybody came into the chamber, they would say they were not there. And according as they counselled them, they crept both into the chest, which anon after they locked. And then anon they buried that chest in a great pit under a stair, which they before had made therefore, and anon cast earth thereon and so buried them quick, which chest was after cast into the black deeps, as is before said.

In Rastell's second version of the fate of the Princes, we now have bodies buried in a chest, indeed buried alive, at the foot of a staircase, though once more, the chest is later dug back up and taken out to sea. This account is important for a number of reasons. Superficially at least it gives some credence to the traditional account; the boys were murdered at the instruction of Richard III, their bodies may have been buried within the Tower grounds or buildings at some point, but they were later removed and finally deposited somewhere else, either a more suitable grave site or jettisoned at sea. The final part is useful because it demonstrates the need to explain away decades of failure to find any bodies. Rastell notes that the story of their disposal at sea is generally believed because 'the said children could never be found buried, neither in the Tower nor in no other place' despite the foot of a stairwell being the most obvious place to look based on these reports. Similarly, Thomas More has them moved by a priest who takes the secret of their location to his own grave so that the failure to locate them can be conveniently explained.

The two versions are interesting too because they do differ. John Rastell was born in Coventry in 1475, joining Middle Temple as a barrister and practising in Coventry, where he also became coroner in 1505 before moving to London in 1508. John took with him his wife and three children, of whom William was the youngest, born the same year as the family moved. John's wife was Elizabeth Rastell, née More, a sister of Sir Thomas. Is it credible that these two brothers-in-law could write accounts of the same events in 1483, living in the same city, both working as lawyers and never discuss the subject? It might seem odd if they had not, yet if they did, how did they still write different versions about which neither was completely certain? Sadly, like so many other questions on this topic, the answer is lost to us but we can reach informed conclusions based on what we know.

Both of these accounts preclude the belief that the bones currently resting within an urn in Henry VII's Lady Chapel in Westminster Abbey, near to the tomb of Elizabeth I, are really those of the Princes in the Tower. In order to accept those remains as being those of the Princes, we must first admit that More and Rastell made errors in their accounts. In accepting this, we must wonder what else is incorrect in such detailed and dramatic tellings. If More is to be believed entirely, then these bones cannot belong to the Princes. The human remains within the urn were discovered in 1674 during some building work within the Tower of London. John Gibbon, Bluemantle Herald, noted that on 'July 17 Anno 1674 in diggin some foundacons in ye Tower, were discovered ye bodies of Edw 5 and his brother murdered in 1483. I my selfe handled ye Bones Especially ye Kings Skull. Ye other wch was lesser was broken in ye digging. Johan Gybbon, Blewmantle.' King Charles II's Principal Surgeon John Knight also recorded:

Ao 1674. In digging down a pair of stone staires leading from the Kings Lodgings to the chappel in the white tower there were found bones of two striplings in (as it seemed) a wooden chest which upon the presumptions that they were the bones of this king and his brother Rich: D. of York, were by the command of King Charles the 2nd put into a marble urn and deposited amongst the R: Family in H: 7th Chappel in Westminster at my importunity. Jo. Knight.

A third, anonymous account gives Knight as the writer's source and records that:

> … in order to the rebuilding of the several Offices in the Tower, and to clear the White Tower from all contiguous buildings, digging down the stairs which led from the King's Lodgings, to the Chappel in the said Tower, about ten foot in the ground were found the Bones of two striplings in (as it seemed) a wooden Chest, which upon them survey were found proportionable to the ages of those two Brothers viz. about thirteen and eleven years. The skul of one being entire, the other broken, as were indeed many of the other Bones, also the Chest, by the violence of the labourers, who … cast the rubbish and them away together, wherefore they were caused to sift the rubbish, and by that means preserved all the bones. The circumstances … being … often discoursed with … Sir Thomas Chichley, Master of the Ordinance, by whose industry the new Buildings were then in carrying on, and by whom this matter was reported to the King.

Another anonymous and undated source noted:

> This day I, standing by the opening, saw working men dig out of a stairway in the White Tower, the bones of those two Princes who were foully murdered by Richard III, … they were small bones, of lads in their teens and there were pieces of rag and velvet about them … Being fully recognised to be the bones of those two Princes, they were carefully put aside in a stone coffin or coffer.

Seven months after the discovery, Sir Christopher Wren was engaged by the king to create a resting place for these remains. A warrant signed by one of the king's ministers, the Earl of Arlington, places an order for 'A Marble Coffin for two princes' and states:

> These are to signifie his Majestes pleasure that you provide a white Marble Coffin for the supposed bodies of ye two Princes lately found in ye Tower of London and that you cause the same to be interred in Henry ye 7th Chappell in such conveient place as the Deane of Westminster shall appoynt. And this shalbe yor warrant. Given under my hand this 18th day of February 1675. ARLINGTON.

Wren later provided an account to the king describing how the bones were found 'about ten feet deep in the ground … as the workmen were taking away the stairs, which led from the royal Lodgings into the Chapel of the White-tower'.

Bones, apparently of two young children, found at the foot of a staircase in the Tower of London were certain to excite interest. It is clear from these accounts though that whilst some bones were dug up, they were thrown onto the rubbish heap initially and only recovered later, the suggestion being after more digging, since one account notes that men 'were caused to sift the rubbish'. The box that might have contained the remains was smashed, if it ever existed, and many of the bones, clearly fragile, may have been lost or destroyed. It has been suggested that the anonymous source recording the presence of velvet near the bones proves both that they were high status and relatively new graves since velvet had only arrived in England around the fourteenth century, yet this need not prove anything since the velvet was merely in a rubbish pile near to the bones. The reference to velvet is not found amongst the other accounts and is not properly referenced elsewhere to assist in finding the source to examine it. Certainly, no velvet was within the urn by 1933 and if it was a key element in identifying royal remains it would surely have been kept with the remains. Any velvet may well have been completely unrelated to the bones and simply ended up near it on a rubbish pile, and when the men were instructed to recover the bones of two princes, a piece of velvet caught the eye as a suitable embellishment, since it had been concluded before the search of the rubbish heap that they were now looking for the bones of the Princes in the Tower. Were the destroyed box and strip of convenient velvet simply the additions of workmen eager to please, doubtless made nervous by the charge that they had tossed aside such royal remains? The existence of velvet has been confidently used to deny that these remains might date back to the Anglo-Saxon, Roman or Iron Age era, or indeed any other age. It may well be a myth. Certainly, there is no real evidence of it.

The political circumstances in which the bones were found, as with the writing of Sir Thomas More, must be placed in the proper context too. Charles II had been on the throne for fourteen years following England's brief flirtation with republicanism. With the Restoration had come bitter reprisals, which Charles had promised he would not seek. Those who had tried and executed his father were ruthlessly persecuted and three of them who were already dead, including Oliver Cromwell, were exhumed, their corpses beheaded and suspended in chains in Westminster Hall, the site of Charles I's trial, before their remains were ignominiously thrown into unmarked pits. By 1674 and into 1675, Charles was at loggerheads with Parliament as it refused to grant taxes he needed for war, forcing him to seek peace where he did not want it. Parliament was, as it had with his father, seeking to tie the hands of the king. When news reached the court of bones found beneath a staircase a memory of More's writing may have been kindled that presented an opportunity. If the nation could be reminded that after the cruel deposition and murder of the innocent Edward V, it had suffered under the cruel tyrant Richard III, and that following the unjust murder of Charles I, Cromwell had again ruled as an oppressive dictator to the country's detriment, it might cause them to think again about opposing their king. The discovery of the remains of the Princes in the Tower would be a timely warning just when Charles needed one. So it was that they were proclaimed to be the bones of those innocent boys and they were placed reverentially in Westminster Abbey bearing an inscription that has echoes of just such a caution when read in the context in which it was written:

> Here lie the relics of Edward V, King of England, and Richard, Duke of York. These brothers being confined in the Tower of London, and there stifled with pillows, were privately and meanly buried, by the order of their perfidious uncle Richard the Usurper; whose bones, long enquired after and wished for, after 191 years in the rubbish of the stairs (those lately leading to the Chapel of the White Tower) were on the 17th day of July 1674, by undoubted proofs discovered, being buried deep in that place. Charles II, a most compassionate prince, pitying their severe fate, ordered these unhappy Princes to be laid amongst the monuments of their predecessors, 1678, in the 30th year of his reign.

The year 1678 can only have been the thirtieth of Charles II's reign if he acceded on his father's death and Cromwell's time in power is utterly discounted. In 1933, the contents of the urn were removed and examined by Professor William Wright, Dean of the London Hospital Medical College and President of the Anatomical Society of Great Britain and Ireland with the assistance of Lawrence Tanner, a man without medical qualification or experience. Amongst the remains they found rubbish, including animal bones, but they also identified two incomplete human skeletons. These findings would tally with the rough treatment the bones initially received but give lie to the assertion in the anonymous account relying on Knight that they 'preserved all the bones'. Perhaps some smaller bones were taken as relics or could not be found and were replaced with animal bones, suggesting a lack of care and reverence at odds with the royal status proclaimed for them. The 1933 report concluded that the bones were those of the Princes and they were returned to their resting place. The primary issue is that the examination seems to have been undertaken with the subjective aim of proving that the bones *were* the Princes, not objectively trying to establish their provenance. In 1955 the results were re-examined by a group of anthropologists and orthodontists, though they were denied access to the remains themselves. This report concluded not only that the age of the children had not been established by a sufficient degree of evidence, but also that no attempt to ascertain the gender of either skeleton had been made. Furthermore, the osteomyelitis present in the older child may have seriously impacted attempts to establish the age of that child. The 1955 findings contradicted those of the 1933 examination, identifying several flaws and concluding that the remains could neither be proved nor disproved as being those of the Princes in the Tower.

The discovery of the bones currently in Westminster Abbey is far from a singular event in the Tower's long history, neither are they the first set of remains to be confidently identified as those of Edward V and his brother Richard, Duke of York. A seventeenth-century edition of Sir Thomas More's *Historie of the Pitifull Life and Unfortunate Death of Edward the Fifth* contains a note on the flyleaf signed 'J. Webb' which reads:

August 17th, 1647, When ye Lord Grey of Wilton and Sir Walter Ralegh were prinsoners in ye Tower, th wall of ye passage to ye Kings Lodgings then sounding hollow, was taken down and at ye place marked A was found a little roome about 7 or 8ft square, wherein there stood a Table and upon it ye aforesaid nobles and all present were credibly beleeved to bee ye carcasses of Edward ye 5th and his brother the then Duke of York. This gent was also an eye witness at ye opening of it with Mr Palmer and Mr Henry Cogan, officers of ye mint and others, with whom having since discoursed hereof they affirmed ye same to me and yt they saw the skeletons.

Lord Grey and Sir Walter Raleigh were simultaneous inmates within the
Tower between 1603 and 1613, placing the alleged discovery between
those dates. Another account by Sir Aubrey de Maurier in his seventeenth-
century *History of Prince Maurice, Prince of Orange* records that:

> The same Prince Maurice likewise told my Father that in Queen
> Elizabeth's time, the Tower of London being full of Prisoners of State,
> on account of the frequent conspiracies against her person, as they
> were troubled to find room for them all, they bethought themselves
> of opening a door of a Chamber that had been walled up for a long
> time; and they found in this Chamber upon a bed the skeletons of King
> Edward V and the Duke of York, his brother, whom their Uncle Richard
> the Cruel had strangled to get the Crown to himself, which Henry VII,
> Grandfather to Queen Elizabeth, deprived him of, together with his
> life. But the prudent Princess, not willing to revive the memory of such
> an action, ordered the door to be walled up as before. Nevertheless, I
> am informed that this same door found in the same place, the King of
> England, out of compassion that these two princes were deprived of
> burial, or from other reasons that I am ignorant of, has resolved to erect
> a Mausoleum to their memory, and have them buried in Westminster
> Abbey among the Kings.

Although this account seems to mix the 1674 discovery with an earlier
room that was found, the two accounts serve to demonstrate that the bones
found in 1674 were not the first recorded discovery of the bones of the
Princes in the Tower. A skeleton found in a tower was swiftly declared to be
that of Edward V, only to turn out to belong to an ape that had escaped the
royal menagerie and become trapped. When the Tower's moat was drained
in the 1830s a wealth of human bones was found, some of which were
confidently declared to belong to the Princes. The remains currently within
Westminster Abbey seem simply to have come to light at an auspicious time,
for Charles II more than anyone else, and so been immortalised. DNA testing may help to shed more light on the identity of the bones and further
modern examination could determine whether there are only two skeletons
there or more, what sex they each are and what period they date from, since
there is no evidence to preclude them being Anglo-Saxon or even Iron Age
remains. They may yet turn out to be the remains of the Princes, but like

so many other pieces of this puzzle, they are not as conclusive as they have been claimed to be, nor as they appear at first glance.

It cannot be denied that, combined with sources written several decades after the events they describe, the combination of the supposed murders, the stories of a burial within the Tower under a staircase and the later discovery of two skeletons confidently declared to be the Princes and interred within Westminster Abbey for over 300 years bearing the confident inscription of their provenance is compelling, but it is far from damning. To believe these, we are forced to accept that More, Rastell and others were wrong in asserting that the bones were moved after their burial. Whilst that may have been an assumption to cover up the fact that decades later they had not been found, it damages the credibility of the accounts if there are acknowledged and unsupported assumptions presented as facts.

Polydore Vergil, the official historian of the Tudor regime, began his writing perhaps as early as 1505. His first manuscript was compiled in 1513, covering events up to that year, but remained unpublished until 1534, when it was cut down to end in 1509, the year of Henry VII's death, and using a version substantially rewritten in the 1520s using the original manuscript as a basis. It is perhaps worth noting that 1534 saw the Act of Supremacy create Henry VIII as head of the Church of England and Pope Clement VII declare that Catherine of Aragon was still the rightful Queen of England more than a year after Henry had married Anne Boleyn. The kingdom, and the Tudor dynasty, was in a state of deep insecurity when this telling of the fate of the Princes emerged into the light.

Vergil's version of the murder, including the part played by Sir James Tyrell, is outlined in the previous chapter and is, in essence, similar to More's version. Vergil, significantly, makes no mention of Tyrell confessing to the deed, a piece of information that was surely crucial to the story. In fact, the confession is only believed to exist because More refers to it and his word is enough for some. However, if More was writing allegory and made several demonstrable and easily corrected errors such as the age of Edward IV at his death, why should his assertion of a confession be taken at face value, particularly when other writers appear to have no knowledge of it? Vergil would have been perfectly placed to access such a critical document, writing after Tyrell's execution but before More began his work, so that it must have existed then if it ever did. Given that such a confession would provide a security the first Tudor king had craved and lacked, its suppression seems counter-productive and unlikely. Indeed, the existence of any confession by Tyrell relating to the Princes must be very seriously doubted. It has been asserted that the presence of Henry VII and Elizabeth of York at the Tower of London during Tyrell's trial shows that he held interesting information that must have related to Elizabeth's brothers. This is to ignore both the fact that he was implicated in a fresh and very serious Yorkist threat to Henry's throne and that Tyrell's trial took place at the Guildhall, not the Tower.

The version of the fate of the Princes given previously is not all that Vergil has to say on the matter. In a statement that suggests there was no official Tudor government line on the matter, Vergil also wrote that 'It was generally reported and believed that the sons of Edward IV were still alive, having been conveyed secretly away and obscurely concealed in some distant region.' Vergil does not say that this is true, only that it is widely reported and believed. He also does not provide detail as to who was responsible for their concealment – Richard III, Henry VII or someone affiliated to the Woodville faction or that of Edward IV – but it is a bold statement to find within the account of an official Tudor historian. Francis Bacon asserted in his 1621 *The History of the Reign of Henry VII* that on Henry's accession:

> Neither wanted there even at that time secret rumours and whisperings, which afterwards gathered strength and turned to great troubles, that the young sons of King Edward the Fourth, or one of them, which were said to be destroyed in the Tower, were not murdered but conveyed secretly away, and were yet living.

Sir George Buck, also writing in the early Stuart period, claimed that:

> some others ... say that these young princes were embarked in a ship at Tower wharf, and that they were conveyed from hence into the seas, and so cast into the deeps and drowned. But others say that they were not drowned, but were set safe on shore beyond the seas.

The Dutch *Devisie Chronicle*, penned around 1500, joined several continental sources in blaming Henry Stafford, Duke of Buckingham for the boys' deaths, believing them to have been starved to death or poisoned, but conceding that there was also a story that Buckingham had murdered one prince but spared the other 'and had him secretly abducted out of the country'.

Of the writers who confidently proclaimed Richard's guilt in near-contemporary accounts, few were without motive and the remainder reported only rumour they could not substantiate. When Diego de Valera wrote to Ferdinand and Isabella in March 1486 that 'it is sufficiently well known to your royal majesty that this Richard killed two innocent nephews' he confidently pronounced something that was demonstrably not well known in England. Queen Isabella had a history with the Yorkist dynasty. There had been rumour of a match with Edward IV, though this was possibly after his marriage to Elizabeth Woodville became public, and more certainly to Richard, Duke of Gloucester, the recently defeated Richard III. Isabella had chosen Ferdinand as her husband and throughout the Yorkist period England had established ever-closer ties with Burgundy and remained close to Portugal. With the dawn of the Tudor era, a closer relationship with Spain seemed of interest to Henry VII, demonstrated by the negotiations for marriage between Prince Arthur and Catherine of Aragon that followed soon after. If Spain remained wary of Yorkist government and saw in the Tudor dynasty a chance for a strong alliance, then they had a vested interest in promoting the story of the death of two Yorkist princes at the hands of their Yorkist uncle, the deposed king.

Similarly, and more definitely, when Guillaume de Rochefort made his report to the French Estates General in January 1484 that King Edward's 'children, already big and courageous, have been slaughtered with impunity, and their murderer, with the support of the people, has received the crown', his motives are not hard to discern. Rochefort again makes a definitive statement of something that was not widely known as a certain truth. Leaving aside the traditional enmity between England and France, there are very particular reasons to be suspicious of this story at this time. During 1475, Edward IV had launched an invasion of France that had promised much and delivered nothing in the way of glory, in part because the Duke of Burgundy had abandoned the scheme in favour of an attack on a distant town even before Edward had landed. Louis XI, King of France, was known as the Universal Spider for the webs of intrigue that he span. Careful to know his enemies, Louis saw the opportunity to buy off Edward's invasion with cold hard cash. Amongst other inducements, Edward received 75,000 crowns immediately and an annual pension of 50,000 crowns.

Pensions were also eagerly snapped up by most of the nobles accompanying Edward. One exception was Richard, Duke of Gloucester, then 22, idealistic and bellicose. Richard asserted that they could defeat the French despite Burgundy's absence and that if Edward wanted a swift peace, the terms would be infinitely improved if they were negotiating after just one victory. Richard was overruled, but perhaps captured the feeling of the nation who did not approve of the waste of money and lack of glory the expedition represented. Louis seems to have been intrigued by the king's younger brother, who refused to attend the sealing of the Treaty in what amounted to an official snub. Richard was invited to a private audience with the King of France, which he attended and at which he accepted gifts of horses and plate. Following the meeting, Louis seems to have kept a close eye on Richard, even sending him a gift of a cannon on one occasion.

The importance of this episode nearly a decade earlier lies in Louis' spider-like politicking. It seems likely that he saw in Richard the most serious threat from England whilst Edward, who could be easily paid off, was alive. In 1482, Richard had led the successful campaign against France's auld allies in Scotland, so when Edward died in 1483 and Richard was appointed Lord Protector of the Realm for the new minor king, several threads of Louis' web must have jangled. Richard would be responsible for military policy, both domestic and foreign, and it seems likely that France, who had just reneged on the Treaty of Picquigny and was looking aggressively across the Channel, feared Richard's less relaxed approach after his brother's death. The threat was only magnified when Richard became king with a free hand in all areas of government. Louis XI died on 30 August 1483, but must have left his warnings about Richard resonating in France. Furthermore, Louis' son and heir, Charles VIII, had not long turned 13 years old when his father died. Charles' older sister Anne acted as his regent but the minority allowed factions tightly controlled by Louis to spill into open revolt. Led by the Duke of Orléans, a cousin of Charles who later became Louis XII, the Mad War lasted from 1485–88. The situation when Rochefort gave his report was already frighteningly similar to that in England. The strong king in place since 1461 was dead, the squabbling restrained by his personality was leaking into court, a boy requiring a minority government was taking the throne just when aggression from across the Channel seemed more likely than it had for almost a decade. In England, the boy king had already lost his throne. Those at the centre of power in France, who also

had the most to gain from the vacuum of royal authority a minority presented, had a strong vested interest in protecting Charles VIII. Richard III
of England offered a powerful warning, both of the evil that might follow
the deposition of a child king and also that France was now under threat
and needed to galvanise, not fall into civil war. Such internal division had
allowed Henry V to take over half of their country and have himself legally
declared heir to the throne. Did they want that to happen again? If not,
they needed to unite behind the young king against the evil aggressor in
England. It was a powerful, vital message, which required Richard to be the
darkest character possible. If there was the faintest whisper he might have
killed his nephews, it needed to become fact. It was a scare tactic. It didn't
work in France, where years of civil war followed, but it has stuck against
the reputation of Richard III for centuries. As a reliable source, it should be
dismissed out of hand.

Dominic Mancini left England before the murders are usually believed to
have happened, yet he reported later that year that 'I have seen' men burst
into tears for fear that the Princes had already been put to death before
his departure. An Italian who spoke no English, Mancini makes demonstrable errors about the geography and politics of England and obtained
his information from almost entirely unnamed sources. The integrity of
and motive for supplying Mancini with the details he had when he left
England are therefore hard to establish, though they appear to be entirely
hostile to Richard, suggesting they were Woodville or latent Lancastrian
in sympathies. He does name Dr John Argentine as a source, a physician
attending on Edward V who later became Prince Arthur Tudor's physician, making his sympathies fairly easy to establish. Mancini is believed
to have met Dr Argentine on the continent later in 1483 and it is unclear
when the information was received. Was Dr Argentine applying hindsight
to rumours that had sprung up? Was he simply trying to blacken the name
of a king under whose rule he was an exile, having lost a key position at
court? What Mancini recorded was that 'The physician Argentine, the last
of his attendants whose services the king enjoyed, reported that the young
king, like a victim prepared for sacrifice, sought remission of his sins by daily
confession and penance, because he believed that death was facing him.'
Mancini, or Dr Argentine, neglect to include any explanation of this. The
passage has traditionally been interpreted to suggest that Edward V feared
his uncle was about to have him killed, but an equally likely scenario is

that Edward was ill and feared for his own life. This situation is made more plausible by the very fact that Edward was being attended by his physician, though this might have been more routine than would be expected today and may not necessarily indicate a severe condition. What makes it almost certain that Dr Argentine's report does not refer to the fear of a plot against the boys' lives by Richard is that the report only mentions Edward's fear of death, completely ignoring his brother. If the dread arose from a belief that Richard was about to send murderers against the boys, it seems likely that both would experience that fear, or at least that Edward would express concern for both of their lives rather than just his own. Of course, Dr Argentine was a fugitive from England when he met Mancini on the continent, where he most likely passed on this information. He was already placing his eggs in the basket carried by Henry Tudor at his faux-court in Brittany so had his own strong motive for painting Richard as a villain. Even so, what he says is far from unequivocal, which may tell us all we need to know.

A secondary problem with Mancini's account lies in its current translation by C.A.J. Armstrong. The original Latin title of the work is 'Dominici Mancini, De Occupatione Regni Anglie Per Riccardum Tercium, Ad Angelum Catonem Presulem Viennensium', which is translated as 'Dominic Mancini To Angelo Cato, Archbishop of Vienne, on Richard the Third's Usurpation of the Realm of England'. Occupatione is translated as Usurpation, but that is not quite accurate. Occupatione means occupation. There is a word in Latin that would translate directly as usurpation here; usurpation. Thus the title by which the work has become widely known, *The Usurpation of Richard III*, is incorrect and should read *The Occupation of the Throne by Richard III*. In a passage about the Princes in the Tower, Mancini's words regarding Edward V are translated as:

> I have seen many men burst forth into tears and lamentations when mention is made of him after his removal from men's sight; and already there was suspicion that he had been done away with. Whether, however, he has been done away with, and by what manner of death, so far I have not at all discovered.

The Latin word translated as 'done away with' here is 'sublatem', in both cases, which actually means to remove or take away, though the reference is followed by mention of death, 'mortis', which is more ominous. There is increasing pressure for a fresh translation of Mancini since it is clear that at least in parts, the language used in the present translation is inaccurate and obviously bent to suit a more sinister reading of the text, from the title onwards. It throws into further doubt the reliance that can be placed on a man who didn't know the land, didn't speak the language, was informed by opponents of Richard III and has been translated to throw a darker shadow over the text.

The *Crowland Chronicle* is very interesting on the matter of the fate of the Princes in the Tower. The continuation covering this period was written in early 1486, when the writer, who is openly hostile to Richard III, had nothing to fear from the defeated king and might have been free to explain events. The identity of the writer is not known for certain but he appears to have been a lawyer by training who served Edward IV as an ambassador at least once, on an embassy to Burgundy, and who was politically well informed, perhaps even acting as a councillor to the king. The chronicler has in-depth knowledge of the period he wrote about, offering valuable detail and insight at many points. The writer may have felt restrained either by Henry VII's early policy on the fate of the Princes in the Tower, which appears to have been silence, or by uncertainty about how any information he possessed might have been received. It is also possible that the writer felt some guilt if the boys were murdered that he had not used his position to better protect them. What is contained within the manuscript is worthy of reproduction in full:

In the meantime, and while these things were going on, the two sons of king Edward before-named remained in the Tower of London, in the custody of certain persons appointed for that purpose. In order to deliver them from this captivity, the people of the southern and western parts of the kingdom began to murmur greatly, and to form meetings and confederacies. It soon became known that many things were going on in secret, and some in the face of the world, for the purpose of promoting this object, especially on the part of those who, through fear, had availed themselves of the privilege of sanctuary and franchise. There was also a report that it had been recommended by those men who had taken refuge in the sanctuaries, that some of the king's daughters should leave Westminster, and go in disguise to the parts beyond the sea; in order that, if any fatal mishap should befall the said male children of the late king in the Tower, the kingdom might still, in consequence of the safety of his daughters, some day fall again into the hands of the rightful heirs. On this being discovered, the noble church of the monks of Westminster, and all the neighbouring parts, assumed the appearance of a castle and fortress, while men of the greatest austerity were appointed by king Richard to act as the keepers thereof. The captain and head of these was one John Nesfeld, Esquire, who set a watch upon all the inlets and outlets of the monastery, so that not one of the persons there shut up could go forth, and no one could enter, without his permission.

At last, it was determined by the people in the vicinity of the city of London, throughout the counties of Kent, Essex, Sussex, Hampshire, Dorsetshire, Devonshire, Somersetshire, Wiltshire, and Berkshire, as well as some others of the southern counties of the kingdom, to avenge their grievances before-stated; upon which, public proclamation was made, that Henry, duke of Buckingham, who at this time was living at Brecknock in Wales, had repented of his former conduct, and would be the chief mover in this attempt, while a rumour was spread that the sons of king Edward before-named had died a violent death, but it was uncertain how. Accordingly, all those who had set foot on this insurrection, seeing that if they could find no one to take the lead in their designs, the ruin of all would speedily ensue, turned their thoughts to Henry, earl of Richmond, who had been for many years living in exile in Britany. To him a message was, accordingly, sent, by the duke of Buckingham, by advice of the lord bishop of Ely, who was then his prisoner at Brecknock, requesting him to hasten over to England as soon as he possibly could, for the purpose of marrying Elizabeth, the eldest daughter of the late king, and, at the same time, together with her, taking possession of the throne.

The most politically well-informed contemporary commentary that we have appears to offer no insight whatsoever regarding the fate of the sons of Edward IV. The chronicler only offers that, as part of Buckingham's Rebellion against Richard III in September and October 1483, a rumour was circulated by the rebels that they had been killed. This is critical to the story. The *Crowland Chronicle* might represent the only hope of a contemporary solution to the matter, yet he remains virtually silent, reporting only rumours that were a part of a revolt two and a half years earlier. The purpose of the rumours was to cause the rebels to switch allegiance to Henry Tudor, and it worked. If the boys were dead, why might the Crowland Chronicler have failed to confirm it? Perhaps he, from his central position in the workings of Richard III's government, knew exactly what had happened to them and that they were not dead at all. What remained to be seen was what the early months of Tudor rule would mean for two Princes who might still be alive but were certainly no longer legally illegitimate.

3

The Black Hole Effect

Henry, 'taking the oath of allegiance in some towns in the neighbourhood of London, proclaimed everywhere before his Coronation that if there were anyone of the line of King Edward who had a right to the throne, that he should show himself, and he himself would help to crown him'.

Jean Molinet, *Chroniques*

Jean Molinet's report of Henry Tudor's words after his victory at Bosworth and before his own coronation offer an interesting sense of confidence that soon evaporated. If they are true, they appear to suggest that Henry felt he knew the boys were dead. He surely did not mean to hand his hard-won crown to another. Elizabeth Woodville had agreed to marry her oldest daughter, Elizabeth of York, to Henry as part of a plot to oust Richard III. Why, it has long been asked, would Elizabeth Woodville have done this if she believed her sons were still alive? The reason is simple, as it is frustratingly unverifiable.

The major problem with any attempt to prove the fate of the Princes in the Tower is always the lack of conclusive evidence. There is no smoking gun, or longbow, unless it is yet to come to light. During a recent discussion on Twitter about the Princes I was offered a perfect analogy for the situation, which I will use here with the kind permission of its originator, Michele Walter (@MshellW). The Princes are like black holes in history. They represent the conspicuous lack of, well, anything. Black holes, though, exert a gravitational influence on their surroundings that offer hints of their presence. The Princes in the Tower can be viewed in the same way. If we cease to look only for definitive evidence of their fates and widen our view to encompass those who might be affected by that fate, it is possible to see intriguing hints of an unseen force at work.

In Richard Grafton's continuation of Sir Thomas More's *History of King Richard III* the Duke of Buckingham is reported as having said of Richard 'He promised me, on his fidelity, laying his hand on mine at Baynard's Castle, that the two young princes should live, and that he would provide for them and so maintain them in honourable estate that I and all the realm ought and should be content.' Is it really feasible that Richard would preserve his nephews alive during his reign? For many, no, yet we have already seen that even hostile chroniclers such as Vergil had to admit that their survival was a widely rumoured possibility. However, it is a crucial point for their longer-term survival that one or both of the Princes reached 22 August 1485 alive, either by their uncle's devise or that of another.

One possibility is that the attack on the Tower in late July 1483, whilst Richard was on his royal progress, succeeded in freeing the boys and sending them over the seas. This would leave the question of why Elizabeth Woodville appears to have supported Henry Tudor's claim by September 1483. The other scenario for their survival is that Richard himself, never having any intention of having his nephews killed, had them taken out of harm's way, where they would be less of a distraction to his rule. This leaves many of the same questions unanswered.

Elizabeth Woodville, the mother to both boys, has to be a key figure in understanding the possible gravitational effect on their surroundings of her sons. Born around 1437 at her family's estate of Grafton Regis, Elizabeth was the oldest child of Richard Woodville and Jacquetta of Luxembourg, Duchess of Bedford. Richard's father had been chamberlain to John, Duke of Bedford, the uncle of Henry VI who had acted as Regent of France until his death in 1435. Jacquetta was of strong noble lineage and had been the second wife of the Duke of Bedford. After John's death, she seems to have made a genuine love match with Richard and the pair married, initially in secret. When the union became public knowledge, it caused a scandal, though Richard was made Baron Rivers in an attempt to mitigate the discrepancy between their social positions. Elizabeth was married to Sir John Grey around 1452 and bore him two sons, Thomas and Richard, before his death at the Second Battle of St Albans in 1461, where he was fighting for the Lancastrian cause. The widowed Elizabeth was left in a precarious position and legend tells of her determination to protect her sons' positions. The story goes that Elizabeth waited at the roadside for the new, young, Yorkist king as he hunted near to her home. With the hand of one of her sons in each of hers, she pleaded with Edward to help restore and secure their properties. Edward was reportedly smitten and tried to have his way with Elizabeth but she, unlike many before, resisted the tall, handsome athlete. The flame of Edward's ardour was only made to burn brighter and he tried to force himself on the widow, but she held a knife to her own throat and protested that her honour meant more to her than her life. The king was only enflamed further and eventually, in order to bed the elusive Elizabeth, Edward agreed to marry her in a secret ceremony, possibly on 1 May 1464, which Edward only later revealed to his Council.

Crowned as queen consort, Elizabeth's father was created Earl Rivers and her eleven siblings, six sisters and five brothers, were soon perceived to be cornering the marriage market and gathering to them key appointments at court. Her oldest son Thomas became Marquis of Dorset and the youngest, Richard, was knighted. The Woodvilles became unpopular, seen as parvenu, undeserving of the favour they received as they pushed older, more established families to the peripheries of Edward's court. Henry Stafford, Duke of Buckingham was amongst those married to a Woodville sister of the queen, Catherine. The story of the king's first encounter with Elizabeth is perhaps apocryphal and designed to portray a mother who would never abandon her sons, a myth that would be strong currency during the early Tudor period. The unpopularity of the Woodville faction was doubtless a key feature of Edward's reign and for Elizabeth, her sons by the dead king represented her only route to security as well as being her flesh and blood. There may well be some substance to accusations of a Woodville plot before Richard, Duke of Gloucester arrived in London since the queen was planning an early coronation and trying to bypass a Protectorate in order to exclude Richard, and the old nobility he was likely to allow back in at the expense of her own influence, but evidence is, of course, lacking.

Once Richard III was crowned on 6 July 1483, the story of the Princes in the Tower becomes almost immediately obscured. There is no certain date, or even month, for their last sighting and rumour seems to have run amok. Since rumour can only take hold where there is no definite information, we must assume that very few in London, and none who were willing to talk, knew what had happened. Elizabeth Woodville had taken her daughters, her oldest son Thomas and her youngest son Richard, Duke of York into sanctuary at Westminster Abbey as news of the coup at Stony Stratford reached London. Her brother Anthony and her second son Sir Richard Grey were amongst those arrested and sent north to Richard's castles. It is from here that she surrendered the Duke of York but it is here that she herself remained with the rest of her children. It is therefore important to consider the information with which the former queen made her decisions during the rest of that year.

If all that was known in London outside the inner circle was that no one knew for certain what had happened, for Elizabeth Woodville to have definitive information would rely on one of Richard's inner circle visiting her to tell her, and news of any such visit would surely have made it back to the king if he was keeping a close watch on the dowager queen's location. One visitor that is known to have attended the former queen in her sanctuary is Dr Lewis Caerleon, a physician allowed access to care for Elizabeth and her family. Dr Caerleon was also in the service of Margaret Beaufort, then Lady Stanley and mother to Henry Tudor. It is believed that Dr Caerleon was the medium through which the plot to marry Henry to Princess Elizabeth was negotiated and agreed. Lady Stanley was, despite her husband's presence and brief arrest at the Council meeting of 13 June that had seen Lord Hastings executed, in high favour at court. She had walked behind Queen Anne at the coronation, a position second only to the queen and ahead of Richard's own sister, the Duchess of Suffolk, and she was yet to be exposed as a key part of her son's coming invasion. One of the few sources of information to Elizabeth Woodville in her sanctuary was a physician in the service of Henry Tudor's mother.

Whilst I do not hold with the notion that Margaret Beaufort had a driving ambition to see her son made king from the moment of his birth, or that she clung to some prophetic religious zeal that made her believe it was destined to be so – there is simply no evidence for a such a belief – it is clear that in 1483 she saw an opportunity for her son. Margaret had been near to concluding negotiations with Edward IV for her son to return to England as Earl of Richmond and perhaps even to marry one of Edward's daughters, though probably not the politically valuable Elizabeth. Whether this was a ploy by Edward to trap the last remnants of Lancastrian resistance in exile or a genuine offer of reconciliation is unclear, but the negotiations stalled with Edward's death, and seemed unlikely to proceed with Richard, Duke of Gloucester, as a prominent member of a child king's government with his natural suspicion of Lancastrians and the inherent insecurity of a minority. It must have seemed an impossible dream when Richard became king. It is at this point that I believe the Tudor faction saw its opportunity, with the rich and well-connected Margaret becoming its chief architect.

It is known that Margaret was in contact with Elizabeth Woodville through Dr Caerleon. It is well documented that the original purpose of Buckingham's Rebellion, planned at least as early as September and failing to come to fruition in early October, was to free Edward V and put him back on the throne. The *Crowland Chronicle* informs us that the rumour of the boys' murders, started as part of the rebellion, causing the revolt to move from championing their cause to aiming to put Henry Tudor on the throne. Buckingham was the most senior member of the planned uprising, but appears to have come to it late, coerced by his prisoner Bishop Morton into abandoning Richard. Buckingham's Rebellion is a misnomer that has persisted despite the clear evidence that this was a Tudor plot. A key feature of the plan was to marry Henry to Elizabeth of York, uniting the rival sides of the Wars of the Roses, and this appears to have secured the approval of her mother, Elizabeth Woodville. How could Elizabeth have agreed to this if she did not know with some degree of certainty that her sons with Edward IV were dead?

A more pertinent, and more easily addressed, question is: how could Elizabeth Woodville have known with any degree of certainty that her sons were dead from sanctuary, particularly when no one else appears to have known? Dr Caerleon offers a solution to the problem. If Dr Caerleon sombrely delivered news to the former queen that her brother-in-law Richard, the new king, had put her sons to death, Elizabeth would have little other information available. Such news would also surely have served to fulfil her darkest fears, festering and growing in her seclusion. It would be no great matter for Elizabeth to believe Richard capable of such an act. He had, on 25 June 1483, executed her brother Anthony, Earl Rivers and her second son from her first marriage, Sir Richard Grey. Both had been held in Richard's northern castles after their arrest at Stony Stratford but were taken to Pontefract and executed on Richard's orders.

Elizabeth Woodville would believe Richard III capable of murdering two of her sons in the Tower because he had already ordered the execution of one, along with her brother. Grey was 26 when he was executed, no young boy perhaps, but a child of Elizabeth's nonetheless. On 28 June, Richard had created John Howard Duke of Norfolk, a title previously belonging to Richard, Duke of York, the younger Prince, following his marriage to Anne Mowbray. It has often been suggested that this implies the boys were dead at this early date, but it does not. With both princes declared illegitimate, they were not entitled to what they held; in Edward's case, the crown, in Richard's, his dukedoms of York and Norfolk. Edward IV had, in the way he attached the Mowbray lands to his son, subverted the laws of inheritance, which would have made the Howard family heirs to Anne Mowbray's lands and titles on her death without issue. Prince Richard had lost the Norfolk lands and titles with the declaration of his illegitimacy. In handing the inheritance to John Howard, Richard was not suggesting that his nephew was dead, he was correcting what he saw as an unfairness perpetrated by his brother, the kind of thing that the petition asking him to take the throne had railed against the old king for.

If the dowager queen had been nurturing a nagging fear that Richard might kill her sons, it must have been easy for Dr Caerleon to simply confirm what she already thought. When the physician then offered not only a pathway to vengeance but also a route back to something like the power she had known before, as mother to the queen consort, Elizabeth must have jumped at the chance – perhaps her only chance. This situation does not presuppose that the Princes were dead, or that Margaret had murdered them to further her scheme. She did not need them to be dead. In fact, she may have been as uncertain as everyone else as to their location or fate. Margaret only needed Elizabeth to believe them lost and in an instant, the Woodville faction and those of Edward IV's supporters who could not be reconciled to Richard's regime would mobilise to see the person they now considered Edward IV's rightful heir – Princess Elizabeth – on the throne. It is also worth considering that, from her seclusion, Elizabeth may not have realised the full extent of what she was agreeing to. It is possible she was induced to believe that the rebellion would reinstate her son as Edward V, who was alive and well and would be rescued, and that the agreement to allow Henry Tudor to return to England and marry her oldest daughter was simply the price of bringing Beaufort money and Stanley muscle to bear, a completion of something that had been the subject of negotiation earlier that same year. For the Tudor faction, it gave

Henry a national platform with dynastic support from which an unknown exile might grasp at the crown of England.

The October revolt ultimately failed. The Kentish portion of the rebels launched their attack on London ten days early and enough were captured by John Howard, Duke of Norfolk for details of their plan to be extracted and forwarded to the king. Richard, then at Lincoln, wrote to Bishop Russell, the Chancellor, for the royal seal to be sent, adding to his letter:

> Here, loved be God, is all well and truly determined, and for to resist the malice of him that had best cause to be true, the Duke of Buckingham, the most untrue creature living; whom with God's grace we shall not be long till that we will be in those parts, and subdue his malice. We assure you there was never false traitor better purveyed for, as this bearer, Gloucester, shall show you.

On the same day, Richard wrote to the city of York, describing Buckingham as 'a vile traitor'. It has been frequently suggested that this episode, and the vitriol poured down on Buckingham by Richard, might be the result of the duke having arranged the murder of the Princes, either thinking he did Richard's will and expecting rewards only to receive horrified condemnation, or for his own reasons, as part of the plot to unseat the new king. Buckingham himself possessed a far stronger claim to the throne than Henry Tudor, so perhaps had one eye on the main prize for himself. This would explain the emergence of the rumour of the Princes' deaths as part of the revolt, if Buckingham had engineered it to be so, but it seems far more likely that the intractable and unsubtle Richard felt the searing pain of Buckingham's betrayal when they had been so close.

Henry Stafford, 2nd Duke of Buckingham, was beheaded in Salisbury marketplace on 2 November 1483. This is a key moment in the story of the Princes in the Tower, the importance of which cannot be overstated. In the instant that Buckingham's head was removed from his neck, Richard was presented with a golden opportunity. If the Princes were dead, this was the moment to break the sad news. Whether Richard had arranged their murders or Buckingham had killed them for his own reasons, whether the bodies could be recovered, were lost at sea or lay in an unknown grave, now was the king's chance to put the matter to bed for the remainder of his reign. Richard had only to blame the executed duke and lament the loss of his nephews to a rebellion in Henry Tudor's name. Implicating Henry in the deaths of Edward IV's sons would cause him to lose the Yorkist support that was the very lifeblood of his cause. A confession by the duke could be fabricated, the bodies could be produced or announced as lost and the boys could be openly mourned, any threat they might pose laid to rest with the revelation of their fate. Instead, silence from the king and those closest to him was maintained. Richard was presented with the perfect moment to resolve the matter of the death of the Princes, if it had happened, in his favour. There may have been some suspicion and rumour, but there already was. With Buckingham blamed and the death of the boys widely known, the matter would slip from public concern. The only obvious reason that Richard would fail to seize this moment was that the boys were still alive and their murder had never even crossed their uncle's mind.

If the Princes survived into 1484, there should be more signs of the gravitational effect of their presence on those around them. Hard written evidence is severely lacking, though this is not without explanation in the fragile early months of Henry VII's rule. Before arriving at August 1485, there are some interesting snippets that have survived as well as the continued actions of others to examine. Horace Walpole, 4th Earl of Orford was a notable art historian and politician who, in 1768, published his *Historic Doubts on the Life and Reign of King Richard III* and became one of the most famous defenders of King Richard. Walpole recorded a note in the Coronation Rolls (though it actually originated from the Wardrobe Accounts) for quantities of fabric in various colours for 'Lorde Edward, son of the late Kyng Edward the Fourthe'. This would not be a form of address used if the entries related to Edward V's coronation, since he had already been proclaimed king. 'Lord Edward' may be appropriate for an illegitimate son who was still Earl of Chester in his own right. The entry is suggestive of an intention that 'Lorde Edward' should be present at Richard III's coronation, or at the very least that fabric was being purchased for him after he had been declared illegitimate.

Further evidence from within the Wardrobe Accounts offers more tantalising incites whilst stopping short of providing proof of anything. Folio 88 marks the point at which the entries, which may have been added some months after the event, begin to refer to 'Deliveree of stuff delivered to, for and ayenst … the moost noble coronations awal of oure souverayne lorde King Richard the Third as of our Lady the Quene'. At Folio 115, with no change of subject, appears the subheading 'yit the deliveree off sylkes and also other stuff', listing materials to be provided for various minor persons including 'two chamberers of our said souverayne Lady the Quene' and 'many dyverse persons' that had been ordered 'in haste' by 'my Lorde of Bukkingham'. Immediately after this list is another headed 'To Lorde Edward, son of the late Kyng Edward the Fourthe, for his apparaill and array'. The list continues through Folios 115, 115b and 116, with Folio 116b listing apparel for 'henxemen of the said Lorde Edward'. Folio 117 demonstrates that the records still refer to the coronation by discussing 'Deliveree off divers clothes off gold and sylkes' ordered for 'knyghtes and other divers persons ayenst the saide mooste noble coronation of oure said souverayne lady the quene' and 'for oure said souverayne lorde the kynges mooste noble coronation'. The list ends at Folio 118b without any clear change of topic. It has been suggested that these records refer to Edward V's own coronation and have been entered out of order, but the references throughout to 'Lorde Edward' rather than King Edward mean that this interpretation is highly unlikely and reference to a queen can only mean the coronation was that of Richard and Anne.

The obvious interpretation is that Edward V was being provided for to attend the coronation of his uncle Richard III. Whilst this does not prove that the elder of the Princes survived into 1484, it at least suggests that he was not a state prisoner and was permitted to retain henchmen in late June and early July 1483 as an earl. The records of the Wardrobe Accounts were compiled by Peter Curtys some months after the coronation and if Edward's name had since become an anathema, it would surely have been removed or obscured in the records, or he might have been noted as 'late' if he was known to be dead. If these records are read without the prejudices of centuries, they offer a suggestion that Edward was alive, well treated and expected to attend Richard III's coronation on 6 July 1483. The records also suggest that when they were compiled some months after the coronation, Edward could still be openly referred to in official records. This does not tally with a traditional view that Edward was a prisoner in the darkest recesses of the Tower who could not be mentioned by a government trying to cover up his death.

On 18 July 1483, a warrant was issued for the payment of fourteen men who had provided service to Edward IV and 'Edward Bastard late called King Edward the Vth'. Whilst this single item is not particularly instructive in itself, it offers another mention of Edward V as he might have been referenced following the declaration of his illegitimacy. It was not deemed necessary to avoid mention of his proclamation as King Edward V and Edward Bastard, along with Lord Edward, were forms of address used for the boy. Another question that presents itself in relation to the coronation is the role played by Thomas Bourchier, Archbishop of Canterbury. The elderly prelate was nearing 80 and had been Archbishop of Canterbury for nearly thirty years, throughout the changing fortunes of the Wars of the Roses. Cardinal Bourchier was the man who had gone to Elizabeth Woodville in sanctuary to convince her to release Richard, Duke of York so that he might join his older brother in the Tower. The Archbishop had given his word to the queen that no harm would befall the boy and if either of Edward IV's sons were in any apparent danger from Richard by 6 July 1483, it seems hard to believe that the old Cardinal would have willingly placed the crown onto Richard's head. The suggestion is that, by the coronation at least, they were not in any danger.

It is at this point that another example of the gravitational effect of the survival of the Princes in the Tower might be perceived. Elizabeth Woodville allowed her daughters to leave sanctuary and join the court of their uncle Richard. Although the records make no mention of the dowager queen herself leaving sanctuary, it seems unlikely that she would release her daughters whilst maintaining her own uncomfortable confinement to which she had initially retreated ostensibly for their protection. It is beyond doubt that there was still some concern on the part of the former queen because Richard read aloud a proclamation on 1 March 1484 before the Mayor and Aldermen of London and those lords spiritual and temporal still in the city:

I Richard … promise and swear, verbo regio, that if the daughters of Elizabeth Grey, late calling herself Queen of England … will come to me out of the Sanctuary of Westminster, and be guided, ruled, and demeaned after me, then I shall see that they shall be in surety of their lives and also not suffer any manner hurt … nor them nor any of them imprison … but I shall put them into honest places of good name and fame, and them honestly and courteously shall see to be founden and entreated, and to have all things requisite and necessary for their exhibitions and findings as my kinswomen; and that I shall do marry … them to gentlemen born, and every of them give in marriage lands and tenements to the yearly value of

200 marks for term of their lives … And such gentlemen as shall hap to marry with them I shall straitly charge lovingly to love and entreat them, as wives and my kinswomen, as they will avoid and eschew my displeasure.

And over this, that I shall yearly … pay … for the exhibition and finding of the same Dame Elizabeth Grey, during her natural life … to John Nesfeld, one of the esquires of my body, for his finding to attend upon her, the sum of 700 marks … and moreover I promise to them that if any surmise or evil report be made to me of them by any person … that then I shall not give thereunto faith nor credence, nor therefore put them to any manner punishment, before that they or any of them so accused may be at their lawful defence and answer …

In short, Richard promised not to harm his nieces, which is strong suggestion of a fear that he would do just that. However, it was also an offer, and a generous one. Elizabeth herself would receive a comfortable income – more generous than she would enjoy under her son-in-law Henry VII – and her daughters would be married well and provided for by the king. How could Elizabeth Woodville thrust her daughters into the arms of a man she knew had killed their brothers? It has been argued that after almost a year in sanctuary with little hope of her position improving, she was forced to accept that she had no option but to submit to Richard, but that ignores several key facts. Elizabeth had, by agreeing to let her daughter become the intended wife of Henry Tudor, implicated herself in a rebellion and might be guilty of treason. In leaving sanctuary, she risked exposing herself to such a charge. Her daughter was still promised to Henry Tudor, who was still at large in Brittany and was still planning to take Richard's crown. After the failure of his October invasion, on Christmas Day 1483 Henry had taken a solemn oath at Rennes Cathedral in Brittany to marry Elizabeth and eject Richard. Henry's cause might not seem to hold much hope at this point, but if Elizabeth was looking for something to cling to, her arrangement with Margaret Beaufort remained intact.

Although she may not have wished to remain in the relative discomfort of her sanctuary, Elizabeth could have done just that, particularly if the option was to send her daughters into the arms of a vicious killer. Elizabeth knew Richard was capable of killing her children because he had ordered the execution of Richard Grey. Rumours of the murders of her sons with Edward IV seem to have driven her to pin her hopes on Henry Tudor's unlikely plot. How could she now hand the king her daughters? Richard promised not to harm them, but if he was a desperate child killer who could not rest while a threat to his crown remained, surely his word was worthless. It is not possible to argue that his nieces posed less of a threat than his nephews had either. The oldest, Elizabeth, was the very key to Tudor's attempts to unlock the kingdom. He was making much of marrying her to unite their houses and bring peace and a substantial amount of those making for Henry's court-in-exile were Edwardian Yorkists, drawn to him by their allegiance to Edward IV's senior heir (assuming her brothers were dead), Princess Elizabeth. Edward IV's daughters were a clear and present danger to Richard when he made his offer to bring them to court. He knew it and so did Elizabeth Woodville. Unless Elizabeth believed that Richard was the kind of man to only do half a job, to stop exterminating threats before they were all gone, the only explanation that comes close to making sense of this spectacular rapprochement is that Elizabeth Woodville did not believe Richard had killed his nephews.

This interpretation presents two significant problems for the story of the Princes' survival. First, it does not mean they had not died, only that their mother was satisfied Richard was not responsible. Natural causes may have claimed one or both of them, the attempts on the Tower earlier in the summer of 1483 might have led to their accidental or deliberate deaths or Buckingham might have been behind their demise, but Richard must have been able to convince his sister-in-law of his own blamelessness in the matter. Second, it seems to ignore the execution of Richard Grey, a son of Elizabeth's for whose death Richard absolutely had been responsible. Although this must have been hard for Elizabeth to look beyond, her family had been blighted by such acts before. Her father and brother had been executed by the Earl of Warwick during the Wars of the Roses. Now, another brother and one of her sons had been executed, though perhaps importantly, not illegally. Some form of trial appears to have taken place at Pontefract under the Earl of Northumberland, probably under the jurisdiction of the Constable's court, which was inequitable and brutal, but entirely legal. Why would the men have been gathered from several locations to Pontefract if not for the purposes of a trial of some kind? It is possible that the men were taken north to act as hostages against the Woodville plot Richard had been advised of prior to his arrival in London. Richard was, at least technically, entitled to execute them on the spot for treason as Constable of England had that been his wish. If Elizabeth called his bluff, she may have felt some degree of responsibility for their ultimate fate herself. Richard Grey was a grown man executed, legally, for treason. That makes his a very different case to the secret murder of two young boys.

It seems unlikely that Richard could have produced sufficient material to convince Elizabeth Woodville of his innocence if her sons were dead by 1 March 1484. She would know that he could concoct any evidence. The only thing that he could possibly do to convince her of his innocence which might cause her to willingly release her daughters to him is show her that her sons were not, in fact, dead at all, despite the ugly rumours she had been fed in sanctuary. It would have been simple to do and a great relief to the former queen. Richard cannot, however, have smuggled the boys into Westminster Abbey to show them to their mother, so she may only have had assurances from people she sufficiently trusted. That would explain the need for the public oath from the king but also her willingness to be reconciled. It is also at this point that Sir James Tyrell may make an appearance in the story that could have led to his eventual condemnation as a murderer.

James Tyrell was born around 1445, the eldest son of Sir William Tyrell of Gipping, Suffolk. Sir William was a staunch Lancastrian and was executed in February 1462, the same month as the Earl of Oxford and his oldest son, for his part in an alleged plot to murder Edward IV. By 1471, James was fighting in the Yorkist army at the Battle of Tewkesbury, following which he was knighted by Edward IV (contrary to More's assertion that Tyrell was knighted for the service of killing the Princes). Just after this, Sir James entered the service of Richard, Duke of Gloucester, the future King Richard III. Tyrell accompanied his lord on the expedition to Scotland in 1482, after the success of which Richard made him a knight banneret. These years of service also give the lie to More's suggestion that an unknown page had to suggest Tyrell to the king for a task as though he was some-one unknown to Richard. An undated letter probably written between 1480 and 1482 demonstrates the relationship between the lord and knight. Contained within the *Stonor Letters and Papers* is a note from Sir James Tyrell to Sir William Stonor, a relative of Tyrell's wife, in which Sir James explains that he has intervened with his lord on behalf of William's brother so that 'my lorde hath herde the excuse of my cosyn, your brother' and forgiven him the unmentioned offence. Sir James was clearly able to ask favours of Richard and have them granted.

Following Richard and Anne's coronation, which he is listed as attending, Sir James was made Master of the Horse and Master of the King's Henchmen (meaning retainers rather than anything sinister). Following the collapse of Buckingham's Rebellion and the duke's flight into hiding it appears to be James who recovered the duke and escorted him to Salisbury, following which he was made Commissioner of Array for Wales and Steward of the Duchy of Cornwall for life. Tyrell would later be remembered as the man who murdered the Princes in the Tower, and his appointments seen as rewards for that evil service, but that was twenty years away and he may have become the fall guy for another reason. Audrey Williamson, in her *Mystery of the Princes*, unearthed a story which, though lacking any supporting evidence, is interesting. The story was an old family legend, the kind impossible to prove or disprove, which came from Kathleen Margaret Drewe, a descendant of a son adopted by the Tyrell family in the eighteenth century and which held that Gipping Hall, Tyrell's family home, had been used to host Elizabeth Woodville and her children, including her sons. It was claimed that 'the princes and their mother Elizabeth Woodville lived in the hall by permission of the uncle', clearly demonstrating that this fell within the reign of Richard – 'the uncle' – and that Tyrell was in fact responsible not for the murder of the Princes, but for their care, particularly during time they were permitted to spend with their mother and sisters. Gipping was in Suffolk, close to London, but not too close, and near to the coast if a flight to Burgundy should become necessary, as it had for Richard in the past. Only 20 miles south-west of Wingfield, Gipping was also close to the seat of Richard's sister the Duchess of Suffolk, her husband and their children, one of whom, the Earl of Lincoln, was becoming a foundation stone of Richard's rule. With John Howard, Duke of Norfolk also holding great authority in the region, it was a safe, secure, sufficiently secluded but suitably accessible location for the boys to meet with their mother.

These all make compelling pieces of a jigsaw that seems to fit together. From her isolated position in sanctuary, Elizabeth Woodville was led to believe her sons had been killed to induce her to offer her daughter in marriage as part of a plot to unseat Richard III, who she had been told was the killer of her sons. It would have seemed plausible given the executions of her brother and Richard Grey and may have confirmed her worst fears. If Richard had murdered the Princes, Elizabeth's emergence and the handing over of her daughters is not only unfathomable, but also unforgivable. Richard's only Parliament sat between 23 January and 20 February 1484 and during that period, *Titulus Regius* was passed into law. The statute outlined Richard's right to the crown because of the illegitimacy of Edward IV's children and the attainder against his brother George, Duke of Clarence. The statute purported to be the same wording used in the document presented to Richard asking him to take the throne in June 1483, but it finally made the illegitimacy of the Princes, and their sisters, legal. Richard's position was more secure than ever, with one rebellion crushed and his legal title enshrined in Parliamentary statute. If he was going to show his hand and close down the rumours about his nephews that caused his sister-in-law to use his niece against him, he was only now in a position to do it without further endangering himself. The only situation in which these actions, at this time, make any sense is if the Princes were alive and it had been proven to Elizabeth Woodville so that, when combined with the additional good faith assurance of Richard's oath, she felt confident that she could bring her daughters out of sanctuary. If she was promised that she would see her sons, the former queen may have been relieved and amazed as they stayed at Gipping Hall together for a time under the watchful gaze of one of Richard's most trusted men. It was likely that this arrangement allowed short periods of time together and was not meant to be a permanent solution though.

So where were the Princes? If the boys were alive and there had been plots in London to free them, or even to murder them, then the natural response for Richard would have been to send them to one of two places. His sister Margaret, Dowager Duchess of Burgundy could offer a safe refuge, though that relied on the uncertainty of a sea voyage, the distance of a foreign country and the insecurity for Richard of relinquishing close control of his nephews. The other place was the north, the old Neville heartland that had been Richard's own home for more than ten years, where he was known and loved and where he could find men he knew and trusted to rely on. Richard re-established the Council of the North that he had run for his brother, Edward IV. Perhaps to the chagrin of Henry Percy, Earl of Northumberland, who may have hoped for an increase in his own regional influence as Richard moved south, the new king placed his oldest nephew John, Earl of Lincoln in charge of the Council. John de la Pole, the oldest son of Richard's sister Elizabeth, Duchess of Suffolk, was around 22 in 1484 and was clearly identified by his uncle as a key plank of his new government. On 23 July 1484, King Richard set down ordinances for the household in the north that includes more tantalising but inconclusive references. The household was to be structured so that 'my lord of Lincolne and my lord Morley to be at oon brekefast, the Children togeder at oon brekefast [and] suche as be present of the Counsaille at oon brekefast'. Who were these 'children'? Richard sent his other young nephew, the 9-year-old Edward, Earl of Warwick and possibly several of the daughters of Elizabeth Woodville to this household a few weeks after the ordinances were established, so it is possible that the provisions were laid down in preparation for their arrival, though it is equally possible that one or both of the Princes were already there.

The separation of the Princes at this point is perhaps more likely than them being kept together. Although it meant two places to keep an eye on, it also kept the king from placing both these delicate eggs in one basket, particularly if they were targets of assassination or release attempts by others. The Princes in the Tower have become, in the collective imagination, a single unit, two blond-haired little children clinging together in fear and dread, an image conjured in so many later portraits. This ignores the fact that they were boys who would have barely known each other. Edward V was raised at Ludlow in his own small court whilst Richard, Duke of York, remained with his mother and sisters around London. They would have seen each other only infrequently, at times such as Prince Richard's wedding. When Richard arrived at the Tower some weeks after his brother, Edward may have been able to offer some solace and company to his 9-year-old brother, but they had not previously spent much time together as Edward soberly prepared for power and Richard ran the corridors of London palaces. The king had two perfect places for two potential problems he wanted kept discretely secure. That begins to sound like providence.

Sir James Tyrell was appointed commander of the Castle of Guisnes, a fortress that shielded the English enclave of Calais, in January 1485. The appointment would probably save his life in August since he was not in England to fight at Bosworth, but some mystery surrounds his activity early in that fateful year. The Register of Grants contained in Harleian MSS 433 contain an entry dated 13 January 1485 which states:

Where as we of late sent oure righte trusty knighte for oure body and Counsailloure Sir James Tyrelle over the See into the parties of Flaundres for diverse maters concernyng gretely oure wele. Whoo in his Retornyng ayen unto us landed in oure poort of Dover the charges whereof amounting to the somme of iiii markes as we certainly knowe were borne by the maire and othre inhabitauntes of our said Towne if Dovor ...

During January, Richard sent to James Tyrell at Calais a vast sum of money, believed to equate to the annual revenue of the crown at the time, for an undisclosed purpose at the same time as Tyrell was given a permanent post with military authority on the continent. It seems unlikely that this was a war chest for an early invasion of France since Richard was unprepared in any other way. Shipping such a vast amount of money to his enemy's doorstep was probably not a good first move. Perhaps the most likely purpose of the money was a bribe to Pierre Landlais, the chief minister to Duke Francis II of Brittany. Francis was increasingly ill and Landlais' power grew in proportion to his master's incapacity. The duke had sworn to protect Henry Tudor but Landlais was interested in the men England might be able to provide to help defend Brittany against French aggression. Agreement was reached later in 1485 to provide 4,000 Welsh and English longbowmen in return for the handover of Henry, his uncle Jasper and any other Lancastrians lingering in Brittany. The plan became known, probably to Bishop Morton, Richard's nemesis, and Henry was tipped off, making his escape to France just in time. The money shipped to Tyrell may have been meant as a bribe to Landlais, though the amount was vastly excessive, or to help pay for the troops Brittany wanted, though that number would have to have been recruited in England and Wales, so sending their wages ahead of them, before they were recruited, seems odd too.

It is simple once more to make sense of this if the continued existence of the sons of Edward IV is accepted, at least as a possibility. If one of the boys was sent to Richard's powerful sister Margaret, Dowager Duchess of Burgundy, several pieces fall into place, which cannot otherwise be satisfactorily explained. On 23 April 1484, a grant is recorded in Harleian MSS 433 to Sir Philip Goguet, 'Chapelyn to the duchesse of Burgoyne [Burgundy] and for iii persones with him. Yeven [Given] at Nottingham the xxiii day of Aprile Anno etc. primo'. The reference is innocuous but on 6 December 1484 a further entry records that 'Clement Goguet hath a like lettre to passe & repasse to my lady Burgoyn with a servant with him/ & ii horses without any Serche etc Yevene at Westminster the vi day of Decembre Anno ii'. It is possible that Philip and Clement Goguet were related, possibly they were brothers, but both were clearly in the service of Margaret, Duchess of Burgundy and Richard III was in secretive contact with his sister throughout 1484 and into 1485. Clement was taking a message and was to await a reply but significantly he was given an exemption from any search, suggesting that the information he carried was of the most sensitive nature possible.

Stories of at least one of the Princes being spirited abroad would persist for decades after Henry Tudor's victory at Bosworth and resisted fiercely the official story of their murders. Sir Thomas More's account, during the time that Elizabeth Woodville sent her youngest son out of sanctuary to join his brother at the Tower, puts into the mouth of Archbishop Bourchier as he discusses the matter with the former queen the words:

> No man denies … but that your Grace were of all folk most necessary about your children, and so would all the Council not only be content but also glad that you were, if it might stand with your pleasure to be in such place as might stand with their honour.

The Archbishop expresses the belief that the former queen could live somewhere with her children in security and perhaps More only has the timing of this option wrong. With Parliament finished, his legal title settled and sufficient time elapsed since the plot to unseat him the previous October, Richard III, as has been discussed, was only now able to feel secure enough to confront the issue of his brother's family.

An Easter amnesty that reflected his new confidence might have been at the root of the timing too. The king could now offer his sister-in-law precisely what Archbishop Bourchier had referred to in More's version of the story: a home with her sons and daughters to live in security, at least for a time. Elizabeth had been separated from Prince Edward for most of his life and though Prince Richard had remained close until this point, he was, at 9, of an age at which he might have entered the household of a lord for training. Perhaps the family spent some time at Gipping, Elizabeth sorry that her sons would have to leave soon, but elated to find them alive beyond her hope. It is possible that Richard involved her in discussions about the best way to deal with them. Edward was little known outside Ludlow, having been only rarely at court, so perhaps the household of the Council of the

North, under the watchful eye of his older cousin the Earl of Lincoln, would be appropriate, allowing him to be kept at a safe distance but, as a potential figurehead for any future revolt, close enough to be carefully managed by the king. Prince Richard, a boy much better known around the capital and its palaces, might have been destined for an upbringing in the opulent, metropolitan court of his aunt Margaret in Burgundy, kept a little further distant but hardly less secure. This arrangement would serve to explain Elizabeth's emergence from sanctuary with her daughters in March 1484, the references to children in the Ordinances of the Council of the North, the secretive correspondence between Richard and his sister Margaret that lasted through the year and into the next, James Tyrell's equally secretive and mysterious trip to the continent, the vast sum of money he was sent and his appointment at Guisnes Castle. This interpretation also offers an explanation for Tyrell's close association with the fate of the Princes over the decades and centuries that have followed. Proof remains elusive, but there is no less evidence for this situation at Henry Tudor's accession than of the murder of the Princes in 1483, and only with their survival can otherwise inexplicable events be made coherent.

If further evidence to support the notion that Richard III had no interest in destroying the Princes in the Tower is required, it is provided by the fates of his other nieces and nephews. Edward IV's daughters were welcomed out of sanctuary in March 1484, though significantly don't appear to be recorded at court until Christmas that year, offering support to the theory that a period at Gipping Hall as a family might have followed their emergence. Of the five daughters alive at Edward IV's death in April 1483, all five survived their uncle's rule. Within *Rymer's Foedera* (texts of agreements made between England and foreign powers) is a note of a commission given by James III of Scotland to Colin, Earl of Argyle, the Chancellor of Scotland, and seven other men to negotiate the marriage of his eldest son, the future James IV, to 'Anne, niece of the K. of England'. Richard had three nieces named Anne; Anne de la Pole, who became a nun, Anne St Ledger and Anne of York, the daughter of Edward IV who was just two years younger than James. Another of Edward IV's daughters, Cecily, was married to Ralph Scrope of Upsall, a younger brother of Baron Scrope of Masham. Henry VII would have the marriage dissolved on his accession, but it is clear that Richard was in the process of honouring his pledge to find his brother's daughters good marriages. The ugly rumour of Richard planning to marry his brother's oldest daughter Princess Elizabeth is at best dubious and at worst the repetition of malicious slander as if it were fact. After the death of Richard's wife Anne on 16 March 1485, the king stepped up negotiations to marry into either the Portuguese or Spanish royal lines, both of which significantly possessed a strong Lancastrian descent. The Portuguese match seems to have been the most likely and the arrangements included a union between Princess Elizabeth and the first cousin of King John II of Portugal, who would later become King Manuel I.

Richard III had a dozen other nephews and nieces alive in April 1483 in addition to the children of Edward IV. His sister Anne, Duchess of Exeter had one daughter, Anne St Ledger. Another sister, Elizabeth, Duchess of Suffolk, had six sons, the oldest being John, Earl of Lincoln, and three daughters. Richard's brother George, Duke of Clarence, who had been executed for treason in 1478, had a daughter, Margaret, and a son Edward, Earl of Warwick who survived him. Of these twelve nephews and nieces and the five daughters of Edward IV, not one failed to survive until the end of Richard III's reign. The obvious question is why the sons of Edward IV would be singled out for destruction. It has been argued that they posed the greatest threat to Richard as male line descendants of the House of York with a better claim than Richard. This is true. Edward, Earl of Warwick, possessed a claim superior, in the same way, to that of Richard III too. He had been disqualified from the succession because of his father's attainder, though this could be reversed in Parliament as easily as the illegitimacy of Edward V and Prince Richard might be. The little earl, in part due to his father's execution, had little natural or cultivated support of his own, which might diminish his threat. Significantly, the oldest daughter of Edward IV, Princess Elizabeth, was a very real and present danger, even as Richard III welcomed her out of sanctuary in March 1484. Henry Tudor had sworn to marry her on Christmas Day 1483 and that vow was drawing the support of disaffected Edwardian Yorkists to his cause. Yet Elizabeth survived too.

If Richard had the Princes in the Tower murdered, he removed two threats to his rule but left seventeen further threats, promoted by the deaths of the Princes, utterly intact until the day of his death. At least one was a direct threat for the duration of Richard's reign, yet all were allowed to survive. This does not appear to be the belated clemency of a man so terrified for his position that he would kill two boys, his own nephews. Why not complete the task, at least of destroying the blood of Edward IV? If security was so frantically sought as to drive the king to kill his nephews, why were other nephews, one of a senior male line to his own, treated with favour and every sign that they were intended to become mainstays of Ricardian Yorkist rule? The events of 1483, 1484 and 1485 make perfect sense if the survival of the Princes in the Tower is accepted, but become harder to understand if they were dead. Without direct evidence, the gravitational effects of their continued existence are the only clues, but they are compelling, not least in the case of their mother. The best lies are constructed around a kernel of truth, so Tyrell's involvement became that of a murderer and stories of a flight abroad were woven through later events as lies told as part of plots against Henry VII.

The single biggest problem with the belief that Richard III had his nephews murdered, that they died at the hands of another or even of some natural cause is the loud and significant lack of a public statement during his reign that they were dead. If the boys were dead, it removed any potential for them to become figureheads for a future rebellion. If they died at the hands of another faction, then Richard could mourn them openly, perhaps taking criticism for failing to protect them more fully, but he would ultimately be blameless in their deaths. If natural causes claimed them both – perhaps the plague – he could again mourn them free from blame, though some might whisper of its convenience. If Richard ordered their deaths, then in October he was presented with a golden opportunity to declare them murdered by Buckingham as part of his revolt in Henry Tudor's name, freeing him of guilt and besmirching his enemy's cause into the bargain. Whatever the public believed, the world would know the boys were dead, ideally confirmed by the displaying of the bodies. The traditional argument is that Richard killed his nephews in order to secure his position, but keeping it secret would not meet that aim; in fact, allowing rumour to spread and persist made the situation worse. The silence is traditionally explained by Richard's unwillingness to shine a light on such a dark deed but that is still counter-productive. The death of the Princes in the Tower only brought an end to any potential threat they might have been if everyone knew they were dead and could no longer be a threat. Rumours of their deaths existed, but so did tales of their survival. Killing them demanded the publication of the deed for it to be effective. Whatever backlash Richard might suffer could not breathe life back into two dead bodies. Failing to display the corpses or publicise the death of his nephews is a strong indication that they were both alive, well, safe and secure when Richard met his end at the Battle of Bosworth.

As Richard III lay in a shallow grave at the Grey Friars in Leicester, Henry Tudor entered London as King Henry VII. If the Princes in the Tower survived to this date, what did the new king find when he arrived in a capital he had not seen in fifteen years? Molinet suggested that he offered a challenge for the sons of Edward IV to come and receive the crown from him. Was he confident they were dead? Did he not know either way? Was his challenge a dare to them to show themselves? Dead or alive, the Princes were to haunt the new king for nearly fifteen years at least.

4

Colchester's Secrets

His body was slender but well built and strong; his height above the average. His appearance was remarkably attractive and his face was cheerful especially when speaking; his eyes were small and blue; his teeth few, poor and blackish; his hair was thin and grey; his complexion pale.

Polydore Vergil describing Henry VII in *Anglica Historia*

Henry VII holds a reputation as a wily miser. That is, at least in part, unfair. Henry was capable of lavish outlay, particularly on his family or when it came to displaying the splendour of his own position. As his reign progressed, the people and the nobility would feel the ever-increasing weight of his fiscal policy, but this was almost always a defensive response to shadows and threats that Henry never really freed his mind of.

Henry was crowned at Westminster Abbey on 30 October 1485 and, on the surface, it may have appeared that he was secure, with old Lancastrians and Yorkist supporters of Edward IV gathered at his back, relieved by the vanquishing of the tyrant King Richard III. The truth was far more complex and nuanced, not least because Richard III fit none of the measures of a tyrant, having ruled in the interests of his people rather than himself. There was a Tudor faction, which largely encompassed the old Lancastrian cause, that viewed Henry as their last hope of restoration. There was also a faction that remained loyal to the progeny of Edward IV and had been unable to reconcile themselves with the rule of Richard III for several reasons. Although currently allied to the Tudor faction, their aims were not necessarily the same. This group appears to have accepted that Edward V and Richard, Duke of York were dead and their support for the Tudor cause was a means to an end – that end being the restoration of Edward's line through his daughter, Princess Elizabeth.

There remained a substantial, though weakened, Woodville faction aware both that marriage to the new Tudor king represented their best path back to power, at least in the immediate term, but also that their position would be significantly diminished and more precarious without Edward IV to throw a strong, protective arm about them. The Tudor cause served their immediate needs, or at least their allegiance to it offered them some protection, but if the Princes had survived, this faction's priorities would lie elsewhere and their motives, whilst needing to remain secret, would be a threat to Tudor's crown, complicated further by his intention to marry one of their number.

Some remained more broadly loyal to the House of York, personification of this wider aim being most notable in Margaret, Duchess of Burgundy, sister of Edward IV and Richard III. As well as those Yorkists who remained pro-Edward and anti-Richard must be added groups who were still pro-Richard and therefore anti-Edward, whose rule Richard had berated, and also those, however small in number, who retained affection for the offspring of George, Duke of Clarence, unsympathetic to Edward IV's cause but perhaps willing to tolerate Richard, though he had passed over Clarence's son in the line of succession. After the initial hot glow of victory had passed, this splintered and opaque set of factions was the political reality that Henry VII had to try and bend to his will. The new king seems to have begun in a spirit of optimism.

Henry VII was aware of at least some of the internal problems that he would face. One of his first warrants as king, issued on the day of Bosworth, was for the arrest of Robert Stillington, Bishop of Bath and Wells, the man believed to have broken the story of Edward IV's pre-contract to Richard III. The bishop was pardoned on 22 November 1485, apparently due to 'his grete age, long infirmitie, and feblenes', though in reality Henry must have spent several weeks trying to understand what Stillington knew and, perhaps more importantly, what he was likely to repeat.

The first Parliament of Henry VII's reign opened on 7 November 1485 and one piece of its business is highly significant to the fate of the Princes in the Tower. Henry ordered that *Titulus Regius*, the act confirming

Richard III's legal title and making the children of Edward IV illegitimate, should be removed from the statute books and every copy of it should be returned for destruction. The statute was not simply repealed, it was removed from the records without being read in Parliament contrary to the usual process and copies were to be returned on pain of imprisonment. The only reason the contents of this key piece of legislation are still known is because a stray copy was located in the library of Crowland Abbey that seems somehow to have been overlooked until it was discovered by Sir George Buck at the beginning of the seventeenth century. During the Tudor period, though, the suppression of *Titulus Regius* was so complete that Sir Thomas More does not appear, if his testimony is to be believed, to have known the identity of the woman Edward IV was alleged to have been pre-contracted to marry.

One petition from James Stanley, dean of the chapel at St Martin le Grand in London, refers explicitly to the 'horrible and heinous offences plotted and committed by the bishop of Bath', but the most interesting record in the Parliament Rolls refers to the man Henry had supplanted on the throne. The new king had been in his capital for over two months by this point. He had kept the Bishop of Bath and Wells in custody until satisfied that it was safe to release him. There had been time for extensive searches of the Tower and other London palaces for traces of the Princes, dead or alive, but there is no record of any such search nor of Henry offering a public statement about the fate of the boys. He could surely accuse Richard of their murder openly now and make sure the entire kingdom knew that they were gone, their cause lost. The *Parliament Rolls* record a condemnation of Richard III which, like so many other pieces of evidence in this story, is tantalisingly obscure and frustratingly imprecise. The Rolls record that Henry was:

> not oblivious or unmindful of the unnatural, wicked and great perjuries, treasons, homicides and murders, in shedding infants' blood, with many other wrongs, odious offences and abominations against God and man, and in particular against our said sovereign lord, committed and done by Richard, late duke of Gloucester, calling and naming himself, by usurpation, King Richard III.

The reference to 'shedding infants' blood' has long been asserted as a reference to his murder of the Princes in the Tower. Medieval records did not use apostrophes and the placement after as a plural is here taken from www.british-history.ac.uk. The original English read 'shedyng of infantes blode', so it is not entirely clear whether it should read 'infants'' or 'infant's' blood, though that is perhaps a distraction, since if Henry knew anything for certain, it was not that both Princes were dead. The series of charges paint a dastardly picture but they are also so general as to be useless in the case of the Princes. There is not a single specific charge of perjury, treason, murder or any other offence or abomination beyond appearing on the field of battle against Henry, and even this was a sleight of hand. Henry dated his reign from the day before Bosworth so that he could attaint anyone on Richard's side for treason, though he later had to rethink his position when the precedent threatened his own ability to put an army in the field if his men feared his loss would mean that they were guilty of treason. If Henry knew in November 1485 that the Princes in the Tower were dead, why would he not say so? He could lay the specific charge against Richard and also free himself from the potential threat the boys would represent, a more potent menace to a king who did not know the land he now ruled and who possessed no power base of his own within England. Henry's reliance on the faction that followed him because of who he promised to marry would abandon him in an instant if Edward V or his brother Richard were available to sit upon the throne.

It has been argued that Henry might wish to keep the fate of the Princes as obscure as Richard had for similar reasons, but Henry had even more cause to make the matter unequivocal since he had just made both the sons of Edward IV legitimate along with his intended bride, making Edward V, if he were still alive, the legitimate king. Henry's need for the boys to be dead was more pressing than Richard's had been. It seems unlikely that Henry found the boys in the Tower on his arrival in London and had them killed only to fail to publicise their certain deaths for the same reason that Richard would have needed to make it widely known. If Princess Elizabeth had known her brothers were alive and well before August 1485, she would surely have found it impossible to accept Henry as her husband when they were dead immediately after his victory. The real problem for Henry was most likely that he didn't know anything for certain. Henry could not announce their deaths and produce fresh bodies without incriminating himself and alienating the larger portion of his own support. Announcing that they were simply missing invited others, those more loyal to Edward V than Henry VII, to find them and use them against Henry. Proclaiming them dead but the locations of their bodies unknown similarly left open the possibility that they were not really dead.

Perhaps silence was the lesser of several evils in late 1485 as the dust kicked up at Bosworth settled. It has been suggested that Henry remained silent to avoid creating a cult around the boys similar to that which had sprung up around Henry VI, but that implies a long-term outlook when more serious issues were pressing in the immediate term. It was Henry who refocused attention on the cult of Henry VI, who he tried to have beatified, so more innocents who he was avenging would actually have fit his narrative rather than been opposed to it. Ignoring centuries of received wisdom, the most likely explanation is that Henry knew or believed that both Princes were still alive and either didn't know exactly where they were or decided to continue with the arrangements Richard had put in place to keep them out of the public eye, thus preventing them from becoming a threat.

Less easily explained is the continued silence of Elizabeth Woodville and her daughters on the politically significant fate of her sons. The former queen had been made comfortable by Richard after her emergence from sanctuary and, true to his word, he had also provided well for her daughters. This matriarch would become significantly less affluent under her son-in-law and her final fate will prove as interesting and hard to decipher as every other piece of this puzzle, particularly if she believed that both her sons with Edward IV were dead by August 1485. At no point before her death in 1492 did Elizabeth Woodville accuse her brother-in-law of killing his nephews. For seven years after his death, she said nothing to incriminate him, even when it might have served to sure up her daughter's and grand-children's positions. In fact, the very opposite will become clear over the years that followed 1485. As significant is the lack of any recorded masses or funerary services for the Princes to speed the passage of their souls through purgatory. Such services may have been kept secret, off the books, if Henry wanted no public mention of the boys to be made, but these were the immortal souls of two of her sons, murdered without receiving the last rites and probably not buried on consecrated ground. It seems impossible that their mother would not seek to mitigate their problematic state in purga-tory. One simple answer is that Elizabeth had no need to accuse Richard because she knew he had done nothing. Not only would she perjure herself in accusing him but by confirming that her sons were dead if they were really alive, she gave Henry the freedom to have them destroyed quietly and escape any blame. She also gave away her own hand, her greatest secret, if Henry did not know where her sons were. There is also the additional problem that saying masses for the soul of those who are still alive as if they were dead was sinful and harmful to their souls. It is unlikely that any threat would induce Elizabeth to endanger her sons' immortal souls in such a way if she knew they were living still.

There are several glimpses again of what might be the gravitational effect of the survival of the Princes which, in the absence of any evidence of their deaths or survival, offer the only hint at their fates. A strong focal point for such anomalies centres on the town of Colchester in Essex. The burgeoning and ancient town boasted a Norman castle and no fewer than eight churches within the town walls, including houses of Augustinians, Franciscans, Benedictines and Crouched friars. The town boasted two large annual fayres and a grammar school for the education of local boys. The focal point of interesting activity in late 1485 was the Church of St John, founded in 1095 and granted rights of sanctuary in 1109, which had been officially confirmed as recently as 13 May 1453 by Henry VI. The Abbot at this time was Walter Stansted, a man in place since 1468 whose position entitled him to sit in the House of Lords amongst the Lords Spiritual.

Probably four or five days after the Battle of Bosworth, a man initially reported to have been killed in the field arrived at Colchester and claimed sanctuary at Abbot Stansted's St John's Church. The dusty traveller had at least two companions, but he was no mere fleeing soldier. Francis Lovell could boast a string of titles and was the wealthiest man in England not holding an earldom or dukedom. Viscount Lovell, Baron Holland, Baron Deincourt, Baron Grey of Rotherfield and Baron Bedale were the least crucial titles he held in the days following the battle, for Francis was also the oldest and probably closest friend of the fallen King Richard III. They had spent time together in the household of Richard Neville, Earl of Warwick as boys and although Lovell was around four years Richard's junior, they seem to have formed a lifelong bond in the cold northern castles of the Kingmaker that would last beyond Richard's death.

Lord Lovell's participation at Bosworth is not recorded. He was reported as amongst the dead in early lists from the field, but that may have been an assumption based on the charge and destruction of Richard's household cavalry, which encompassed his closest friends, including, perhaps most interestingly, Sir Robert Brackenbury, who was still willing to fight and die for a man history records ordered him to murder two boys, a task he found so odious that he refused his king. Odd, then, that such a man would still fight for a king who he knew had done the deed anyway. The assumption of Lovell's death as part of that action, unless it was deliberate misinformation, which seems unlikely, as it would allow a fugitive to escape unsought, is of interest because it suggests that some significant reason must have kept Lovell out of the fighting. Amongst the confused versions that exist it has been suggested that Lovell was sent to watch Milford on the south coast, east of Bournemouth, since Richard had received information that Tudor intended to land at Milford and simply picked the wrong one, overlooking Milford Haven in south-west Wales. If this was the case, there was time – fifteen days in fact – between Tudor's landing and Bosworth for Lovell to reach his friend. If he was at the battle, why did he fail to take a part significant enough to see him fall amongst the rest of Richard's friends? It is possible that he held back for a vitally important reason.

Colchester is around 130 miles from Market Bosworth. It was by no means the closest route to sanctuary; indeed, Lovell must have ridden past several potential havens if safety in the arms of the church was all that he sought. Colchester was, however, on a straight line that might end in Flanders, at the court of Richard's sister Margaret, but if that had been his intention, why stop at Colchester, so close to the coast and an escape? Significantly, Gipping is only 30 miles from Colchester and St John's, with its recently confirmed rights of sanctuary, might have been the perfect predesignated meeting place if things went wrong at Bosworth. The plan might have been to recover one of the Princes, perhaps Edward, who was still in England and take him to safety at Margaret's court to join his brother, perhaps even to rekindle their cause. Richard's own son and heir had died in 1484, leaving the succession unclear. Whilst it is frequently suggested that Richard named either his brother George's son Edward, Earl of Warwick or his sister's son John de la Pole, Earl of Lincoln as heir, there is no evidence that he named anyone. Negotiations for another marriage suggest a belief that he could father more children of his own and promoting a family member only to later strip them of that promotion was likely to breed resentment. Since Warwick remained debarred by his father's attainder, it is likely that John, upon whom Richard was relying heavily in the north, would have been considered Richard's heir presumptive if he had died suddenly still without a son. However, subsequent events suggest that the issue of the planned succession may not have been quite so clear-cut. If the sons of Edward IV were still alive, Richard may have planned to re-legitimise them in time if he did not have further sons to follow him, knowing that they would present the best hope for the continuance in power of the House of York. Perhaps their mother had spent her time convincing him of the benefits of that course of action. Certainly, Richard sent Thomas Langton, Bishop of St David's, and Sir John Kendall, Prior of the Order of St John, to Rome and both men would become key activists after Richard's death on behalf of Perkin Warbeck. It is possible that Richard was quietly investigating the possibility of legally restoring the boys in the future if it became necessary, or even desirable. There may have been a plan to remove the stain of his father's attainder from Edward, Earl of Warwick in order to keep the succession within the male line. Although nothing was officially recorded on the matter, events early in Henry VII's reign suggest activity in that area.

Lovell arrived in Colchester with Sir Humphrey and Thomas Stafford, two brothers from a junior branch of the Duke of Buckingham's family whose heartland lay around the city of Worcester in the west, near to the border with Wales. The Stafford brothers had remained fiercely loyal to Richard III and are believed to have fought at Bosworth, perhaps fleeing with Lovell or meeting on the road at an agreed rendezvous point. It was not long before Henry discovered the presence of these Ricardian remnants within the walls of St John's. The new king's response was surprising, but had been predicted by at least one man. Sir William Catesby was a lawyer who had transferred his allegiance from Lord Hastings to Richard following the former's execution and proved himself very valuable to his new master. He rose so high in the service of the new king that he was one of the triumvirate identified in the famous couplet pinned to the door of St Paul's by William Collingbourne in July 1484 which read 'The Catte, the Ratte and Lovell our dogge rulyth all Englande under a hogge.' Catesby was the cat, Sir Richard Ratcliffe, who died alongside Richard at Bosworth, the rat and Lovell, whose family crest included a hound, was the dog to Richard's hog, taken from the king's personal badge of a boar. Catesby had been apprehended in Leicester after the battle and executed three days later on 25 August. In his hastily prepared will, the lawyer, amongst other sentiments and jibes, most notably at the Stanley family of Henry's step-father, included an expression of hope, if not belief, that 'my lord Lovell come to grace'. Did Catesby know that Lovell now held a critically important secret?

Traditionally, the laws of sanctuary permitted the claimant forty days free from the attention of the law. At the end of that period, the alleged criminal was required to make a choice either to answer charges in court or be exiled from England forever. Some larger sanctuaries, including Westminster Abbey, were in a position to protect those claiming sanctuary for longer and the observance of this rule might also rely on the will of the law to apprehend the suspect. In Lovell's case, that will was curiously lacking. Lord Lovell and the Stafford brothers remained in sanctuary at St John's for around six months, during which time they were not subjected to any attempt by Henry to remove them. It is not known whether Lovell met someone else at Colchester, a Prince perhaps, or simply used the time to clear his head and make his plans. It is possible that he waited there for Prince Edward and perhaps the Earl of Warwick too, only to be dismayed when his charges did not arrive. The Earl of Lincoln was summoned south by Henry, and Princess Elizabeth and Edward, Earl of Warwick were to be delivered to London and into Henry's care. In Elizabeth's case, it was for her marriage. Edward was destined for a cell in the Tower. If the plan was for Lincoln to use someone from amongst his men to deliver Edward V to Lovell in Colchester, he may have found himself unable to complete the plan under the intense glare of the new regime. Colchester was close to Gipping, but also to Lincoln's family home in Wingfield, so the plan would have seen him moving the Prince into lands Lincoln and his men knew well. Lincoln's father, John de la Pole, Duke of Suffolk managed to negotiate the choppy political waters throughout the Wars of the Roses and the early Tudor years without loss or damage, a knack that may have been at the root of his nickname of 'The Trimming Duke', trimming his sails to meet prevailing political winds. It could be that Suffolk, ever cautious, put the brakes on his son's plans and refused to allow such a dangerous prize to pass through his lands in case it brought trouble to his own doorstep.

Within the second volume of *Letters and Papers Illustrative of the Reigns of Richard III and Henry VII*, edited by James Gairdner, is an account by John Flamank of a conversation he had with Sir Hugh Conway in which the latter recalled his treatment at Henry's hands during the period of Lovell's sojourn at Colchester. It seems that Conway had received word that Lovell planned to leave sanctuary and instigate a rebellion against Henry, but when Conway passed this intelligence to the new king, he was ignored, even sneered at. Flamank wrote that Conway had said to him that during 'that tyme that the lord Lovell lay in Colchester a trysty frend of myn Came to me and shewed me in councell the day and tyme of hys departyng'. Although Conway swore to his source that he would not pass the information on to any man, Conway felt obliged 'by cause of myn alegens' to inform the king. Conway went to Sir Reginald Bray who, on hearing the information, took Conway before the king to repeat it, but 'the kynge said that hyt could not be so, and resoned with me always to the contrary of my said sayynges'. Henry refused to believe Conway's intelligence report on Lovell's plans, though it was soon proven to be true. It seems likely that during the six months Lovell and the Stafford brothers spent in sanctuary, a channel of communication was opened by the new regime, or at least an attempt to initiate some negotiations had taken place, though the nature of such efforts mean that there is no surviving record of them.

Lord Lovell left Colchester some time early in 1486 and headed north to Yorkshire. At the same time, the Stafford brothers moved back to their lands in Worcestershire and began to foment revolt. The brothers managed to enter Worcester and briefly hold it before their cause broke and they fled into sanctuary again at Cullum. This time, Henry ordered Sir John Savage, who had been one of the coffin bearers at Edward IV's funeral, to break into the church and remove the brothers. Sir Humphrey was executed and Thomas vanished from the historical record, though the case led to Henry requesting that the Pope remove the right of sanctuary for cases of treason, a change that the Pope granted, excusing Henry for the violence used at Cullum. In Yorkshire, it was reported that Lovell tried to raise a rebellion in Richard's old heartlands, planning to snatch the new king as he travelled north to the city of York. It was an odd plan that never really got off the ground, but it might not have been the truth of Lovell's flight north. If one of the Princes was still in the north, protected in Richard's old stronghold by lingering affection for an old lord, Lovell may have been forced to make a dash to recover the boy when he failed to appear in Colchester. Henry may have had the same reason for his own progress north at that time. He may have learned from Lincoln or Suffolk, or perhaps even from his own negotiations with Lovell, of the boy's presence there and set off to take charge of this most dangerous young man. When Lovell was spotted around Yorkshire,

Henry could hardly disclose the reason that they were both in the same place without endangering his own precarious hold on the crown, so the story of a kidnap plot might have been built around the kernel of truth that Lovell did rush north to take custody of someone. It just wasn't Henry VII. This possibility seems to be reinforced by Lovell's immediate departure from Yorkshire to Margaret's court in Flanders, perhaps in the company of one, or both, of the sons of Edward IV.

Colchester remained a focus of attention for Henry that is hard to explain, unless it is all complete coincidence. A record within *Materials For A History of the Reign of Henry VII, Volume II*, edited by W. Campbell, notes that Philip Knighton, described as one of four 'messengers of the Exchequer', was despatched to Colchester in June or July 1486, after Lovell had left the town, 'with secret letters from the king's council'. Between 2 and 10 April 1487, Henry was on progress around East Anglia and his journey included a visit to Colchester, where he approved the appointment of a John Fynney to the parish of All Hallows the Great in London. Henry was in Colchester again in March 1489. David Baldwin noted an interesting entry in the *Calendar of Patent Rolls* in his book *The Lost Prince*. The item was a pardon issued on 5 February 1491 and the entry records:

> General pardon to Eleanor Kechyn, alias Kechen, alias Kechyne, late of Colchester, co. Essex, widow, alias 'huswyf', for offences before 18 December last, provided that she find security not to go at large during the rest of her life, but remain in the custody of her parents or nearest kinfolks.

Eleanor appears to have been the widow of Thomas Kechyn, a free burgess of Colchester in 1468 but clearly deceased by 1491. Eleanor had been in trouble with a Mark Walker, a grocer from London who claimed he was owed money, £14 10s, by Eleanor's late husband that he demanded she should pay. There is no record of the outcome of that claim, but the pardon is odd in several respects. The entry of such a pardon within the *Calendar of Patent Rolls* suggests that Eleanor had in some way offended the king. Her offence is not specified, except that it happened before 18 December 1490 and the condition that she should remain under effective house arrest for the rest of her life in the custody of her family is extraordinarily draconian. The fact that Eleanor's parents were still alive suggests that she was still quite young, but even when her parents died, she was to be required to find other close relatives to keep watch over her. It is hard to think what she may have done to warrant what might be decades of house arrest. Is it possible that she knew something about the Princes in the Tower and their possible connection to Colchester? Had she known the boys, who might have been close to her own age, when they had been in the region after 1483? Is it even possible that she had had a relationship with one of them as late as 1490, or at a time unclear to the authorities, and if so, what might it mean if she had fallen pregnant? That might warrant the harsh imposition of house arrest and a restriction on her attempts to travel. Equally, it may have no relation to the Princes in the Tower, but the accumulation of coincidences is intriguing.

Henry was in Colchester again on 19 and 20 July 1491. Abbot Stansted died in 1497 and was succeeded by William Lyndesey. The scraps of information from Colchester continued into the reign of Henry's son, Henry VIII. Within the *Letters and Papers, Foreign and Domestic, of the Reign of Henry VIII* is a note of a pardon uncovered by David Baldwin granted on 31 January 1512 to 'Richard Grey, of Colchester, alias of North Creke, Norf, yeoman or labourer. Pardon. Greenwich, 31 Jan. 3 Hen. VIII'. Grey had been the married name of Elizabeth Woodville during her first marriage and in Richard III's Parliament of 1484 she had been referred to as 'Elizabeth, late the wyf of Sir John Grey, knyght, and late callyng her selfe quene of Englond' and *Titulus Regius*, enacted by the same Parliament, mentions the 'mariage bitwixt the abovenamed King Edward and Elizabeth Grey'. It is possible that the sons of Edward IV, if they lived into Henry VII's reign, were referred to as Edward and Richard Grey in order to keep them secret, given their mother's former name (though legal name once more whilst *Titulus Regius* was in force) which their half-brother Thomas Grey, Marquis of Dorset had. The succinct pardon, again making no mention of the offence, might simply mean that this was a trivial issue barely worthy of record, or that it was so sensitive that no more information could safely be recorded.

If this Richard Grey was connected to the story of the Princes in the Tower it presents two options. It is possible the youngest Prince had made the rendezvous with Lovell at Colchester but his older brother had not. Richard may have been at Gipping with his mother and sisters at the time of Bosworth, perhaps on one of his visits back from Flanders to enjoy the familiar company of his mother and to keep the former queen assured of his continued good health and education over the sea. When news of King Richard's defeat at Bosworth arrived, it would have been no effort for him to be whisked the short distance to St John's to await Lovell and his return to Flanders. The prolonged stay in Colchester may have been enforced by the failure of Prince Edward to arrive and perhaps Henry's discovery of the younger prince's presence there with Lovell. That would explain the light hand given to Lovell, since drawing too much attention to Colchester risked exposing the secret that would cost Henry the throne he had only just won. Bishop Morton seems to have been possessed of an uncanny ability to discover the most secret information. The skill had allowed him to help Henry avoid being handed over by Pierre Landlais in Brittany and the well-informed bishop may have uncovered the secret that drew Lovell to Colchester. If so, it would have been made all but impossible for the younger Prince to slip away. Henry's belief that he had Lovell pinned down in the town, perhaps hoping to negotiate the handover of the boy, may be behind Sir Hugh Conway's complaint that Henry refused to believe Lovell would flee Colchester and incite trouble. Lord Lovell may have been forced to leave himself to recover Prince Edward as the only leverage to keep Prince Richard safe as the net tightened around them in sanctuary. If this was the case, Richard may have been left in Colchester in 1486 and could have remained there for some time.

By the time of Richard Grey's pardon in 1512, Prince Richard would have been thirty-eight. The other possibility is that the person in Colchester was a son of one of the Princes, born of a relationship with Eleanor Kechyn before 1491, placing him in his early twenties by 1512 and explaining not only the harsh terms of Eleanor's incarceration but also the king's visit to the town in July 1491, a date that might coincide with the birth of a baby conceived before 18 December 1490, the only clue to the time of Eleanor's otherwise unknown offence. The youngest, Richard, would have been 17 years old by this point, so both would have been capable of a lusty affair in their youth that produced a child. If neither Prince remained in Colchester at this time, and the timing is perhaps significant, then the presence of a baby boy born to one of them in the town was a threat, which the Tudor government would be hard pressed to deal with. Killing a baby risked losing the restraint that kept Eleanor Kechyn silent, not to mention tarnishing Henry's regime with the same brush currently being used to darken Richard III's reputation. If a close watch was kept on Colchester and the boy's progress, he might grow up ignorant of his true parentage, just another boy abandoned to the monastery, and his threat would pass. If he ever did present a hazard to the Tudor crown, he could be dealt with then, hopefully as a man, and could be discredited as a nobody. It is hard to believe the fearful and careful first Tudor king failing to deal with such a potential threat, but his treatment of others soon to appear in this story suggest that he was not cruel to children even when they did threaten him directly, so, if he felt that he had a close enough watch on Colchester, he may have allowed the boy to grow, hopeful that he would mature into obscurity.

In *The Story of Colchester*, G.H. Martin noted that Catherine of Aragon, then queen consort to Henry VIII, passed through the town 'on a pilgrimage to the shrine at Walsingham in Norfolk'. Assuming that Catherine was travelling from London, the journey to Colchester took her in almost the opposite direction to Walsingham. The queen was reportedly escorted to the Church of St John by the town bailiffs. At this early stage of his reign, Henry VIII was years away from the overweight, paranoid man who would tear a country apart in his quest for a son. In the early years, the young, athletic king was confident, enjoying his new-found freedom from his father's overbearing protectiveness and was utterly besotted by Catherine. Henry VII must have left his son aware of the Colchester issue if there was one. It is not unlikely that the cocksure Henry would spill such a secret to the woman he was blindly in love with. After all, what better way to express confidence in your position than to list the potential threats you are willing and able to comfortably tolerate? A pilgrimage to the Shrine of Our Lady of Walsingham suggests that children were on Catherine's mind, since it was traditionally a place to pray for the conception and birth of a healthy child. By 1515, Catherine had suffered the devastating loss of four babies, three sons and a daughter. If her grief led her to fear for the future if she could not produce a healthy son and heir, Our Lady of Walsingham was the natural place for her to reach out to. In February 1516, Catherine would be delivered of the future Queen Mary I. The significance of a visit to St John's in Colchester may lie in the same fear that a secret the town had held for years was becoming an ever-increasing risk to her own future and that of her husband.

5

The First Pretender

kepe due watche and warde for the suritie therof, as well by day as
by night.

Henry VII to the City of York, ordering the officials to be prepared
against the threat of a Yorkist invasion

Francis, Viscount Lovell did not remain in the shadows for long. On 16 June
1487, he took part in the Battle of Stoke Field, 6 miles south-west of
Newark-upon-Trent in Nottinghamshire. This engagement was the last
pitched battle of the Wars of the Roses, though a more traditional version
would see the struggles end in 1485, creating a neat thirty-year conflict
ended by a victorious Henry Tudor. The battle that took place two years
into his reign is frequently glossed over and whilst it might appear desirable to the Tudor king to try and ignore an armed invasion so similar to his
own less than two years after he had won the crown, the real reason that it
has been discounted as part of the long, dynastic civil war, which neither
began in 1455 nor ended in 1485, may be that it was more terrifying and
threatening than the new king wanted to let on.

Before embarking on the retelling of the adventures of a series of men and
boys who became known as 'pretenders' to Henry's throne, it is important
to establish the true meaning of the term applied to them. To modern ears,
a pretender is someone who is playing a part, acting a character. At the time
of Henry's reign, the word pretender was derived from the French word
pretendre, meaning to claim. A pretender was not the same as an imposter.

The word retained this meaning into the eighteenth century when James Stuart, son of James II, acquired the nickname of the Old Pretender. There was no accusation in this term that James was not really the son of King James II. It meant only that he claimed the crown. The blanket use of the term pretender for those who sought to depose Henry VII should therefore be taken in the same context. It does not imply that they were not who they claimed to be. In that instance, the word imposter is more fitting.

The figurehead for the rebellion Lovell was now embroiled in was a boy who had been crowned as King of England in Dublin before leaving Ireland to invade England. Tradition tells us that this boy was Lambert Simnel, an Oxford lad trained and encouraged to impersonate Edward, Earl of Warwick, the 12-year-old son of George, Duke of Clarence held in the Tower of London by Henry VII, but this story took time to crystallise and varied wildly in sources written close to the uprising. The sequence of events, at least, is clear enough. After his flight from Yorkshire, Lord Lovell reached the court of Margaret, Duchess of Burgundy. He was later joined by John de la Pole, Earl of Lincoln, who fled Henry VII's court to Flanders where Margaret plotted with them the invasion of England, providing 2,000 Swiss mercenaries under the command of the experienced Colonel Martin Schwartz.

Initially, the rebels sought to harness the affection that Ireland still held for the House of York and were warmly received. On Ascension Day, 24 May 1487, the boy they had with them as their figurehead was crowned King Edward in Dublin Cathedral before a large contingent of Irish kerns, fighters wearing no armour and hardly any clothes, joined the invasion. On 4 June, the army landed at Furness Falls in the north-west and headed for York, only to be denied entry or assistance. Forced to march south, they met Henry VII's army, commanded by John de Vere, Earl of Oxford, as it had been at Bosworth, at Stoke Field on 16 June 1487. The invaders were crushed. Lincoln was killed, Lovell was never seen again and their Irish king was captured, along with his priest-tutor. The boy was spared as a poor innocent pawn of evil men and put to work in the royal kitchens. He was identified as Lambert Simnel of Oxford and Henry was able to dismiss the plot as a farcical nonsense, particularly since the real Warwick, who the boy had been impersonating, was in Henry's custody in the Tower.

This story has long been accepted, almost unquestioned, and crucially the success of the scheme to handle the plot may have established it as a template for the dismissal and ridicule of future plots against Henry. A closer examination of the details throws up many questions and problems with this official version of events, not only with the claim that Simnel was an imposter rather than a pretender, but even with the identity he was claimed to have adopted. King Henry's response and the effect of the plot on others, as with the gravitational effect of the continued existence of the Princes in the Tower, or perhaps because of it, are key features of a reassessment of what is remembered as the Lambert Simnel Affair.

Edward, Earl of Warwick can rightfully be regarded as the third of the Princes in the Tower. His story is a sad one, tragic even, but the one that is widely known may not be the whole truth. Edward was born on 25 February 1475, the second surviving child of George, Duke of Clarence and Isabel Neville. Edward's older sister Margaret was eighteen months older than her brother. On 6 October 1476, Isabel gave birth to another boy, Richard, but her second son died on 1 January 1477. Isabel did not live to see this tragedy. She died herself on 22 December 1476, probably from consumption – tuberculosis – though her husband George would fly into a rage that ultimately led to his downfall, claiming she had been poisoned. On 12 April 1477, eighty of George's men fell upon Keyford Manor in the West Country and arrested Ankarette Twynyho, one of his late wife's ladies-in-waiting, who the duke claimed was behind her murder. Ankarette was taken to Bath, then to Cirencester the following day and by the end of the third day, she was in Warwick at George's seat of power. At nine o'clock the next morning, Ankarette stood trial for murder before the duke and was found guilty by a jury who would later insist they were forced to reach the verdict the duke demanded. Ankarette was hanged at the gallows at Myton in Warwick.

George had exercised an authority reserved for the king and his Constable, but he did not stop there. When he burst into a Council meeting to protest at his brother King Edward's execution of two men accused of sorcery at Tyburn it was simply too much. George was arrested, tried in Parliament at the beginning of 1478, attainted and executed on 18 February 1478. According to legend, he elected to be drowned in a vat of his brother's malmsey wine, though, as befit his rank, the execution took place in private and the method is not recorded. A week before his third birthday, Edward and his older sister Margaret were orphaned. Shortly after his father's execution, Edward was created Earl of Warwick by his uncle the king, a title plucked from amongst his father's but acquired through his maternal grandfather Richard Neville, Earl of Warwick, remembered as the Kingmaker. The young earl was placed under the care of Thomas Grey, Marquis of Dorset, Elizabeth Woodville's oldest son, and it is believed that he was kept in the Tower of London during the years that followed, since Dorset was Constable there, though there is no real evidence to assist in placing Edward during the five years between his father's execution and his uncle's death in 1483. When Dorset fled in 1483, Edward was taken into the care of his other uncle Richard III and, according to Mancini, was initially placed in the household of his aunt, Richard's wife, and then into the household of the Council of the North under the care of his cousin John de la Pole, Earl of Lincoln.

If Warwick had been a virtual prisoner before, he was to enjoy what appears to be a rehabilitation and liberty that must have been refreshing, though which was doomed to be short-lived. In September 1483, Richard III knighted his 8-year-old nephew at York as he accompanied his aunt and uncle on their northern progress. During the boy's time in the north there is evidence that he was being trained for a position of power that his relationship to the king might, attainder of his father aside, merit. A record in the York House Books refers to an issue upon which 'it was determyned that a letter should be consaved to be direct to the lordes of Warwik and Lincoln and othre of the counsail at Sheriff Hoton ffrome the maire and his bretherne'. Warwick's position was surely no more than nominal, but he is considered important enough here to be named as a recipient of the city's letter, even appearing ahead of Lincoln. It would seem that Richard's plan was to nurture his nephew into loyalty, perhaps even intending in the future to lift the burden of his father's attainder, since the sins of the father should not be made to weigh upon the son. Richard appears to have got on reasonably well with George. The two were raised together, being close in age and much younger than their two older brothers Edward and Edmund. The pair had shared a terrifying abandonment before an enemy army by their father at Ludlow in 1459 and a spell in exile in 1460 as the Yorkist cause faltered. The brothers had married sisters, the two daughters of Warwick the Kingmaker, who had been George's co-conspirator in deposing Edward and was Richard's former mentor. Whilst they seem to have indulged in some sibling rivalry regarding the dissection of Warwick's lands between them, it was with Edward that George fell out and whilst Richard may have disliked, perhaps even failed to understand, his brother's betrayal, *The Arrival of King Edward IV* makes it clear that Richard was instrumental in bringing his two brothers to terms when Edward and Richard returned from exile to end the Lancastrian readeption.

Any rehabilitation of the king's little nephew would need to be carefully handled. *Titulus Regius* made it clear, by explicitly passing over Warwick because of the attainder, that the boy's claim was senior to Richard's. Removal of this barrier would surely need to make it explicit that Edward was still prevented from pressing a claim to his uncle's throne. Richard's own (and only legitimate) son died in 1484, to the reported devastation of his parents. The Crowland Chronicler, generally unsympathetic to Richard, allows that when they heard of the loss whilst staying at Nottingham 'you might have seen his father and mother in a state almost bordering on madness, by reason of their sudden grief.' As has been discussed, Richard made no recorded definitive statement on the succession after this crushing blow. Lincoln would surely have been heir presumptive and Richard was negotiating another marriage which he might hope would bring another heir, but he would know that the Yorkist male line would always be preferable. The rehabilitation of Edward might have moved further to the front of his mind, as well as the possibility of Papal approval for the legitimisation of the sons of Edward IV. The real problem for young Warwick was that he lacked a personal affinity, having been orphaned at a young age, tainted by his father's treason and then consigned to obscurity for several years.

Any plans that may have been forming in the mind of King Richard for his nephews were abruptly shattered in August 1485. As previously discussed, he may have made contingency plans for his loss at Bosworth to see them safely whisked away, though they may not have succeeded. Warwick was delivered to Henry VII in London and, if it had been his home before, returned to the Tower of London, though now much more clearly as a detainee of the new regime. From 1485, at the age of 10, until his execution in 1499 aged 24, with only a brief moment in the limelight during the rebellion of 1487, Warwick was to remain a hidden, jealously guarded prisoner for fourteen years before being offered as a sacrifice to the security of the Tudor dynasty as it sought an alliance with Spanish monarchs unwilling to accept any continued Yorkist threat to the Tudor crown that courted one of their daughters. The long-held belief that Warwick was affected by some degree of learning difficulties is almost certainly untrue. The story seems to stem solely from a passage in Hall's *Chronicle*, published in 1548, melded to a Tudor willingness to allow this boy to be ridiculed and then forgotten, passing over completely any idea of him as a potential king. Hall wrote that:

> Edward Plantagenet erle of Warwike, of whome ye have heard before, beyng kept in the Towre almost fro his tender age, that is to saye, fro his first yere of the kyng to thys xv. yere, out of al copany of men & sight of beastes, in so much that he coulde not descerne a Goose from a Capon.

It is likely that Hall simply implied that a lifetime of seclusion, deprived of company and education, had left Warwick unworldly and unlikely to have tried to arrange an escape, but easy to dupe into falling for the scheme that ultimately led to his death. There is certainly no trace of any hesitation in Richard III's treatment of his nephew, preparing him for authority within the Council of the North.

On 29 November 1486, Thomas Betanson, a priest at St Sepulchre-without-Newgate, wrote to Sir Robert Plumpton that:

> Sir, as for tidings, here there are only a few. The king & queen are staying at Greenwich; the Lord Percy is at Winchester; the Earl of Oxford is in Essex; the Earl of Derby and his son are with the king. Also there is but little talk here of the Earl of Warwick now, but after Christmas they say there will be more talk of [him]. Also there are many enemies on the sea, & divers ships taken, & there are many of the kings house taken for thieves.

Quite what Betanson knew is unclear, but he was correct in his prediction that Edward, Earl of Warwick would hit the headlines in 1487. He may have been aware that Henry planned to use Warwick to negate the coming threat. Before examining his greatest impact on the national stage, it is worth considering how certain the Tudor government can have been, and even if they were certain, how correct they might have been, that the boy in the Tower was really the Earl of Warwick. A frequently neglected episode in his past adds to the feasibility of the theory of the survival of his two cousins, Edward V and Richard, Duke of York.

The attainder against George, Duke of Clarence entered in the Parliament Rolls offers two significant insights. First, it states that 'He secured an exemplification under the great seal of an agreement made between him and Queen Margaret promising him the crown if Henry VI's line failed.' The attainder recalls the fact that the Kingmaker had previously tried to replace Edward IV with George and had then abandoned that scheme in favour of a revival of the Lancastrian cause, which led to the readeption of Henry VI. The final version of this plan appointed George as the Lancastrian heir in the event that Henry VI and his son Edward of Westminster died without further issue, as both did. This made George the Lancastrian heir, as appointed by the last Lancastrian government, and after his death, that baton passed to his son, Edward, Earl of Warwick. Edward IV had reason to keep a close watch on his nephew since he was the legitimate Lancastrian heir, subject perhaps to his father's attainder. Indeed, that fact may have been at the heart of the unending rupture between Edward IV and George. Henry VII had made great play of his claim to be the heir of Lancaster, uniting the warring houses by his marriage to Princess Elizabeth. The existence of Edward, Earl of Warwick meant that Lancaster had another, far better qualified heir and more than any other reason, including his Yorkist claim, this may have been the cause of the earl's prolonged extraction from the world under the first Tudor.

The second issue revealed by the attainder may offer an explanation both for the uprising of 1487 and for the lack of record of George's location between his wife's death in December 1476 and Ankarette Twynyho's arrest in mid-April 1477. The attainder mentions a plan that George had sought to enact to protect his young son, having:

> willed and desired the Abbot of Tweybury, Mayster John Tapton, Clerk, and Roger Harewell Esquier, to cause a straunge childe to have be brought into his Castell of Warwyk, and there to have putte and kept in likelinesse of his Sonne and Heire, and that they shulde have conveyed and sent his said Sonne and Heire into Ireland, or into Flaundres, oute of this Lande, whereby he myght have goten hym assistaunce and favoure agaynst oure said Sovereigne Lorde; and for the execution of the same, sent oon John Taylour, his Servaunte, to have had delyveraunce of his said Sonne and Heire, for to have conveyed hym; the whiche Mayster John Tapton and Roger Harewell denyed the delyveraunce of the said Childe, and soo by Goddes grace his said false and untrue entent was lette and undoon.

The Abbot of 'Tweybury' was the Abbot of Tewkesbury, who had strong connections to George and had stood godfather to little Edward, Earl of Warwick
at his baptism. George and his wife Isabel's bodies would be interred at
Tewkesbury Abbey, where the bones can still be seen today in a glass box
within the Clarence Vault. It appears that George had planned to replace his
young son with a 'strange child'. Significantly, there is no mention of a need
for the boy to look like little Edward, perhaps because he was not yet well
recognised and would change as he grew so that none need know of the
imposture. The plan was that the Abbot, John Tapton and an esquire, Roger
Harewell should find a suitable boy and deliver him to Warwick Castle to
take the little boy's place. John Taylor, a servant of Clarence's, was to oversee
the smuggling away of George's real son either to Ireland or Flanders, it
seems that King Edward's information was not certain which, where he was
to be kept safe from the retribution George must have known was coming.

From the attainder, it seems that Abbot Tapton and Roger Harewell had
not found and delivered a boy to replace the earl, though it remains silent
as to whether John Taylor fulfilled his part of the plan by whisking the boy
away. Tapton and Harewell appear to have been questioned to extract their
information and it is possible that Taylor could not be found, particularly if
he went to ground after completing his task, or remained abroad with his
master's young son. The intended destination for Edward is also significant,
since Ireland and Flanders would both play a significant role in the events
of 1487 and were considered safe hiding places for the boy as early as 1478.
It is possible that Clarence travelled to Ireland during the months that his
location could not be pinpointed between December 1476 and April 1477
in order to lay the groundwork for his son's arrival, if not to deliver the boy
himself. George had been born in Dublin Castle on 21 October 1449 and
the traditionally unruly lands at least nominally governed by the kings of
England held the House of York in special regard. George's father had served
as Lord Lieutenant of Ireland and his time there was generally regarded
by the Anglo-Irish as a golden age, still close enough in the recent past to
be almost tangible. George may have seemed a natural heir to his father's
affection there and indeed he had held the position of Lord Lieutenant
since 1462. The ready support of the Earl of Kildare was a key feature of the
rebellion in 1487 and it seems possible that this most powerful of Anglo-
Irish lords would have made the perfect guardian for George's son. If this
was the purpose of George's several months off the map, then it suggests he

knew what would follow was going to be dangerous enough to be a risk to his life and the safety of his young son.

Edward IV may have been uncertain of the boy he gave custody of to his step-son Thomas Grey, Marquis of Dorset, or he may have felt certain his brother had not been able to complete his plan, but there must have been a reason for the months of delay between Isabel's death and George's out-raged response. If the story of George's plan was well known, which it must have been amongst the gentry, nobility and Lords Spiritual who attended Parliament or were connected with the government, then Henry VII may have had cause to wonder about the boy he held in the Tower, though Richard III didn't seem to doubt his identity and that may have been suffi-cient for Henry to have ignored any lingering doubt, if he knew of any. This fascinating incident, though, adds another layer to the events of 1487 that helps explain why Henry VII may have felt so threatened. One final piece of evidence that makes the matter even less clear is an entry in Margaret of Burgundy's household accounts at Mechlen that records eight flagons of wine bought for the St Rombout's Day feast in 1486 as a gift for 'the son of Clarence from England'. There is no other mention of this boy, who could conceivably have been an illegitimate son of Clarence, though no such child is ever mentioned anywhere else, or a fabricated entry to support a later conspiracy, but an apparently innocuous entry in a household account would hardly be a stirring contribution to a plot to unseat a king.

The possibility that Warwick had been spirited away is given further weight by the Burgundian chronicler Jean Molinet, who may have had access to information from Margaret, Duchess of Burgundy. Molinet wrote towards the end of the fifteenth century that 'one little branch, engendered by a Royal tree, had been nurtured amongst the fruitful and lordly shrubs of Ireland', before identifying his 'little branch' as Edward, Earl of Warwick, who was also the figurehead for the planned revolt. *The Annals of Ulster* also record that a 'son', presumably meaning grandson, of the Duke of York, presumably Richard, the father of Edward IV, George and Richard III, amongst others, 'was exiled at this time with the Earl of Kildare' during the year 1487, though it does not offer a name to help identify the boy, who might have been Warwick, but could also have been Edward V or Richard, Duke of York.

Worrying news must have begun to arrive at Henry's court in the early part of January 1487. When Council met at Sheen Palace it was surrounded

by a series of events that betray a mounting sense of concern at the increasing threat. Henry issued a proclamation that 'pardoned and excused from
punishment all who were accused of treason or any other crime' in what
must have been an attempt to offer those either already embroiled in the
plot or considering joining it a way out with the comfort of a royal pardon.
Messengers were despatched to Ireland and to the court of Margaret of
Burgundy to discourage those who might seek to aid Henry's Yorkist enemies and to protest to Margaret at her part in the brewing threat. Polydore
Vergil records that shortly after the Council meeting the Earl of Warwick
was brought out of the Tower to a service at St Paul's that was little more
than a staged exercise to exhibit the boy and so curtail any uprising in his
name. If Henry had received news that he was under threat from Edward,
Earl of Warwick, who was at large and on the brink of invading, he must
have been slightly confused since he knew he was holding that very boy
within the Tower.

There is another possible explanation that is worth a close examination
and which ties in, from this point onwards, with the fate of the Princes
in the Tower. Vergil records that following the service at St Paul's, the earl
'spoke with many important people, and especially with those of whom the
king was suspicious, so that they might the more readily understand that
the Irish had based their new rebellion on an empty and spurious cause'.
This appears a natural enough response to a threat in the boy's name that
relied on a belief that he was free, but the conspirators surely knew that
Henry might take this apparently obvious step and that their entire plan
would be undermined with the simplest of single strokes. It is not clear
exactly what information was widely known in London, but it is certain
that Henry and his government, not least his Chancellor John Morton, who
was also Archbishop of Canterbury by this date, would have been keeping
as tight a lid on the flow of rumour and truth as they possibly could. It is
not impossible that the Tudor government employed smoke and mirrors to
try and undermine the very serious threat that their reaction betrays was
understood to be in full flow. Edward, Earl of Warwick may have been used
as a part of that deception.

Thomas Betanson's note at the end of 1486 was apparently proving pro-
phetic as early as 13 February 1487, when *Concilia Marnae Britanniae et
Hiberniae* records a trial at a convocation of the Province of Canterbury at
St Paul's Cathedral in London. The entry explains:

A certain Sir William Symonds, was produced, a priest, of the age of twenty-eight years, as he declared, in the presence of the said lords and prelates and clergy who were there, as well as the mayor, aldermen, and sheriffs of the city of London. He publicly admitted and confessed that he took and carried off to Ireland the son of a certain [blank], organ maker of the University of Oxford, the which son was there reputed to be the Earl of Warwick, and that afterwards he was with Lord Lovell in Furness Falls. These, and other things were admitted by him in the same place. The said most reverend father in Christ asked the aforesaid mayor and sheriffs, that the above mentioned Will. Symonds be brought unto the Tower of London, to be kept there for him, since the same most reverend father was holding another of the company of the said William, and had [space for] but one person in his manor of Lambeth.

This trial is dated as taking place before the invasion that would follow in the summer but holds several significant pieces of information. First, the priest produced was named as William Symonds and the later, official story would name Richard Symons as the lone priest who would pluck Lambert from the obscurity of his Oxford tradesman father's house to train him to pretend to be a Yorkist heir. The name of Lambert Simnel's father is left blank and in fact, the name Lambert Simnel is not mentioned at all, only the imposture as Edward, Earl of Warwick. The reference to being 'with Lord Lovell in Furness Falls' is odd, since that is where the invasion landed, so unless the pair met there some months earlier, before Lovell left for Flanders, perhaps to sound out support in the area, it makes little sense. The 'most reverend father in Christ' referred to is John Morton, Archbishop of Canterbury and he requests that the priest be held at the Tower because he only has room for one detainee at Lambeth and the suggestion is clearly that this space is already filled by a prisoner more valuable or dangerous than this priest.

It seems entirely likely that this account was written up later and has been ascribed, either at the time or in later reproductions, to the wrong year. This is possible, since the medieval New Year fell on 25 March rather than 1 January, or because the misinformation machinery of early Tudor government chose to ascribe to itself a degree of control over the revolt that it did not in fact possess. If the trial was a year later, in February 1488, then William Symonds would in fact be the 'Richard Symons' who had supposedly led

Lambert Simnel on his quest for a crown. The reference to being at Furness Falls with Lord Lovell would refer to the invasion's landing in 1487 and the presence of a more senior prisoner in Morton's household can only be a boy who might be king. Who else would be more important than the man who steered the boy to this fate? If the boy was well known to be a commoner, not least because the true Earl of Warwick was demonstrably in the Tower already, then why the need to keep him so close to the chief agent of Tudor government? There remain more questions than answers, but if this trial did take place in 1488, then the meat of the uprising has been skipped.

Following the Council meeting at Sheen Palace, at which the bulk of the business appears to have been concerned with the plot that the king knew was in motion, there were several occurrences that make little sense. John de la Pole, Earl of Lincoln, who had been heir presumptive to Richard III, was at court under close watch. Vergil wrote that Henry caused Edward to talk 'especially with those of whom the king was suspicious' and Lincoln must have been right at the very top of that list. John de la Pole had been Warwick's guardian in the north during Richard III's reign and would surely have known the boy better than any other at court. The new king must have held his breath as Lincoln spoke with his former ward, desperately trying to discern any sign of deceit or concern in Lincoln. It was almost immediately after this performance at St Paul's that Lincoln fled from court and made a dash across the Channel to his aunt Margaret in Flanders. What Henry made of this sudden turn of events and why Lincoln ran are matters of conjecture. When Lincoln met the boy at St Paul's, it was either the Warwick he had known or it was not the same boy.

If he recognised his former ward, then his flight might mean he feared the suspicion he was under as eyes drilled into the pair whilst they spoke. If the boy was not the same one he had known, then perhaps his task was to ensure that the Tudor government accepted the wrong boy, delivered by Lincoln from the north whilst the real Warwick was whisked away to safety. It may also be that Margaret, now in a position to challenge a man she would devote the rest of her life to removing from her family's throne, was ready to play a hand previously unknown to most. If George had succeeded in smuggling his son away in 1478, he must have told someone he trusted. Richard was too close to Edward IV perhaps, but Margaret was also close to George in age and they had spent most of their childhood growing up together at Fotheringhay. The confusion about George's intentions relating to Ireland or Flanders may have been because he sent his son to the Earl of Kildare in Ireland but let Margaret know of the plan in case he should fail to survive his challenge to Edward IV. The only other unlikely possibility is that Lincoln snatched Warwick away with him, and there were some rumours before and after this point that Warwick had been murdered or had escaped the Tower, which the government was hardly likely to verify. Whatever the reason, it was a serious increase in the threat posed by the plot and a severe setback to Henry.

Another key feature that must have been discussed at the Council meeting at Sheen was Elizabeth Woodville. Amid all the other activity after the meeting closely related to the problems brewing for Henry, he stripped his mother-in-law of all her possessions, saw her retired to Bermondsey Abbey and left her so poorly provided for there that, according to her will, she was all but penniless, with nothing to leave her daughters but her blessings. Elizabeth withdrew to Bermondsey on 12 February 1487 and, apart from rare visits to court for state occasions, remained there until her death on 8 June 1492. Polydore Vergil wrote that the treatment of the queen's mother was a direct result of Henry's outrage that she had allowed her daughters to be placed into the danger of Richard III's custody after promising the oldest to Henry in marriage. Three years after the event and eighteen months after becoming king seems a prolonged period of simmering for such a burning disgust at his mother-in-law's behaviour. All the former queen's properties were taken from her and given to her daughter, the current queen, though to all intents and purposes, this meant that as her husband they were Henry's. In the absence of some corroboration, Vergil's story simply does not ring true and the timing is suggestive at least that the decision was related to the growing threat Henry was about to confront. Francis Bacon's analysis in the early seventeenth century that it was 'very probable there was some great matter against her, which the king, upon reason of policie, and to avoid envy, would not publish' seems far more likely. Add to this that Thomas Grey, Marquis of Dorset, Elizabeth's oldest son, was also arrested and placed in the Tower and the belief that the Woodville faction were associated with the plot becomes more certain. Henry reportedly asserted that if Thomas was as faithful as he protested, then he would not object to a little time as a prisoner to prove his loyalty to the king.

The apparent involvement of the Woodville faction, or at least the fear of it, returns us to the potential gravitational effect of the continued existence of the Princes in the Tower, working on those who were aware of it and affecting their actions. The first problem with the traditional story of an imposter posing as Edward, Earl of Warwick, or even with the real Earl of Warwick having been hidden away or freed after Henry became king, is simply that the Woodville family would have no interest whatsoever in such a scheme. If her sons with Edward IV were dead, Elizabeth probably had the best position she could hope for as mother to the king's wife. It is unthinkable that Elizabeth would risk that position to favour the cause of a boy just nearing his twelfth birthday who was the son of a man who had tried to destroy her. The extent of any personal hatred between Elizabeth and George is not well documented, but George had certainly tried to unseat her husband, dispossessing her children in the process. He may have given air to the story of Edward's illegitimacy and cast aspersions upon the validity of Elizabeth's marriage to Edward. Bishop Stillington, who reportedly revealed the pre-contract story to Richard III, was an associate of George's after the fall of his previous patron, the Kingmaker Earl of Warwick, and would spend time in prison when George was arrested. It has long been suspected that Edward IV was pressed to deal with his perennially troublesome brother by his wife. There was no reason at all for Elizabeth and her oldest son to risk their positions to try and place the son of George, Duke of Clarence on the throne. If it was feared, rumoured or by now known that the rebellion would be led by one of Edward IV's sons, the fear of Woodville involvement makes perfect sense. Henry VII may have exhibited Edward, Earl of Warwick at St Paul's as a destabilising diversion against a plot he knew favoured another Edward: Edward V.

Bernard André, the blind French friar-poet who would become tutor to Henry's son Prince Arthur, epitomises the confused messages surrounding this episode before the traditional story took its more solid and enduring form. Writing of the lead up to the Lambert Simnel revolt, André explains with some disdain that:

> While the cruel murder of King Edward the Fourth's sons was yet vexing the people, behold another new scheme that seditious men contrived. To cloak their fiction in a lie, they publicly proclaimed with wicked intent that a certain boy born the son of a miller or cobbler was the son of Edward the Fourth. This audacious claim so overcame them that they dreaded neither God nor man as they plotted their evil design against

the king. Then, after they had hatched the fraud among themselves, word came back that the second son of Edward had been crowned king in Ireland. When a rumour of this kind had been reported to the king, he shrewdly questioned those messengers about every detail. Specifically, he carefully investigated how the boy was brought there and by whom, where he was educated, where he had lived for such a long time, who his friends were, and many other things of this sort. Various messengers were sent for a variety of reasons. At last [blank space] was sent across, who claimed that he would easily recognise him if he were who he claimed to be. But the boy had already been tutored with evil cunning by persons who were familiar with the days of Edward, and he very readily answered all the herald's questions. To make a long story short, through the deceptive tutelage of his advisors, he was finally accepted as Edward's son by many prudent men, and so strong was this belief that many did not even hesitate to die for him.

This version of the story is confusing. André is clear earlier in his writing and in this passage that Richard III had murdered his nephews, lamenting 'After the tyrant, safe in his London stronghold, slew the lords he knew were faithful to his brother, he ordered that his unprotected nephews secretly be dispatched with the sword.' Here, André offers another version of the fate of the Princes in the Tower, but asserts that they were certainly dead in 1483. Despite such certainty, he explains that people were prepared to believe that the threatened revolt was, in fact, in the name of a son of Edward IV. André compiled his work between 1500 and 1502, but he had been in England for some months by the time of the rumours he reports, so was an eyewitness to the events. Although he claims that the second son of Edward IV was the figurehead of this uprising, it is well documented that the boy making an attempt on Henry's crown was called Edward, as will be seen as the story progresses. This can only mean Edward V. André appears uncertain of the boy's father's occupation and makes no mention of Oxford, the priest Richard (or William) Symons or even the name Lambert Simnel.

An interesting feature of this account is the recollection that someone, probably a herald, was sent to Ireland with the express purpose of identifying the boy held up as a son of Edward IV. The blank space was meant to be filled if André could recall or rediscover the name of the herald, but it was never completed. The space might also have been left blank because the man possessed information none wanted him sought out to discover. Strikingly, the man was the last of a stream of messengers sent and he claimed that he could definitively identify the boy, suggesting that he knew at least one of the sons of Edward IV well enough to be trusted to identify him, as a royal herald of some years' experience might have. Far from returning and dismissing the boy as an imposter, André is compelled to record that the boy was accepted as a son of Edward IV, perhaps even by this herald who had known him, by 'many prudent men'. For one such as André who wrote, and was employed to write, effusive panegyric about the first Tudor king, the admission that so many believed the boy who sought to unseat Henry VII was the true son of Edward IV – and that can only have been Edward V – is conspicuous and important. André was in England at the time of the events he describes, was writing a decade later, when the official story should have been well established and was writing for the man with the highest interest possible in portraying the boy as an imposter, yet the blind poet tells us he was acknowledged, seemingly by men who would have known, as the son of Edward IV.

Easter 1487 saw Henry stepping up preparations for the invasion he knew was coming. The king moved into the east, visiting Bury St Edmonds, then Norwich and afterwards making a pilgrimage to the Shrine of Our Lady of Walsingham. The Duke of Suffolk, Lincoln's father, escorted Henry as far as Norwich and on 7 April the king ordered that the beacons on the east coast be repaired and fully manned as he assembled a fleet at Harwich. It was clear that he expected a landing from Flanders in Norfolk or Suffolk, lands Lincoln knew well and could rely upon for strong support. The duke was surely led around behind the king to offer some sense of security against his son's landing. After his pilgrimage, Henry travelled to Cambridge and then to Huntingdon, where he wrote a letter to York recorded in the city's Civic Records instructing the officials there to keep a close watch for rebels who 'might by some crafty meanes and by espiell doo som reproche or vilany to our Citie' and to 'kepe due watche and warde for the suritie therof, as well by day as by night'.

Having moved to Northampton and on to Coventry, Henry wrote again to York on 3 May advising them that he had received intelligence that the rebels had left Flanders heading west, so that a landing in the east and an immediate threat to York were no longer likely. Henry gave them permission to stand down their watches but the tone of his letter seems to betray a degree of concern at the lingering threat as he asked the city to remain loyal and promised the officials there they could 'assure yourself that for this true acquitail ye have beene of unto us, wherin we pray you to continewe, we shal be soo good and gracious souverain lord unto you'. By 8 May, Henry was at Kenilworth Castle, writing again to York to thank them for 'the good provision and preparacion of vitaill and othre stuff for such men of wirship and theire retenues, as we late commaunded to goo thidder for the surtye and defense of our Citie', demonstrating that Henry had been gathering lords and men at York in preparation for a threat to the city, believing it a likely and perhaps susceptible target for the rebels. With the threat moved westward, most of the men were ordered that way, Henry telling the mayor 'we have licensid suche personnes as we comaunded to make ther repar thiddre, to depart thens for a season and to resort to you agene if the caas shall so require'. However, the king also advised the city that 'our cousin the Erle of Northumberland entendeth hastily to be in the cuntrey nigh unto you, which we doubt not wol gladly assiste and strength you at all tymes if ye desire hym so to doo'. It seems the king did not feel entirely able to trust York if it were put to the test but also that he didn't want Northumberland at his side following his performance, or lack thereof, at Bosworth twenty-one months earlier.

6

A King in Dublin

My Masters of Ireland, you will crown apes at length.
King Henry VI to the Lords of Ireland, recorded in
The Book of Howth

On 5 May 1487, Lincoln, Lovell and the boy they championed landed in Dublin to a rapturous welcome. Only the town of Waterford and Thomas Butler, Earl of Ormond, son of the staunchly Lancastrian James Butler, held out against the new authority. The Yorkists brought with them 2,000 professional mercenaries bankrolled by Margaret, Duchess of Burgundy and commanded by Martin Schwartz. Their positive welcome was largely due to Gerald FitzGerald, 8th Earl of Kildare. Earls of Kildare had a strong association with the Yorkist cause from Richard, Duke of York's time as Lord Lieutenant and it was the present Earl who was rumoured to have taken in the son of George, Duke of Clarence. The welcome might be explained by Kildare's knowledge that George's son was the true Earl of Warwick but he would have offered a similar welcome to Edward V as a grandson of Richard, Duke of York if that was who landed in Ireland with his cousin Lincoln. If Clarence's son had been in Flanders before they left, it is possible that he travelled with them as well as Edward V, his father's connection to Ireland and his personal connection to Kildare bolstering his older cousin's position. If there were two Yorkist boys in Ireland, that would serve to explain later confusion over the pretender's age and identity, but it would have represented a huge risk to place two such important eggs in one basket, unless it was the weight of those eggs combined that was to give the best chance of victory.

A key event referred to by André, and which places the visit of the messenger intended to identify the pretender as a fraud he mentions shortly after this date, was a coronation ceremony at Dublin Cathedral on 24 May 1487, the day of the Feast of the Ascension. A gold circlet was taken from a statue of the Virgin Mary to act as a crown and later reports confirm that the ceremony was well attended. As well as Lincoln and Lord Lovell, Kildare played a prominent role and several Anglo-Irish lords were present. The Irish clergy were well represented, with Ottaviano Spinelli del Palacio, Archbishop of Armagh, Walter FitzSimon, Archbishop of Dublin and the bishops of Meath, Roche, Cloyne and Kildare in attendance. The Pope would later acquiesce to Henry's request for a bull of excommunication for all those involved in Ireland, only to be lifted if offenders submitted to Henry and received his pardon. It was reported that the crowned boy was carried on the shoulders of the giant William Darcy of Platten, nicknamed Great Darcy, a cousin of Lord Darcy of Knayth, so that the crowd could see their new king better.

The boy was certainly crowned King Edward, though the use of regnal numbers, which might confirm whether this was Edward V or Edward VI, is sadly lacking in the Irish records. The existence of two personalities named Edward who might be used to unseat Henry frustratingly muddies the matter and cannot easily be cleared up to definitely confirm who this figurehead was, or was meant to be. The solitary contemporary record that uses a regnal number appears in the *York House Book* and refers to the letter sent to that city by the pretender. The note above the entry identifies it as a copy of a letter sent 'in the name of their King calling himself King Edward the vj*t*.' The problem with this account is that York was known to be under close watch and would have been hard pressed to deviate from the official story that the invader was posing as Edward, Earl of Warwick and so would have been crowned Edward VI in Dublin. The entry may date from just after the rebellion, when taking such a risk would have been pointless, but it is also possible that a reference to Edward V was doctored. It was hardly a stretch to add a 'I' after the original reference to keep Henry's retribution at bay. Without any other reference to a regnal number it is hard to be entirely clear who this Edward was, or was supposed to be. There is an interesting passage in Vergil on this rebellion, which explains 'se uenisse ad

restituendum in regnum Edwardum puerum nuper in Hybernia coronatum'
in relation to the plot to replace Henry with Edward. The verb 'restituere'
that Vergil used means to restore, reinstate or re-establish. It is an odd choice
of verb to describe what was meant to be the use of an imposter to place
Edward, Earl of Warwick on the throne, since he would not be restored to
anything, but established anew. Only Edward V would have been reinstated
to the throne, and a coronation in Dublin would not have been out of place
since Edward V was proclaimed king but never crowned in England before
being set aside in favour of his uncle. There is suggestive evidence both that
the boy-king was crowned Edward V and Edward VI with no clear resolution available. That André and Vergil, two Tudor-sponsored writers, chose to
claim that the boy was meant to be, and was confirmed by many as being,
a son of Edward IV, as André insisted, and that the plot aimed to *restore* him
to the throne, as Vergil noted, are indications that the traditional story of a
plot in favour of Edward, Earl of Warwick was perhaps a red herring, meant
to throw a shadow over an attempt to bring Edward V out of hiding to take
back his throne.

Within a fortnight of the coronation in Dublin, the Yorkist force had
landed at Furness Falls in the north-west on Whit Monday, 4 May, where
they were met by Sir Thomas Broughton and a few others, but the response
was somewhat lacklustre. The Swiss mercenary contingent had been swol-
len by around 5,000 Irish kerns supplied by Kildare and led by his brother
Thomas FitzGerald. Lightly armed and barely armoured, many bare chested
and bare legged, the Irish warriors must have appeared wild and probably
discouraged many from taking up the Yorkist cause. Two days later the Earl
of Northumberland wrote to York to tell them he was on his way to them
following the landing of the rebels:

> which God helping I entend to resist, and for the same intent wolbe in
> the citie of York toward them upon sonday next comyng; therfore I desire
> and pray you to cause provision of vitaill to be redy ayenst that tyme for
> such people as shall come and be ther with me, also that ye incontinent
> after the sight herof woll provide for the sure keping and saufgard of the
> said Citie.

The close watch on York was swiftly resumed in what must have been an
attempt to block the city from offering any support to the Yorkists.

The uncertainty and fear of being under such intense scrutiny must have been heightened as the Yorkist army moved east toward the surest hope of assistance and a letter from 'King Edward' was received in York:

By the King.
To our trusty and wellbiloved the Maiour, his brethren and comunaltye of our Citie of York.

Trusty and wellbiloved we grete you wele, and for somoch as we beene comen within this oure realme, not oonlly, by goddes grace, to atteyne oure right of the same, but also for the relief and well of our said realme, you and all othre our true subgiettes, whiche hath bene gretely injurid and oppressid in default of nowne ministracon of good rules and justice, desire therfor, and in our right herty wise pray you that in the behalve ye woll shew unto us your good aides and favourez. And where we and such power as we have broght with us, by meane of travayle of the see and upon land, beene gretely weryed and laboured, it woll like you that we may have relief and ease of logeing and vitailles within oure citie ther, and soo to depart and truly pay for that as we shall take. And in your soo dooing ye shall doo things unto us of right acceptable pleaser, and for the same find us your good and souverain lord at all tymes herafter. And of your disposicions herin to acertain us by the bringer. Yevene undre our signet at Masham the viii day of Juyn.

This was the letter noted in the *York House Book* as being from the person calling himself 'King Edward VI', though the letter itself gives no name or regnal number and provides no insight into whether it was from a king returning to reclaim his realm or to press a previously untested claim to the throne. Copies of the letter were swiftly sent in all directions, including to Northumberland and the king. The city was instructed, as recorded in the *York Civic Records*, to prepare its defences and to deny entry to any of the Yorkist force.

Two days later, the same records tell of a skirmish at Tadcaster, just 10 miles south-west of York. Lord Clifford, heir to an inveterate enemy to the House of York, led his men toward Bramham Moor where the Yorkists were encamped. This Lord Clifford was Henry, the 10th Baron, son of the Lord Clifford who had avenged his own father's death at the First Battle of St Albans in 1455 by killing the 17-year-old Edmund, Earl of Rutland, brother of Edward IV and Richard III. The 9th Baron Clifford, John, had been killed at Ferrybridge before the Battle of Towton in 1461 when his son Henry was 7 years old. John Clifford was attainted and his son Henry was sent into hiding by those loyal to Clifford, remaining utterly incognito for twenty-four years, until his father's attainder was reversed after Bosworth. Henry Clifford therefore had deeply personal reasons for going after a potential scion of the House of York. His story also shows that it was perfectly possible for a noble boy to vanish from medieval England for a quarter of a century if needed.

Lord Clifford lodged at Tadcaster, near to the rebels, 'but the same night the Kinges ennymes lying negh to the same towne, cam upon the said Lord Clifford folkes and made a grete skrymisse ther'. In the confusion, many men from York were killed as the rest escaped back to the city and Lord Clifford's cases were stolen away. A further two days later, on 12 June, two Lords Scrope, of Bolton and Masham, tried to launch an attack on York but failed to break through the barred gates. The Scrope lords were both loyal Yorkists; Lord Scrope of Bolton's second wife was godmother to Edward V and the younger brother of Lord Scrope of Masham had been married to Edward IV's daughter Cecily during Richard III's reign, but the union had been dissolved by Henry VII. The attack may only have been meant as a diversion, though, as it was swiftly withdrawn, but caused Lord Clifford and the Earl of Northumberland to turn back north to protect the city. Perhaps it also offered Northumberland a chance to avoid the battle that was by now inevitable.

As it traversed Sherwood Forest, the Yorkist army bumped into some of King Henry's cavalry and defeated them in another small skirmish that must have further increased their confidence. On 15 June, the army crossed the Trent and camped at East Stoke. The following morning, the two armies faced each other at East Stoke and the better-armed and organised Tudor army, commanded by the Earl of Oxford, eventually routed the Yorkist force. Many of the Irish fell, as did Martin Schwartz, Thomas FitzGerald and John de le Pole, Earl of Lincoln. The aftermath of what André described as 'the second triumph of Henry the Seventh' is as interesting as what came before and serves to demonstrate again the holes in the traditional story of Lambert Simnel's invasion. The *York City Records* offer their account of the battle as follows:

The Satterday next after the fest of Corpus Christi, the King lying with a grete powre divyded in three hostez beyond Newark, the wayward of the same in which th'erl of Oxford, the Lord Straunge, Sir John Chyney, th'erl of Shrewsbury, and many othre to the nombre of xMl met with the Lordes of Lincolne and Lovell with othre many noblez, as well of Ynglisshmen as Irisshmen, and othres to the nombre of xx Ml, of the more beyond Newauk, and there was a soore batell, in the which th'erl of Lincolne and many othre, as well Ynglisshmen as Irish, to the nombre of v Ml were slayne and murdred; the Lord Lovell was discomfotid and fled, with Sir Thomas Broghton and many othre, and the child which they callid ther King was takyn and broght unto the Kinges grace, and many othre in grete nombre which was juged to deth at Lincolne and othre placs theraboute.

André offered scornfully that:

That miserable kinglet of scoundrels, who had been crowned in Ireland, as I said before, was captured there in battle. When asked what audacity had possessed him to dare commit such a great crime, he admitted that infamous persons of his own rank had coerced him. Then, questioned about his family and the status of his parents, he confessed that they were thoroughly mean individuals every one, with low occupations. In fact, they are not worthy to be included in this history.

André contradicts himself by claiming the boy and his family did not merit recording, since he had already described him as 'the son of a miller or cobbler', and although he informs his reader that the boy confessed his family were 'thoroughly mean individuals every one, with low occupations', he also claims that the boy was coerced by 'infamous persons of his own rank' when the invasion had been instigated, planned, financed and supported by Margaret, Duchess of Burgundy and John de la Pole, Earl of Lincoln, both members of the House of York. Was this the boy's 'own rank'?

Vergil recorded of the aftermath of the battle that:

Young Lambert the pretender was taken, together with his tutor Richard, but the lives of both of them were spared, because the former was innocent and, thanks to his youth, had done no wrong, as being incapable of doing anything in his own right, and the latter was a priest. And yet, so that he might learn (as they say) that a rock hangs over the head of the man who has cast it aloft, he was remanded to perpetual darkness and chains. Lambert is still alive, made a falconer by the king after he had turned the spit for a while in the royal kitchen and performed other base tasks.

This represents the official version of the falling apart of the revolt, written twenty-five years later and not published for a further twenty years. The account within *Leland's Collectania* states that 'ther was taken the Lad that his Rebells called King Edwarde, whos name was indeed Lambert, by a Vaylent – and a gentle Esquier of the King's Howse, called Robert Bellingham.' A more contemporary version contained within the *Heralds' Memoir* also refers to the boy's capture by Robert Bellingham, but states that the boy's name was given as John.

A continental chronicle written by Adrien de But suggests that the boy was not captured at all, claiming that:

> the Earl of Lincoln and Martin Zwarte fell with about 5,000 men. But the king, who acted in a kindly way towards foreigners, commanded that all the prisoners from Ireland should be strangled. The young Duke of Clarence was also captured, whom the Earl of Suffolk, carefully delivered, and he fell back with him to Guisnes.

The use of the title Earl of Suffolk dates the account to some years after the battle, since it refers to Lincoln's younger brother Edmund de la Pole, who did not obtain that title until some time later. Nevertheless, the account names the pretender as Warwick, though using his father's title of Duke of Clarence, and has the boy spirited away to Guisnes by Edmund, where James Tyrell had been posted by Richard III. The possibility that the boy at the head of this invasion was in fact Edward V is dealt a further blow by the fact that Sir Edward Woodville, brother of Elizabeth the former queen, took the field for the king. Whilst he is unlikely to have done so in opposition to his nephew, he perhaps had little choice and clearly his sister had enough involvement in the plot to warrant her retirement to a monastery.

The official account of Lambert Simnel's life after the revolt is as described by Vergil. After a period in the royal kitchens, he is recorded as a falconer to Henry VII, probably to Henry VIII and to Sir Thomas Lovell, at whose funeral in May 1525 a 'Lambert Symnell, yeoman' was recorded in attendance. The list of yeomen issued with livery cloth for the funeral recorded in *Letters and Papers, Foreign and Domestic, Henry VIII, Vol. IV* ends 'broche turners, scullions, housekeepers, labourers, carters, Lambert Symnell, the schoolmaster, and Jack the lad in the kitchen'. Francis Bacon, in *The Reign of Henry VII*, believed that this boy was kept alive and at court 'as a continual spectacle before peoples' eyes of how they had been fooled, and as a kind of remedy against the like enchantments of people in time to come' and it seems entirely possible that Henry and the wily Morton might concoct a scheme by which a threat from Edward V was destabilised by official statements linking it instead to Edward, Earl of Warwick, serving both to undermine the plot and to mark Warwick as a threat in order to justify his continued detention. If the government remained uncertain as to the fate of the Princes in the Tower and feared a future uprising in their name, if indeed this was not already the first, then this established a template to use again in future attempts. A simple roll of the eyes, a tut, a throw away 'Not another one' and a later revelation of humble origins and a baseless lie would serve as a shield against future threats that might be lifted in protection at any time. It is also possible that the Yorkist invasion of 1487 had in its possession the real Earl of Warwick and that Henry held a counterfeit boy inserted a decade earlier to pretend to be the Earl of Warwick. Alternatively, this was a case of a boy from Oxford impersonating a senior member of the House of York well enough to fool men who would have known better. Each scenario leaves unanswerable questions.

The support for the uprising is curious and cannot be satisfactorily reconciled. If Elizabeth Woodville's loss of her possessions and retirement to a monastery relate to this uprising, as seems likely, it can only have been in the belief that it would place one of her sons with Edward IV on the throne. Even ignoring the animosity between her and George, Duke of Clarence, she would never have championed Edward, Earl of Warwick at the expense of her own daughter's and new grandson's positions. The only route that increased her authority was if one of her sons was seated on the throne and her belief in that outcome is the only reasonable explanation for her perceived support of this rebellion. However, this aim cannot be reconciled with her brother Sir Edward Woodville's appearance amongst the king's army at the Battle of Stoke Field, unless Sir Edward only knew the king's official version of events and Elizabeth Woodville had been successfully silenced very early in the affair. Just as with her emergence from sanctuary in 1484, the former queen's fate in 1487 is easy to understand if we believe, as plenty still did then, not least Henry VII, that her sons might still be alive. The Burgundian chronicler Molinet mentions an episode that may have been overlooked by Tudor sponsored writers in which Sir Edward Woodville was leading men through Sherwood Forest to meet up with Northumberland before the latter's volte-face and return to York caused Sir Edward to retreat slowly through Sherwood back to the king, suggesting that he was unwilling to directly attack the Yorkist force. Had he been making for Northumberland's contingent to support his nephew's invasion, only for the earl to back out at the last moment?

Even harder to fathom is the decision of John de la Pole, Earl of Lincoln to support a rebellion if it was in favour of an imposter pretending to be Warwick. Lincoln and his family appeared, in the early months of Henry's reign, to have ridden out the storm. They were not deprived of lands or titles and can hardly have expected anything other than the close watch they were subjected to, but time would relax that glare. Instead, after the exhibition of Henry's Earl of Warwick at St Paul's, Lincoln ran for the coast to join a revolt instigated by his aunt in Burgundy. Simply by leaving England he was risking everything that he and his entire family had. To do so for a boy that he knew was an imposter is unfathomable, unless he had only stayed in England to make sure the real Warwick was alive and well to be made king if they succeeded, but he would also know then that they crowned and proclaimed a fake king in Dublin. If Lincoln wanted Warwick as king, it can only have been a demonstration of the utmost loyalty to the male line of the House of York. Warwick was a boy with no powerbase and no support in the country, which would be Henry's reason for claiming that he was the figurehead chosen by the revolt. Not only that, but Warwick was still barred from the succession by his father's attainder. Lincoln himself, by now in his mid-twenties, had been Richard III's heir presumptive after the death of the Prince of Wales. His own claim was far superior to Warwick's, albeit through a female line, and he had a regional powerbase both in the north and the east. Why would Lincoln not press his own claim? There were only two figures with better Yorkist claims to the throne than Lincoln: Edward V and Richard, Duke of York. If Lincoln supported an Edward, it seems far more likely to have been Edward V, now conveniently re-legitimised by Henry VII, than Edward, Earl of Warwick, who at best might provide Lincoln a few years in which to act as Lord Protector, but after that, the future would be far less certain. The only circumstance in which Lincoln's bid for an imposter might make sense is if he wanted the crown for himself, but that aim would have been better served in the open.

The motives for the Earl of Kildare's ready involvement, which drew in most of the Anglo-Irish lords, is perhaps less difficult to fathom but presents two clear and distinct versions. If George, Duke of Clarence had succeeded in smuggling his son away to Kildare's household in the early months of 1478, then Kildare knew, or at least firmly believed, that he had the real Warwick. In this scenario, Kildare's support was born of an affection for the House of York, and the Clarence branch of that tree in particular, having the closest connection to Ireland. If Kildare knew the boy was a fake, then he was surely most interested in his own authority in Ireland. The advent of a new dynasty in England presented a golden opportunity to try and assert the freedom from English rule that Ireland had wanted for so long, but in this scenario, the decision to send thousands of troops into England, led by his own brother, seems counter-productive. Bacon asserts that there was a desire to keep the new king in Ireland and draw Henry there, but not the funds to support such a plan in the short or medium term. If Kildare knew he had a fake then he risked, and lost, his brother's life and shone a spotlight on his own authority in Ireland for little real hope of gain. Only with a legitimate restoration of the House of York could he have hoped for real progress.

The boy who slipped into the royal kitchens and eventually rose to act as a falconer presents several problematical questions too. The name Lambert Simnel only appears in later, official reports that follow, sometimes by decades, the Battle of Stoke Field. To modern eyes, the name might look odd and it was equally out of place amongst medieval names. The *Heralds' Memoirs* record that the boy was named John, but everywhere else the identity of Lambert Simnel emerged. Lambert was not a common forename, though it is a possible one. Interestingly, Lambert was the maiden name of Edward IV's most famous mistress, Jane Shore, whose forename was actually Elizabeth and was changed for Elizabeth Woodville's sake. Simnel is a type of grain, and may have tied in with the idea in some sources that the boy's father was a miller or baker. Simnel cakes were eaten at Easter time, during Lent, and it is an odd coincidence that such a name became attached to a rebellion that emerged over Easter 1487, with the boy crowned on Ascension Day and the army landing on Whit Monday. Did Henry's government simply invent an odd sounding name, easily remembered and unlikely to be duplicated, with which to pass off this boy as a fraud? Is there even a hint that this boy was an illegitimate son of Edward IV by Jane Shore, used because of his Plantagenet resemblance and bearing, or is that insinuation simply more smoke and mirrors? When Henry wrote to the Pope asking him to punish the Irish clergy involved in the coronation in Dublin, the Pope's reply condemning their actions described 'a boy of illegitimate birth, whom the said king already had in his hands'.

The background of Lambert Simnel seems far more uncertain than it should have been. Bacon described him more than a century later as 'a baker's son' who was a pupil of Richard Symons, the priest. André wrote that the boy was 'the son of a miller or cobbler' and Vergil does not mention an occupation for the boy's father, though Lincoln's attainder in Parliament lists him as a joiner named Thomas. Such confusion amongst official sources is concerning. Both André and Vergil wrote for Henry and surely had access either to official records of Simnel's background or to the man himself, since Vergil notes he was still alive and prospering as a falconer when he wrote. A further identity as an organ maker has been ascribed to Lambert's father and there is no certainty at all offered as to his background, particularly before 1486. It is possible that different writers were muddled, misinformed or too lazy to discover the truth, but that in itself should cause concern about the accuracy of their work. If Lambert was a fabricated persona foisted on to a boy who would act a part in return for comfortable progression within the royal household, the confusion becomes understandable, but no less destructive to the official version of events.

The matter of the age of the pretender involved in the Yorkist uprising also throws up several interesting issues. Lincoln's attainder within the Parliament Rolls of November 1487 describes how the earl had 'caused one Lambert Simnel, a child of ten years of age, son of Thomas Simnel late of Oxford, joiner, to be proclaimed, set up and acknowledged as king of this realm, and did faith and homage to him, to the great dishonour and shame of the whole realm'. The implication is that the boy was 10 years of age around the time of his coronation, since it then goes on to describe the subsequent landing at Furness Falls. At the time of the coronation in Dublin on 24 May 1487, Edward, Earl of Warwick was 12 years old, Richard, Duke of York was 13 and Edward V 16. It would have been impossible to pass a 10-year-old boy off as a 16-year-old but just possible to convince some that he was 12. Vergil offers no precise age for his king from Ireland, but his Latin manuscript shows an alteration from describing the pretender as a *puer* – boy – to an *adolescens* – a word more suggestive of a young man or an adolescent, certainly someone older than 10. Bacon, over a century later, claimed that the boy was 'of the age of some fifteen years, a comely youth, and well favoured, not without some extraordinary dignity and grace of aspect'. In this passage, Bacon refers to the plucking of the student by Richard Symons sometime in 1485 or 1486, making him around 16 at the time of the Dublin coronation. Though Bacon did not repeat this in an attempt to link the plot with Edward V, the age puts the boy well beyond a passable facsimile of Edward, Earl of Warwick.

The only other piece of evidence suggestive of an older Lambert Simnel comes from what may have been a slip by Henry VII's own envoys. In 1493, as a second pretender worried the first Tudor king, Sir Edward Poynings and Dr William Warham were sent to Margaret, Duchess of Burgundy where, in the presence of the new pretender, Warham, who would later become Archbishop of Canterbury, accused Margaret of giving birth to two princes aged 180 months; 15 years old. Richard, Duke of York, subject of this second and most famous conspiracy, would have been 15 between August 1488 and August 1489, though there is no evidence extant that Margaret recognised him this early. The other prince was the one crowned in Dublin, who Margaret was supporting from 1486. If aged 10 at the Battle of Stoke Field, the boy would by this date have been 15 or 16, but hardly just given birth to by Margaret. Edward V was 15 from November 1485 until November 1486, and thus was 15 when Margaret started planning the Yorkist invasion of 1487. It is possible that Warham referred to the age of the boy in 1493 clumsily, but perhaps it is more likely that in trying to be clever, Warham unwittingly slipped up and made the boy older than the official story of six years earlier had allowed.

A final reference to this boy, captured at the Battle of Stoke Field, can be found in the *Book of Howth*, a chronicle which, at the time of these events, detailed the life of Nicholas St Lawrence, 4th Baron Howth. Two years after Stoke Field, the bulk of the Anglo-Irish nobility were summoned to England where the Book of Howth describes an odd scene that is not corroborated by any other source but remains interesting. During a feast, King

Henry ordered the boy captured at Stoke Field to serve wine to the gathered Irish lords but no one seemed to recognise him. The lords were told 'that their new King Lambarte Symenell brought them wine to drink'. For a long moment, none would take the drink, 'but bade the great Devil of Hell him take before that ever they saw him' until Baron Howth told this Simnel to serve him 'and I shall drink it off for the wine's sake and mine own sake also; and for thee, as thou art, so I leave thee, a poor innocent'. Lord Howth was one of the few Anglo-Irish lords who had not acknowledged the boy crowned at Dublin and appears not to have attended the event or been involved in the government in the boy's name, so it seems improbable that, unlike all of the others in the room, he would have ever seen the boy in Ireland. Those who had seen the boy crowned in Dublin did not reconcile that person with the one now serving them wine. If the episode took place, it has the strong odour of a stage-managed piece of theatre organised by Henry. The meeting may have been engineered to force the Anglo-Irish lords to acknowledge that they had supported an imposter, in which case it backfired spectacularly. The alternative intention was for Henry to test whether the boy in his possession was in fact the one crowned in Ireland, in which case his worst fears were confirmed. It was during this event that the *Book of Howth* records Henry quipping 'My Masters of Ireland, you will crown apes at length', but the response to the entrance of his Lambert Simnel may have wiped the smile from his face.

Francis Bacon recorded that Henry VII lamented the death of John de la Pole, Earl of Lincoln at the Battle of Stoke Field. He had hoped to have the earl taken alive in order to understand 'the bottom of his danger'. This suggests that Henry did not know what dangers still lurked in the shadows for him, surely pointing to a belief that the Princes in the Tower were not gone. Evidence relating to the Yorkist invasion of 1487 is sadly lacking but the official, Tudor, story took time to crystallise and even then varied hugely, even among those hired by the Tudor king to write his history. There are tantalising hints that the rebellion might have been spearheaded by the real Edward, Earl of Warwick, who could have been hidden in Ireland since 1478. Even more interesting is the possibility that the figurehead was in fact Edward V, some years older than the boy later claimed to have been crowned in Ireland and seeking, as Vergil wrote, to reclaim his kingdom. There is no official, definitive evidence of the Yorkist rebels claiming their leader was Edward V, but it would seem unlikely that such a reference would survive.

Just like evidence of their continued existence after 1483, Henry VII had an interest in ensuring the destruction of anything that could prove the greatest threats to his throne were still alive. The government published an official version, that this was an imposter claiming to be Edward, Earl of Warwick, early in the affair so anyone claiming otherwise risked persecution for it. André claims there was knowledge in London that the boy claimed to be a son of Edward IV and was identified as such. It is known that Henry ordered the records of the Irish Parliament of 1487 destroyed on pain of prosecution for treason.

The official story has been universally accepted for hundreds of years simply because it was the version published by a Tudor government best served by a laughable imposture. So many questions surround the affair that it is far from clear who the boy crowned in Dublin was, who he claimed to be or even how old he was. If the Princes in the Tower survived beyond 1485, Edward V was the natural choice to lead this rebellion and nothing but his involvement can explain his mother's suspected collusion. It would make little sense for Yorkists to rise in favour of a boy held prisoner, since his execution was only made more likely by such an enterprise. Warwick had no power base of his own and had been isolated for his whole life. If the Yorkists who refused to support Henry Tudor sought an experienced, capable leader they had the perfect option in Lincoln, who passed over his own position as Richard III's heir presumptive to support this revolt in another's name. The only legitimate Yorkist claims better than Lincoln's were those of Edward V and his brother Richard, though Warwick's attainder might be reversed if he won the throne. An extreme interpretation of the revolt might have Edward V as its leader, with the real Warwick collected from his hiding place in Kildare's household in Ireland before the invasion. There might have been any number of young boys in the train of the army who might have been captured afterward. We only have Henry VII's word that the boy he mercifully spared was the one crowned in Dublin. One boy caught by Sir Robert Bellingham was called John, but might have been used to present the beheading of the rebellion. Adrien de But believed that at least one boy was whisked away to Guisnes Castle after the battle. Francis, Lord Lovell famously vanished from the historical record after being seen escaping across the River Trent.

The events of 1486 and 1487 might have provided Henry Tudor with a template for dealing with such threats; assert the use of an imposter with an obscure name and background and challenge anyone to disagree. It has worked for over 500 years so far, but Henry was a man haunted by his worries. What is remembered as the Lambert Simnel Affair may have exposed to Henry just how clear and present the dangers he faced were. It is possible that the revolt was aimed at putting Edward V back on his throne and it is possible then that, if he was present at the Battle of Stoke Field, Edward V was either killed along with Lincoln, Thomas FitzGerald and Martin Schwartz, captured, which presented the problem of what to do with the teenager next, or escaped. If Henry now knew that Edward V had survived Richard III's reign, he must also have known that his younger brother Richard, Duke of York probably survived too. Accepting this serves to explain the increasing fear and uncertainty that wrapped itself around Henry's shoulders, weighing him down and ageing him. If the Yorkists had waited until Edward V was 16 to launch their invasion, he might have expected more trouble in three or four years' time when Richard would reach a similar age. He had a brief respite to gather himself and prepare to defend his crown from the House of York once more.

7

Richard of England

The news thereof came blazing and thundering over into England, that the Duke of York was sure alive.

Sir Francis Bacon, *The History of Henry VII*

King Henry VII had some years of respite from Yorkist threats after the successful quelling of the first full-blooded attempt to unseat him from his hard-won throne. Even the Earl of Kildare, during the visit of the Irish lords, had astonished everyone by shaking Henry by the hand and telling him jokes like an old friend, helping to secure his own position in Ireland with his roguish charm. The *Book of Howth* recalls that when Henry was told that all Ireland could not rule the lovable scoundrel Kildare, the king replied 'Then he is meet to rule all Ireland, seeing all Ireland cannot rule him.' By the end of 1490, when the second son of Edward IV would be due to turn 17 and might have been considered old enough to lead a fresh offensive against the Tudor crown, Henry had a healthy 4-year-old son and heir, Prince Arthur, a daughter, Margaret, who turned 1 in November, and his wife Elizabeth of York was coming to the end of the first trimester of another pregnancy. Henry's dynasty was shaping up nicely and that fortified his position in the country, allowing him to demonstrate that he could be a dynastic force for stability after all the recent troubles. He still had a long way to go, though, and it is doubtful that he found much peace in the respite he was granted as the Yorkist threat was far from destroyed. It merely licked its wounds, openly defying him from Flanders but more worryingly, perhaps only slumbering, waiting for the right moment, all about him at court and in the country.

The traditional story of the second prolonged and deeply threatening affair is peppered with the same kind of questions, ambiguities and problems that afflict the story of Lambert Simnel, yet is still similarly considered the unquestionable truth, handed down to us by the same government that had the most to fear from the plot. A new pretender, labelled an imposter, would dog Henry VII for almost a decade throughout the 1490s. Explained to the world as Perkin Warbeck, the well-travelled son of a burgess from Tournai who was coerced into impersonating Richard, Duke of York, the younger of the Princes in the Tower, the success he enjoyed and the genuine terror his career inflicted on Henry reveal at the very least that no one was so certain that the younger Prince was dead that he could simply be dismissed and laughed away into the annals of history.

Stepping off a boat at Cork harbour in the autumn of 1491, a lad in his late teens, wearing the expensive, fine silks sold by his master, the merchant Pregent Meno, set the town to whispering at his uncanny resemblance to those of the House of York who were still held close to Irish hearts. Professor S.B. Chrimes asserts that this boy's appearance in Cork at this moment was no mere accident, but had been planned by Margaret of Burgundy and Charles VIII of France, who meant to use this young man to try once more to unseat King Henry VII. Charles VIII's government had financed and supported Henry Tudor's own assault on the throne of Richard III in 1485, yet appeared now to be nudging forward an enemy to torment him. Henry's widespread network of spies soon began to feed information back to their master in England that a new threat was emerging in Ireland. Bacon wrote that 'As for the name of Perkin Warbeck, it was not at that time come to light, but all the news ran upon the Duke of York, that he was being entertained in Ireland; bought and sold in France, and was now plainly avowed and in great honour, in Flanders.' Henry would have to face down another Yorkist plot, just as he might have expected.

The complex web of European politics was being woven in ever longer, stronger and more intricate strands. Charles VIII had emerged from his own minority and had an eye on the expansion of French influence. In 1489, Pope Innocent VIII had offered Charles the Kingdom of Naples if he would unseat Ferdinand I there. Innocent's successor, Alexander VI, dreamed of an Italian state controlled from Rome and by 1493, Ludovico Sforza, Duke of Milan was asking Charles for help in defending his territory from the acquisitive Vatican. It was here that Charles planned to focus his attention and early support for Perkin may have served to distract Henry VII in England, but when Henry invaded France, Charles swiftly agreed to the Peace of Étaples in 1492 to see the English withdraw in return for a promise not to support Perkin. The plan may have initially been to use Perkin to keep Henry busy, but the invasion brought a fresh opportunity to agree a peace that would secure France's northern seashores in return for abandoning a cause Charles had little genuine interest in anyway.

In Spain, the powerful will and authority of Ferdinand of Aragon and Isabella of Castile, the husband and wife team gifted the epithet of the 'Catholic Monarchs', were uniting the states of the Iberian Peninsula, crafting the unified nation of Spain as they drove the Moorish population back to northern Africa, expelling the Muslim community that had been resident for more than 700 years and achieving a final victory in January 1492 when the Islamic Kingdom of Granada submitted. As domestic victories paid dividends, the Catholic Monarchs turned their gaze beyond Iberia. By the end of 1492, Christopher Columbus had sailed west under their patronage and a diplomatic alliance with England held a strong appeal as Henry VII looked about for a union for his young son to strengthen his own position.

Brittany and Burgundy were under increasing pressure from France, which eyed them as pieces of a jigsaw required to complete the French state. In 1491, following the death of Duke Francis II of Brittany, who had been Henry Tudor's custodian for most of his fourteen-year exile, Charles VIII married Anne, Duchess of Brittany, Francis' only heir, thereby effectively sealing French control of Brittany and ending that state's independence, though the official absorption would not follow for some years. Burgundy to the east of Paris, with territories stretching north to the coast around Flanders, was the last domino that France needed to see fall. Although it teetered for many years, its Dukes had stubbornly refused to allow it to topple. Margaret of York's husband Charles the Bold had died in 1477, leaving only one daughter to succeed him, Margaret's stepdaughter Mary, Duchess of Burgundy. Margaret took her 20-year-old ward under her wing and counselled her to complete her father's intended marriage for her to Maximilian I, Holy Roman Emperor.

The Holy Roman Empire represented the other major power block in Europe during the medieval period. The expansive territories that made up the empire encompassed much of modern Germany, Poland, Austria and the northern Balkans, smothering the top of Italy too in a kingdom of diverse cultures nominally sponsored and supported by the Pope, though during its long history, emperors had often been at logger-heads with Rome. With a sprawling territory broken into ethnic pieces it was ruled by the House of Habsburg which would, in the following century, draw even larger swathes of Europe under its wing. In the 1490s it was the protector of Burgundian independence. Margaret retained a great deal of affection in Burgundy that translated into influence over her stepdaughter's husband and his family, which she would not hesitate to use when she needed it. Maximilian is frequently remembered as an ineffectual lightweight who was chronically short of money. Taxation was a universal problem, as Henry VII would find out, but his contemporaries seem to have had a good opinion of him. Niccolò Machiavelli, author of *The Prince*, wrote of Maximilian, 'He governs his country with great justice; he is also a good general, skilful and successful in war' offering the criticism that 'if he could get over two qualities – weakness and his easy nature – he would be a perfect men.' G.E. Waas, in *The Legendary Character of Kaiser Maximilian*, lauded the emperor as 'the most accomplished Prince the House of Habsburg has produced; he had energy and a strong desire to reform abuses, and inherited a striking personality from his vivacious mother', claiming that he 'was able to estimate a person's abilities at a glance, so that he could immediately assign each person for the task for which he was most suited'.

The intricacies of European power politics must always be seen at play in the shadows of the adventures of the man remembered as Perkin Warbeck. He would receive backing that might appear to genuinely suggest men in power believed he was who he claimed to be. Each of these powers had their own reasons to cause problems for, or to help protect, Henry VII, which must be acknowledged as colouring their actions, though by the same token, cannot be taken to utterly undermine their every step. A desire to distract or upset Henry VII might be a motive to lie, but it could also act as an incentive to solidify a desire to help a man genuinely believed to be the second son of Edward IV; a fringe benefit of helping a fellow prince. Those in England who sought to undermine this pretender would call him Perkin Warbeck. He would introduce himself to the international stage as Richard of England.

The winter that Richard spent in Ireland allowed news of his claim to spread on the cold winds. Henry VII wrote to the Earl of Ormond, who was acting as Chamberlain to the queen, that he had 'tidings that our Rebelles landed the vth daye of this Moneth in our land of Irland', demonstrating that the news travelled quickly and was perhaps not unexpected. Henry told Ormond that he had 'sent for our derrest wif and for our derrest moder to come unto us' and asked Ormond to also join them to add his advice to theirs. The reason for calling on Henry's mother, Margaret Beaufort, is not hard to fathom; she was a pillar of the early Tudor establishment and had crafted Henry's current position for him from the most unlikely lump of clay. She was one of the very few in whom Henry had total and unwavering confidence. Ormond was able to provide information specific to Ireland. The queen's summons was either a sign of a close bond blossoming between the king and his wife or it was a defensive reaction. If the Lambert Simnel Affair had been an uprising in favour of Edward V in which Elizabeth Woodville was implicated, a second attempt in the name of Richard, Duke of York, would certainly make Henry nervous enough to feel he needed to watch his wife and make sure she was not tempted into betraying him as the plot moved into the light. The letter is dated 13 May 1492, by which time Richard had been in Ireland for some months if he arrived in autumn 1491, so Henry's information machinery may not have been as efficient as he had hoped.

From France, Charles VIII sent an envoy, Louis de Lucques, and a Burgundian named Stephen Frion who had been French Secretary to Henry VII before defecting to the court of Charles VIII. Frion would remain close to Richard, becoming one of his chief advisors, but the purpose of this visit was to invite Richard to the court of the French king. In March 1492, Richard sent Sir Edward Ormond to France to accept the king's kind invitation to visit during May. Richard arrived in France to a magnificent reception, hailed as Richard, Duke of York, the second son of Edward IV and rightful King of England. It is to be remembered that Charles VIII had previously welcomed Henry Tudor to Paris in 1485 as a true son of Henry VI and rightful heir to the House of Lancaster before subsidising his invasion, so duplicity was not beyond the French government, but even if Henry did not believe the pretender was really Richard, Duke of York, the repetition of such recent history that had ultimately led to him deposing a king must have caused alarm bells to ring in the cautious king's mind.

Henry found ready friends in his hostility to France. Maximilian I was trying to uphold Burgundian independence and any common ground between the king and the emperor would mitigate the influence of Margaret of York that Henry needed to nullify. The Spanish sought to regain counties to their east taken by the French and Rome was feeling the weight of French attention too. It cannot be coincidence alone that saw Richard arrive in France in May 1492 and Henry mount a flash invasion before the end of the same year. James Gairdner's *Henry the Seventh* makes no such connection and finds nothing extraordinary in the issue of proclamations on 2 August 1492 ordering every man capable of fighting to be ready for war at an hour's notice. Before the end of August, an English fleet commanded by Sir Edward Poynings lay siege to Sluys, a centre of piracy and of opposition to Maximilian. As the siege progressed through September, Henry mustered an army in London and marched to the south coast. On 6 October Henry arrived in Calais with his army and moved to Boulogne. News arrived during his journey that, just as Edward IV had found in 1475, his allies were not going to help him. Maximilian wished Henry well but could not spare resources to support him. Even Ferdinand and Isabella were close to concluding a new peace treaty with Charles.

Undaunted, Henry continued, to the shock of many, surprised that he would launch an offensive so late in the year, outside the traditional campaigning season. Within six months of Richard's arrival in Paris, Henry was at the French shores with a hastily assembled army at his back, ready to begin a campaign out of season. Charles swiftly offered peace terms, perhaps also taken aback by the reckless aggression he might not have expected from the Henry Tudor he had known. The Peace of Étaples was quickly reached under which Henry received two years' arrears of the pension Louis XI had given Edward IV in 1475, but withdrawn early in 1483. Maximilian was promised the payment of money owed to him by Charles' wife Anne of Brittany that she had secured to defend the duchy from France. The treaty was sealed at Étaples on 3 November and, once Charles confirmed it three days later, the English army moved back to Calais, entering the town on 7 November and returning to England. It had been a lightning strike that had brought more success and better terms than the circumstances might have warranted.

One key feature of the Peace of Étaples was an agreement extracted from Charles to cease his support for the young man from Ireland and expel him from French territories. Obliged to meet these terms, Charles sent Richard away from his court. This end would seem to make far more sense of Henry VII's actions in the autumn of 1492 than a sudden, all-consuming urge to invade France. The campaign was prepared in an inordinately short time, leaving within two months of the first sign of a plan to invade when such a scheme would more usually have been many months in the planning and preparation. To take an army to a foreign land as winter approached was generally considered a dangerous idea, yet Henry did not hesitate to land in France in October, even though Maximilian and the Spanish monarchs had abandoned the idea of an offensive. Perhaps the telling timescale is the matter of six or eight weeks between Richard's welcome in Paris and Henry's issue of orders to prepare for war. Henry must have received plenty of information from Ireland and surely had spies in the French court feeding him intelligence. The hurried invasion of France makes far more sense if Henry had received certain news that Richard was truly the younger son of Edward IV, verified at least as far as possible by men who may have known the boy in London less than a decade earlier. This driving motivation makes Henry's actions far more understandable as he panicked at the threat and needed to cut it off quickly. A thrust into France drew peace negotiations, which were quickly agreed once they encompassed Charles' promise to divest himself of the pretender to Henry's throne.

If the lad was easily proven a fake, Henry could sit in London and laugh at the foolish French king, duped by an imposter and galvanising his own support amongst Yorkists by aiming their ire at a French king pretending to support a fake claimant of the House of York. Instead, Henry quickly raised an army and rushed to face the threat. Even after the Peace of Étaples saw Richard move from France to Flanders and the court of Margaret, Dowager Duchess of Burgundy, Henry's own writer Polydore Vergil noted that the 'sodeyn newes, more stacke and fretted in hys stomacke, than the battaile which now was late set forwards, and more paine he had (not without ieopardie of him self) to appease and quench this newe spronge conspiracy, then makynge peace with the French kynge hys enemy'. With Richard at Margaret's court, things had gone from bad to worse and Vergil suggests that Henry began to worry himself sick at the threat posed by the young man. Once more, there is some evidence of the suspected, if not well-known, survival of the Princes in the Tower to be discerned in such desperate worry at a threat in the name of one of them. If they were dead and everyone knew it, how could this Richard cause Henry such intense worry?

Richard spent 1493 with Margaret in Burgundy, ostentatiously and visibly surrounded by attendants decked in the murrey and blue of the House of York. Hers is the least difficult motive to understand if Richard was an imposter rather than a genuine pretender. Margaret devoted what remained of her life to trying to remove Henry from his throne. If Edward, Earl of Warwick had slipped from her grasp and Edward V had been lost to her during the 1487 revolt, or indeed if Warwick had always been in the Tower and Edward V had never been under her control, she had no children to champion in this cause, her sister Elizabeth, Duchess of Suffolk had lost her oldest son to the failed attempt of 1487 and no other heir of the House of York showed any sign yet of wanting to take up the mantle of direct and open opposition to Henry. It is feasible that Margaret would use an imposter if she had no better way to trouble Henry, but that in itself is not evidence that she did not believe Richard was her nephew.

Tudor writers became unanimous in their believe that Margaret plucked out this imposter and trained him to be able to impersonate Richard, Duke of York. Edward Hall's *Chronicle* sums up the feeling that Margaret thought 'to have gotten God by the foote, when she had the devell by the tayle', but later writers applied both hindsight and the official story to the events they described. None for over a hundred years after the 1490s would have dared explain that Perkin Warbeck had been the genuine Duke of York. Margaret's ability to school a man approaching 20 years of age must be questioned too at this point. Margaret had left England on 23 June 1468 at the age of 22 and her only recorded visit to England after that came in 1480 when she met her brother Edward IV to try and renew Anglo-Burgundian ties. Margaret left England when Edward IV had two infant daughters and no sons. She may have met her nephew Richard, Duke of York during her visit to London in 1480, but it can only have been a brief acquaintance. Despite a quarter of a century out of her native country, Margaret was charged with coaching Richard to impersonate a boy she barely knew, giving him the information to convincingly describe households she had never seen, routines and even secret passages in palaces that she seems unlikely ever to have known, nevermind recalled fluidly enough to equip this man to lie. It is not impossible, but it seems like a stretching of plausibility required to fit later constructs of the episode.

The young man's appearance is the second issue of note that emerges at this point. There is a pencil sketch of the man later named as Perkin Warbeck believed to date from this period in Flanders. The sketch bears an unerring similarity to portraits of Edward IV, particularly around the nose. The draft has the hair marked as 'Lon', which is believed to mean it was to be blonde. Perkin Warbeck's mother was later discovered to be Nicaise Warbeck, a woman whose Portuguese extraction makes blonde hair deeply unlikely. The portrait may have been intended to resemble Edward IV to aid in the propaganda effort, but it cannot have been too far from the real face it purported to represent as such a deception would soon be uncovered and would destroy the pretender's cause. Horace Walpole, writing his *Historic Doubts on the Life and Reign of King Richard III*, noted that:

> The Earl of Shaftesbury was so good as to inform me that his ancestor the Lady Ashely, who lived to a great age, had conversed with Lady Desmond (that Countess of Desmond who could remember Edward IV and Richard III), with this strong addition that Perkin Warbeck was remarkably like Edward IV.

The portrait is not the only evidence of a strong likeness to the Yorkist king, which must be conceded by the pretender's success in claiming to be the son of Edward IV. This does not mean he was who he claimed to be, but it is strongly suggestive. It is possible that the likeness was genuine because this young man was an illegitimate son of Edward IV either coming from Ireland to Margaret or having been earlier sent in the opposite direction as an opening gambit in Margaret's plan to pass him off as Richard, Duke of York.

On 25 August 1493, both Margaret and Richard sat down at her palace in Dendermonde to pen a letter each to Isabella of Castile, seeking her aid and explaining their situation. Margaret's letter is recorded in Mélanges' *d'histoire offerts à Charles Bemont* and explains that the boy had been brought to her attention by the Earls of Kildare and Desmond the previous year, claiming that 'Richard Plantagenet, Duke of York – whom everyone thought was dead – was still alive', suggesting that she had not been aware of his continued survival. Richard 'was with those earls in Ireland, safe and held in great honour. They affirmed this with letters reinforced with their seals and with a sacred oath.' Margaret's version seems to dispel any idea that she had been involved either in sending Richard to Ireland or in protecting him from 1484 onwards at her brother Richard III's request, but Margaret needed to play a part to convince her cousin in Spain. Isabella would be deeply sceptical and the best way to alleviate such natural concern was for Margaret to express her own reservations, which had been satisfied, thus preventing Isabella from responding with a stream of questions that could have been guessed at. Presenting Richard's sudden appearance, of which she had no previous knowledge, having believed him dead, mirrored Isabella's own position and offered her reassurance that such concerns could easily be laid to rest. Margaret must have felt this course preferable to a claim that she had harboured her nephew for years, which, although it might have allowed for her certainty of his identity, might raise further questions about her prolonged silence and mark her as a long-term schemer, which of course she was.

Richard's own letter to Isabella opens with the greeting 'To the most Serene and Excellent Princess, the Lady Isabel, Queen of Castile, Arragon, Sicily, Granada, &c. my most honored Lady and Cousin' and continues to provide an early explanation of the story under which he would launch his bid for Henry VII's throne:

Most serene and most excellent Princess, my most honored Lady and Cousin, I commend me entirely to your Majesty. Whereas the Prince of Wales, eldest son of Edward formerly King of England, of pious memory, my dearest lord and father, was miserably put to death, and I myself, then nearly nine years of age, was also delivered to a certain lord to be killed, it pleased the Divine Clemency, that that lord, having compassion on my innocence, preserved me alive and in safety; first, however, causing me to swear on the holy sacrament, that to no one should I disclose my name, origin, or family, until a certain number of years had passed. He sent me therefore abroad, with two persons, who should watch over and take charge of me; and thus I, an orphan, bereaved of my royal father and brother, an exile from my kingdom, and deprived of country, inheritance and fortune, a fugitive in the midst of extreme perils, led my miserable life, in fear, and weeping, and grief, and for the space of nearly eight years lay hid in divers provinces. At length, one of those who had charge of me being dead, and the other returned to his country, and never afterwards seen, scarcely had I emerged from childhood, alone and without means,

I remained for a time in the kingdom of Portugal, and thence sailed to Ireland, where being recognised by the illustrious lords, the Earls of Desmond and Kildare, my cousins, as also by other noblemen of the island, I was received with great joy and honor. Thence being invited by the King of France, with many ships and attendants, and having been promised aid and assistance against Henry of Richmond, the wicked usurper of the kingdom of England, I came to the aforesaid King of France, who received me honorably, as a kinsman and friend. But on his failing to afford me the promised assistance, I betook myself to the illustrious Princess, the Lady Duchess of Burgundy, sister of my father, my dearest aunt, who, with her known humanity and virtue, welcomed me with all piety and honor; out of regard also to her, the most Serene King of the Romans, and his son, the Archduke of Austria, and the Duke of Saxony, my dearest cousins, as likewise the Kings of Denmark and Scotland, who sent to me their envoys, for the purpose of friendship and alliance. The great nobles of the kingdom of England did the same, who execrate the proud and wicked tyranny of this Henry of Richmond. But (most Serene Princess, Lady and Cousin) since, on account of our relationship, and your renowned virtues, by which you surpass all other princes of the world, in justice, actions, and prosperity, you ought no less than other princes to compassionate our condition, and succour us with pious love, I pray and implore your Majesty will use your influence with your Serene Spouse, that, together with your Clemency, he may be induced to pity the numerous calamities of our family, and in my right, which is also yours, to further me and mine with his favor, aid, and assistance. For I promise, if the Divine Grace should restore to me my hereditary kingdom, that I will continue with both your Majesties in closer alliance and friendship than ever King Edward was, and that I and my kingdom will be ever ready to fulfil your pleasure, no less than your own realms. Farewell to your noble Majesty! Written from the town of Dendemonde, the 8th calends of September [25th August], 1493.

Of your Excellent Majesty the Cousin, Richard Plantagenet, second son of Edward formerly King, Duke of York, &c. RICHARD.

The Spanish and Portuguese royal families, by virtue of their legitimate descent from John of Gaunt, possessed the greatest well of Lancastrian blood left in Europe. This lay behind Richard III's desire to marry a Spanish or Portuguese princess, made a match between his son Arthur and a daughter of Ferdinand and Isabella even more appealing to Henry VII, since it would bolster the questionable claim of his own line whilst eliminating a potential source of mischief, and may explain why Richard of England made contact with Isabella of Castile now. Spain would find itself courted by both sides of an emerging, or re-emerging, civil war in England, able to play the card of dynastic legitimacy wherever it would prove most beneficial to the Catholic Monarchs.

This letter offers the earliest full explanation of Richard's story still extant. The first point he makes clear is that Edward V is dead, murdered, from the assertion that Richard was 'nearly nine years of age', in 1483. Richard, Duke of York would then have been 9 and approaching 10, not 8, but perhaps a boy removed from his family and spirited away might be forgiven for being unsure of his young age at the time events took place. He may even have been unsure how old he was with no one to provide such basic information as a date of birth. Interestingly, no mention is made of Richard III as murderer or duped guardian. It may be that the boy did not know who was behind what went on, or that his Aunt Margaret writing beside him had made sure that he omitted such a direct accusation against her brother. All that Richard is quoted as saying about King Richard III is a brief line from Bacon, who claims he displayed no ill will to his uncle, recalling 'Although desire of rule did blind him, yet in his other actions, like a true Plantagenet, was noble, and loved the honour of the realm, and the contentment and comfort of his nobles and people.'

If Richard was to launch his assault on the Tudor throne as the younger son of Edward IV, he would have to explain why it was not his older brother making the bid, and that can only have been because he was dead and no longer able to press his own, superior, claim. There are three possibilities in this scenario, whether Richard was who he claimed to be or not. The first possibility is that the version he provides is close to the truth; that Edward V was murdered during 1483, in which case, and for the lack of an excuse made for him, we must presume that Richard III is accused of ordering the act. This requires that the murderers, having killed one boy in cold blood, were suddenly afflicted by cold feet and decided to abandon their nefarious deed half-done. Although entirely possible, this feels unsatisfactory. If men were willing enough to enter a room to kill two boys and had killed one, how likely is it that they would then stop, leaving themselves precariously balanced on a fence, their immortal souls already condemned as murderers but now having to watch their backs on the mortal plane for failing to do as the king instructed in full? In this situation, it is most likely that both boys were killed in 1483 at the order of Richard III, though as we have seen already, there is little evidence that this happened and at least as much, if not more, that it did not.

The second possibility is that neither boy was murdered but they were separated to ensure their safety and to minimise their potential to act as figureheads for rebellion until Richard III's grip on power was tighter. The younger boy, and indeed his older brother, may have been given the story that the other was murdered but they were spared in order to frighten them into obeying the requirement of silence that was placed on them. This would have been cruel, convincing a small boy whose father had recently died and who had been separated from the mother and sisters who had been his constant companions that his older brother had now been a victim of a murder that stalked him into hiding, but it could have been an expedient to deal with immediate problems. If Richard was who he claimed to be and this version was genuine, it negates the possibility that the Princes were permitted to meet with their mother after March 1484, perhaps at James Tyrell's Gipping home, though might fit more neatly with the story that at least one was whisked away over the sea. This must have been a version of events sanctioned by Margaret, if not designed by her, and at least suggests her confidence that Edward V was not going to be forthcoming to lead a future rebellion, though Richard's words do not preclude an error on his part from which his brother might later emerge alive and well. The pressing concern was to present Edward IV's second son as the legitimate heir of the House of York.

The third possible interpretation of this version of the Princes' fate is that Edward V died at Stoke Field, or was a captive of Henry VII and that the 1487 imposture of Lambert Simnel was a Tudor cover thrown over an attempt by Edward V to win back his throne. If this was the case, then Henry VII could hardly say as much. The king was not going to broadcast the fact that the older prince had been killed at Stoke Field for two very pressing reasons; he would jeopardise the Yorkist contingent of his support upon which he was still heavily reliant and thus bolster a rebellion against himself, and admitting this version of events, if true, necessarily dispelled the myth being quietly cultivated that Richard III had murdered both boys. If Edward V had survived to challenge Henry VII, then Richard, Duke of

York probably had too, and men would flock to the boy now in Flanders under his aunt's arm, believing him to be the real Prince. Why would the Yorkists in exile not broadcast this version of events to increase the belief in the possible survival, and therefore the truth of the claimed identity, of Richard, Duke of York? They could not. To do so would be to draw attention to a failed revolt when attempting to launch a fresh one on a strikingly similar premise. Admitting the failure of a previous plot to topple Henry VII would not inspire men to join their cause. Better for this boy to be a chance survivor, plucked by the Almighty from the jaws of an horrendous fate to take back what had been stolen from the House of York.

Whichever explanation, or combination of explanations, caused Margaret and Richard to arrive at this version of events, it is clear that Edward V had to be out of the picture to galvanise support, but that there should be no sense of the Yorkist plotters at the heart of this project having already failed once before. The next part of Richard's tale is equally unsatisfactory. He was apparently abandoned at the cusp of adulthood by a man charged with his care who must surely have had some sense of who he was, the second man tasked with protecting him having died. Finding himself in Portugal, the young man happened, as a servant to a merchant, to land in Ireland where he was almost immediately recognised as the younger son of Edward IV. The remainder of the tale is more authentic but was also the public portion of Richard's career to this date. He was invited to France and received as a true prince, then ejected and entered Margaret's court where he could vicariously draw upon the support of the Hapsburg Holy Roman Emperor and his son the Archduke Philip which Margaret enjoyed, adding the kings of Denmark and Scotland to the list of those supporting his enterprise. In the end, this letter is a pleading one that wants to win the support of the last major monarchy in Europe outside England yet to openly declare a belief in Richard's candidature. Such support was vital, but it would not in itself win Richard a throne. He needed backing from within England, he needed men and he needed money. To date, he had made a promising start, but there was a long way to go.

The greatest and most marked difference between the Yorkist invasion of 1487 and the plot that continued to take form around the persona of Richard, Duke of York is the time taken. What is remembered as the Lambert Simnel Affair has the air of a rush job, trying to slide a new king from his throne before he had time to make himself comfortable and more difficult to dislodge. It is interesting that the invasion came before Henry VII's reign had reached the length of Richard III's, as though that might offer some measure of time within which such an enterprise might hope to succeed and after which it would necessarily become more difficult as old ties slipped, replaced by new, firm knots lashing self-interest to the mast of the Tudor dynasty's ship. If allowed to find calm waters, those aboard would come to trust their captain. The headlong rush to Stoke Field, barely a year in the making, was not now to be repeated. Henry VII had a firmer hand on the tiller and that must be accounted for. Every scrap of time required was taken to help ensure the success of Margaret's plans this time, not least because, whether this lad was truly her nephew or not, it would be her last real chance. She had now painted Edward V as dead and this young man as the last hope of the House of York. He was a card not to be played lightly, a piece on the chessboard that represented their king; he was to be protected as far as possible until the very end of the game.

The campaigning season of 1494 passed with little threat to England, mainly because Richard was on a charm offensive on the continent. Richard's cause took a healthy step forward on 24 August 1494 when Maximilian, the Holy Roman Emperor, and his son Archduke Philip rode to church on St Bartholomew's Day with Richard, who was dressed in royal cloth of gold and flanked by thirty halberdiers wearing the Yorkist murrey and blue. Maximilian now gave a very public endorsement to the world of Richard as the son of Edward IV. This episode can, and has traditionally, been passed off as an act of disingenuous politicking. Henry's peace with France had thwarted the long-established co-operation between England and Burgundy that helped maintain that duchy's independence. Maximilian had little personal control over great portions of his territories. As Henry grew more secure and increasingly wealthy and as his interests began to grow more distant from those of Flanders, and therefore Maximilian and his son Philip, propping up an attempt to unsettle the English king, whether Richard was who he claimed to be or not, had appeal for Maximilian.

By this point, though, Richard had begun to broadcast the fact that he had three distinctive marks about his body that would clearly identify him as the true Richard, Duke of York to anyone who had known the boy. This kind of claim was odd if untrue, since it would just as easily out him as a liar when men who had known the little Duke of York could recall no such birthmarks or blemishes. The pencil sketch of Richard from this period mentioned above shows what might be a defect around his left eye. It may be a trick of perspective, but the left eye appears more heavily lidded, perhaps showing a squint, that might have been one of the three marks Richard spoke of and may have been part of the reason for the portrait. It would have taken little effort for Henry Tudor, surrounded by old Edwardian Yorkists at his court, to establish the truth of the claim that the Duke of York had such telling marks and certainly Henry made no effort to deny the claim. One woman who would certainly have been able to authoritatively confirm or deny such a claim was Elizabeth Woodville, but she had died at Bermondsey Abbey on 8 June 1492. If Richard was who he claimed to be, the timing may be significant, since the Lambert Simnel Affair appears to have cost his mother dearly in 1487 and the first appearance of this lad in Ireland came in autumn 1492, within a few months of the dowager queen's death. The boy's sisters, including the king's wife, might have been able to throw some light on the subject, but would Henry dare to ask them, knowing that it would flood their minds with hope that the boy might be genuine?

The lack of direct action from Margaret's pretender does not mean that concern in England was not reaching a thinly veiled peak. On 20 July 1493, Henry VII wrote a letter recorded in *Ellis's Original Letters Vol. I* to Sir Gilbert Talbot and expressly blamed Margaret for instigating the problems he now faced and tried to dismiss her prince as a 'boy', but it also ordered Talbot to be 'ready to come upon a day's warning for to do us service of war' against the threatened invasion of 'certain aliens, captains of strange nations'. It was all very well for Henry to call this pretender a mere 'boy', but Richard, Duke of York would have been 19 years old by this point, an age at which his father was leading armies and devouring enemies, not only at the Battle of Mortimer's Cross but at the cataclysmic Battle of Towton, the largest battle fought on English soil, which Edward IV won to cement his own position on the throne. Henry would have been all too aware of this so his flippant disregard can only have been a blustering front.

Ellis's Original Letters Vol. II offers further illumination of the concern Henry felt, but needed desperately to hide. This document is a set of instructions given to Clarenceux King of Arms for an embassy to Charles VIII in France. The current holder of the office of Clarenceux King of Arms on 10 August 1494, when these papers were signed by Henry VII at Sheen Palace, was Roger Machado, who had been appointed to the role on 24 January that year. Roger Machado was of Portuguese extraction, which may be important to the tale, and had served Edward IV as Leicester Herald and appears, during the early part of 1485, to have undertaken several journeys on behalf of Thomas Grey, Marquis of Dorset, which may have been in relation to Henry Tudor, then in exile and planning his attack, or might equally have related to one or more of Thomas' half-brothers, the Princes in the Tower, in hiding abroad.

In this instance, Henry VII's instructions remain in full. The first part of the instructions order Machado to let Charles VIII know that his emissary, Messire George le Grec, had been afflicted by gout on his way to England but that Charles' messages had been received from an esquire, Thomyn le Fevre, who had travelled in le Grec's stead. Henry wished Charles to know that he had received the news that an embassy from Charles to Maximilian had returned to Paris with confirmation that the Holy Roman Emperor meant to do all in his power to assist Margaret's pretender and that Maximilian had travelled to Flanders to help champion that cause. Charles appears to have sent Henry an offer of assistance, despite his own efforts to raise an army to assault Naples. France would lay the fleets of Brittany and Normandy at Henry's disposal on the sole condition that he met the costs of running them whilst they served him and Charles, in line with his agreement at the Peace of Étaples, had ordered that none of his subjects should join or aid the pretender's efforts. Henry thanked Charles for this offer, but said that he would not need to avail himself of it because the 'garçon' was of so little importance that Henry was not at all concerned by him. This, of course, was not true, as the king's letter to Gilbert Talbot attests. Henry, though, needed to maintain a calm appearance above the surface as his legs beat furiously below the water against a strengthening tide. The instructions, written in French and containing parts that cannot be clearly read, continue:

> And in regard to the said garcon the King makes no account of him, nor of all his … because he cannot be hurt or annoyed by him; for there is no nobleman, gentleman, or person of any condition in the realm of England, who does not well know that it is a manifest and evident imposture, similar to the other which the Duchess Dowager of Burgundy made, when she sent Martin Swart over to England. And it is notorious, that the said garcon is of no consanguinity or kin to the late king Edward, but is a native of the town of Tournay, and son of a boatman (batellier), who is named Werbec, as the King is certainly assured, as well by those

who are acquainted with his life and habits, as by some others his companions, who are at present with the King; and others still are beyond the sea, who have been brought up with him in their youth, who have publicly declared at length how … [a few words are wanting] the king of the Romans. And therefore the subjects of the King necessarily hold him in great derision, and not without reason. And if it should so be, that the king of the Romans should have the intention to give him assistance to invade England (which the King can scarcely believe, seeing that it is derogatory to the honor of any prince to encourage such an impostor) he will neither gain honor or profit by such an undertaking. And the King is very sure that the said king of the Romans, and the nobility about him, are well aware of the imposition, and that he only does it on account of the displeasure he feels at the treaty made by the King with his said brother and cousin, the king of France.

Here we have Henry's riposte to Richard's pretension: the king claims that the youth is a native of Tournay, the son of a boatman and that his true name is Warbeck, though it is unclear whether this is offered as the imposter's forename or the family name of his father. Henry asserts that he has a wealth of creditable information confirming this and that Maximilian knows he is supporting an imposter, rather than a genuine pretender. This accusation is important for the very reason Henry points out. It should be considered beneath a prince of any nation to undermine the authority innate in royalty by holding up a known impostor, and a commoner from a foreign land to boot, against a fellow prince, whatever their personal quarrels may be. Supporting a legitimate potential alternative was fair game and an important political tool, but to cause a common man to be treated as royalty, allowed to wear royal cloth of gold and be hailed as a rightful king was not something any prince should, or would, do lightly, not least for the harm it would do to their own exalted position. From the descriptions provided earlier, Maximilian does not seem likely to take such an unwise step simply to help the stepmother of his deceased wife keep a personal feud alive. It is possible that Maximilian took the inadvisable step as an expedient to keep Margaret onside and harness her popularity in Burgundy for his son's benefit, or that he turned a blind eye to the possibility that Richard was not Margaret's nephew, at least not the one he claimed to be. One explanation for the family likeness is that this Richard was an illegitimate son of

Edward IV, though a child from Edward's exile in Burgundy in 1470–71 would appear too old and one fathered during his 1475 invasion of France too young to pass off as Richard, Duke of York, born in 1473. It is possible that another illegitimate child was sent to Margaret to be raised in comfort, away from the glare of Elizabeth Woodville, and that Margaret now saw in him the perfect chance, but such an illegitimate child is undocumented and no contemporary is recorded to have made such a suggestion.

Henry went on to offer his mediation in the dispute over Naples, since he and Charles VIII were now firm friends and the King of Naples was also on good terms with Henry, being a knight of the English Order of the Garter. Machado was, if asked about the state of domestic affairs, to assure Charles that England was more peaceful now than at any time in living memory, though Ireland remained something of a lost sheep that the king was resolved to bring back into the fold. In this way, any further input from Ireland into current problems could be written off as typical Irish trouble-making. Henry expressed his intention to send an army to quell the 'Wild Irish' and bring firmer order back to the Pale, where the English writ at least nominally ran. The last instruction to Machado was to thank the King of France for his assurance that if the King of Scotland were to launch an attack on England, Charles would neither condone nor offer any support to the action.

A separate instruction was added to the end, after the main set had been signed, giving Machado authority to show evidence to the King of France that Maximilian knew the pretender he supported was a fake and that his sole motive was anger at the peace now being enjoyed between England and France. Henry expressed a firm belief that he could reach terms with Maximilian if he wished to, but said that he would not for as long as Maximilian continued on his present course, trusting that England and France together could comfortably overcome any storm opposition to the Holy Roman Emperor might bring their way. Early the following year, Machado, having returned from this embassy, was sent back to France with fresh instruction drawn up at Greenwich on 30 December 1494. Henry reminded Charles that the French king had promised to send an envoy to discuss the state of affairs in both their countries but that none had arrived. Machado was therefore returning to France with news that Henry was in fine health and as beloved by his people as any of his predecessors had ever been. All was well in Ireland, where the men of power had submitted to Henry's Lieutenant.

The final instruction to Machado (who, as well as holding the office of Clarenceux King of Arms, was Richmond Herald) was:

> Item, in case that the said brother and cousin of the King, or others about him, should speak at all touching the king of the Romans, and the garçon who is in Flanders, the said Richmond may reply as he did on his former journey. And he shall say, that the King fears them not, because they are in capable of hurting or doing him injury. And it appears each day more and more to every person who the said garçon is, and from what place he came.

It seems that Machado was briefed with a response to be used only if the matter to the pretender was raised by the King of France or any of his ministers. The response was to be repeated as it had been before: Henry was not afraid, but in sending Machado back so quickly on the pretence of a delay in Charles' envoy arriving, Henry betrays a strong sense of concern. He protests too much and perhaps wanted a trusted, experienced pair of eyes at the French court again to make sure that Charles was not double-dealing. The constant reference to Richard as a boy smacks of bluster, an attempt to depict smooth confidence where none really existed. All was not, as Henry tried to make out, quiet in England and this second embassy by Machado was in response to shocking events at home.

In November 1494, Richard made out a deed promising to repay his aunt Margaret various sums of money on the success of their venture. Once king, Richard would pay Margaret the 81,666 crowns still outstanding from her 200,000 crowns dowry and return to her the manor of Hundon, seized from the dowager duchess after the death of Richard III. Margaret was also promised the town of Scarborough, a strategically important port linked to trade with Flanders, and she was promised reimbursement of expenses that she had incurred in the invasion of 1487. Richard was hardly in a position to be too picky, but there is a sense in the terms of this agreement of Margaret feathering her own nest. In order to get those feathers, though, she still needed to put this man on the throne of England.

By this time, Richard had been slowly gathering support for months in much the same way as Henry Tudor had at his faux court in Brittany and then France; a terrifying parallel for the Tudor king. If men could find themselves accepting the possibility that the Princes in the Tower had not been murdered, then those who had attached themselves to Tudor's cause in repulsion at Richard III had found their rightful king. Amongst those who had joined Richard were Sir Robert Clifford and Sir William Barley. Clifford might be counted a diehard Yorkist, though he had been quietly at peace with the new regime. In 1478 he had entered the lists of the jousts to celebrate Richard, Duke of York's marriage to Anne Mowbray and had received a golden 'M' set with emeralds from the little Mowbray princess for one of his successes. Clifford had come to Richard in Malines in 1493 and immediately, enthusiastically, declared him the genuine Duke of York, sending letters home to England to friends he believed would rise for the Yorkist cause telling them the exciting news. The precise cause of Clifford's certainty is unclear. Tudor chroniclers argue at what convinced him, from Stow's assertion that it was because of the young man's 'gesture and manners' to Edward Hall's belief that it was his looks: 'his face and other lineament of his body'. Vergil simply offers that Clifford saw him and believed. Was the fault in the young man's left eye the giveaway?

There is a problem with Clifford's effusive confidence and willingness to spread the news of Richard's confirmed identity. That problem was exposed on 22 December 1494, just before Machado's second set of instructions to visit the King of France were written. On that date, Sir Robert arrived in London and threw himself before the king, receiving and pardon and £500 on 20 January 1495. Henry was keeping Christmas at Greenwich when Clifford burst back on to the London scene but travelled immediately to the Tower of London to hear what the Yorkist knight had to say. Clifford reeled off a list of those in England who had promised support to the pretender, giving them all to the king in return for his pardon. Vergil listed Lord Fitzwalter, Sir Simon Mountford, Sir Thomas Thwaites, William Daubenay, Robert Ratcliffe, Thomas Cressner, Thomas Astwood and William Worsley, the Dean of St Paul's as being amongst those charged by Clifford with treason. The most shocked face in the room probably belonged to Sir William Stanley when he heard his own name included in the list.

The Stanley family were one of the few to emerge from the Wars of the Roses not only unscathed but improved. Thomas Stanley, the head of the clan, had balanced his loyalties carefully, though he had nearly been caught out on more than one occasion. After the Battle of Blore Heath in 1459, the House of Commons entered a petition calling for Thomas to be tried as a traitor for secretly supporting the Yorkist cause and failing to heed the call to arms addressed to him by Henry VI. At Bosworth, Stanley had famously walked the thin line again before the forces of his younger brother, Sir William, had poured down upon the household knights of Richard III and seen to the destruction of the king and his men. Thomas, who was married to Margaret Beaufort, was Henry's stepfather and was created Earl of Derby after the victory at Bosworth, a title that his descendants still hold today. Although there has been rumour that he hoped for more, there has never been any evidence that once his stepson was installed on the throne, Thomas ever deviated from his cause.

William was only slightly younger than his brother and was nearing 60 years old at the end of 1494. His record was less phlegmatic than his brother's, having fought for the Earl of Salisbury at Blore Heath against Henry VI's forces and been more consistent in his Yorkist attitude. William was his brother's right hand, acting as Thomas instructed but allowing him plausible deniability of his little brother's actions if everything went wrong. It meant that William took all the risks whilst Thomas reaped the rewards, but that was perhaps the accepted role of the younger brother in a baronial family making the transition from regional power to national importance. If anyone had reason to feel overlooked and under-rewarded, it might have been William, since his action had been the decisive one at Bosworth. When Sir William petitioned Henry's first parliament to confirm grants he received from Richard III, he only received confirmation of some and was given compensation for others which he lost. William was, however, made Lord Chamberlain and Chamberlain of the Exchequer by a grateful Henry VII and may have counted that as sufficient reward for one who was not the head of his family.

The horror that spread through Sir William's mind might only have been briefly halted by a snort of disbelieving derision, but the ageing knight was swiftly arrested. There have been lingering, but unproven, suggestions that Henry was already aware of Stanley's involvement, yet there was no out-ward sign of mistrust. As Lord Chamberlain, Stanley was in a frighteningly privileged position for one who might have been suspected of plotting with the king's enemies. He was responsible for appointments to Henry's household, for the staff who attended the king in private and for organising the staff for state events. The role made the incumbent a member of the

Privy Council and therefore a close advisor to the monarch who was also able to easily and regularly gain access to the king's person. The thought that one so close, frequently within a knife's length of the king or able to see to the slipping of poison into his food, being a traitor would suggest that for Henry to allow him to remain in such a role when he was aware of any activities linking him to the pretender on the continent would have been uncharacteristically reckless on the part of the king. If Henry had not held some secret knowledge of William Stanley's alleged involvement, he must have been shocked and terrified at the reach of this new threat.

There is no official record of Sir William's trial, which took place before the King's Bench at Westminster Hall on 6 and 7 February 1495. André mentions it only in passing, providing no detail beyond a certainty of Sir William's guilt. *Cobbett's Complete Collection of State Trials* is only able to provide the accounts of Edward Hall and Sir Francis Bacon to shed any light on the matter. Hall records that the Privy Council was tasked with questioning Sir William, 'In whiche examinacion he nothinge denied, but wisely and seriously did astipulate and agree to all thinges layed to hys charge, if he were in any of them culpable or blame worthy.' It seems that Sir William did not deny that he had received communication from Robert Clifford on the subject of the pretender nor that he had stated 'he would never fight nor beare armore against the young man, if he knew of a truthe that he was the indubitate sonne of kyng Edward'. If this account accurately reflects William's responses to questioning, it smacks of a man who felt he had nothing to hide and had done nothing wrong. If convincing word was reaching William that the boy really might be Richard, Duke of York, as Clifford himself was advertising, then the old knight must have been struck by a sense of having been duped into his actions at Bosworth. William appears to have born a more genuine attachment than his brother to the Yorkist cause, at least as represented by Edward IV, and loyalty to Edward's sons may have been at least in part behind his willingness to ride down King Richard III. If he began to harbour doubts, a belief that he had been fooled, then he may have taken against Henry to some degree, but there is no sense in this account of a desire to kill Henry in favour of the pretender, only a reserved assertion that he would not be willing to take the field of battle *if* the boy really was Edward's son.

Bacon records a similar version to Hall's, noting that Sir William 'denied little of that wherewith he was charged, nor endeavoured much to excuse or extenuate his fault'. Bacon thought that the old knight 'trusted much to his former merits, and the interest that his brother had in the king' in 'thinking to make his offence less by confession'. Bacon also suggests that Sir William's vast wealth was a strong motive to Henry, with 40,000 marks in cash, plate and jewels confiscated from Holt Castle to go with his rents of £3,000 per year. Bacon's account also states that Sir William said he would not fight the pretender if he truly was Edward IV's son and Bacon opines that the 'case seems somewhat an hard case, both in respect of the conditional, and in respect of other words', though he suggests the judges 'thought it was a dangerous thing to admit ifs and ands, to qualify words of treason'. The words proved so great a threat to Henry because 'if Stanley would hold that opinion, that a son of king Edward had still the better right, he being so principal a person of authority, and favour about the king; it was to teach all England to say as much', though this can hardly have been a threat unless at least one of the sons of Edward IV was still alive and at large. That Henry felt his title so fragile as to be threatened by the ethereal touch of ghosts after ten years as king would be difficult to believe, unless he knew that their touch was far more tangible.

Sir William Stanley was beheaded on Tower Hill on 16 February 1495, his brother unable or unwilling to save him from his confessed folly. Several chroniclers believed that Henry wrestled long and hard with the notion of killing the man who had gifted him his crown, not to mention saving his life in the process, at Bosworth Field. Concern at the reaction of his powerful stepfather may also have slowed Henry's hand, but in the end, Thomas did not move to protect his brother and Henry must have felt that the circumstances, with an enemy at the gate who a member of his household might feel affection for, left him no choice but to order William's death. The greatest concern must have been that if Sir William, a man high in the favour of Edward IV, as was his brother Thomas, could not be so certain that Richard, Duke of York was dead as to laugh off an uprising in the boy's name, how could Henry possibly know himself? More than ever he might have hoped Lord Lovell had fallen into his hands or Lincoln had lived to tell him 'the bottom of his troubles'.

On 11 February, the *Calendar of State Papers of Milan* record a report from Erasmo Brascha, a Milanese ambassador to Flanders, which relates an odd story Maximilian seems to have passed on. Erasmo wrote to the Duke of Milan, Ludovico Sforza, that 'the first man who had this son of King Edward, when he was in England, has run away', adding that many men, including the Bishop of London, had been arrested in England because of this flight. The report continues to explain that 'His Majesty told me that this man, when he was in England, divulged that this Duke of York was not the son of King Edward, but is the son of the Dowager Duchess of Burgundy and of the Bishop of Cambrai', noting also that he was making for Ireland to harness the support he had there. This is the only mention of a man who had taken the pretender to England as a boy and who had fled, though the news was no doubt meant to make sense of the rash of arrests and executions taking place. Henry would hardly wish to broadcast the uncovering of a terrifying plot at the centre of his own household. The news most likely reached Maximilian through the whispers of Henry's spies, serving to both draw a veil over the threat to Henry's position and to sow a small seed of doubt in Maximilian's mind that could explain both Margaret's attachment to the young man and his undoubted Plantagenet looks. King Henry was, perhaps, testing the waters to see which story might cause the most damage to the pretender's cause: bastard son of a Yorkist duchess and a bishop, or commoner from Tournai. Alternatively, the confusion was deliberate to make the uncertainty over Richard's origins plain.

Whether or not Clifford had been in Henry VII's service as a spy for part or all of his time with the pretender is impossible to determine. Both Hall and Bacon did not think it likely, since Clifford was not in high favour after his return. André mentions only that Clifford 'had defected from the king and had fled to Flanders', seemingly unaware of any duplicity on Clifford's part. John Flamank wrote to Henry in a letter recorded in the *Letters and Papers Illustrative of the Reigns of Richard III and Henry VII, Vol. I* that 'a nodre tyme I dyd wryt unto his hygnes that oone hade shewed me that Sir Robert Clyfford should say here in this toune to a lady that Perken Warbeke was kynge Edwardes sone', suggesting that Clifford was openly broadcasting the opinion that Richard was who he claimed to be, an act perhaps too conspicuous and damaging to Henry for a spy. Whether Clifford perceived some fatal weakness in Richard's cause or came to doubt the identity he had so confidently attested to cannot be known, but that he was a spy for Henry seems doubtful. Like so much of this episode, including the details of Sir William Stanley's trial, no record remains of the deep questioning that Clifford must have undergone to earn Henry's pardon, but there was no news of a confirmed imposture circulated based on Clifford's information. If Henry learned anything from Clifford, it may have unsettled his mind even more.

On 30 November 1494, just before Clifford's return to spill his story, Henry had overseen the creation of his second son, Prince Henry, as Duke of York, having been created a Knight of the Bath the day before. The king's second son was just 3 years old and was already Constable of Dover Castle, Lord Warden of the Cinque Ports, Earl Marshal of England and Lord Lieutenant of Ireland. His creation as Duke of York has often been suggested to prove the fact that the previous holder of that title was dead, but it does not prove Richard, Duke of York's death any more than John Howard's creation as Duke of Norfolk in 1483 did. It was, instead, a defensive manoeuvre by Henry VII that betrays the threat he perceived in this fresh revolt. Henry clearly hoped that giving the title the pretender claimed was his own to his second son would somehow end the belief that he could be the real son of Edward IV. Clifford's news and Stanley's execution must have shown King Henry that this foe would not be so easily swatted away. Buck wrote that 200 men were executed as a result of Clifford's betrayal of Richard's cause and the young man's support in England was, at least for the moment, destroyed sufficiently to prevent the invasion that might otherwise have been imminent, but this was no half-hearted pretence. The young man Henry labelled an imposter and called Perkin Warbeck would prove the most persistent and serious threat of his entire reign.

8

A Prince Among Kings

With regard to the Duke of York we entertain great hopes that after obtaining the kingdom of England he will soon attack the King of France; and to this effect have we received every promise and certainty from the Duke aforesaid.

Maximilian I to Venetian Ambassadors Contarini and Trevisano
Calendar of State Papers of Venice, Vol. I

Richard of England's cause stalled after the losses inflicted on his support in England by Clifford's betrayal, though André insists that still 'False prophets spread prophesies far and wide about that deceiver, which completely blinded the eyes of the lower classes and common people,' demonstrating that he did not vanish and the threat he posed did not diminish in Henry's eyes. Instead, the involvement of William Stanley had caused Henry no small amount of panic as to how far, how wide and how deep this conspiracy now ran. Having won the throne for himself in a not dissimilar fashion, he was particularly sensitive to the fact that a plot that may appear weak might still undo a king if its foundations were solid enough.

The head had, quite literally in some cases, been cut off Richard's English support and Henry's ruthlessness was no doubt designed to, and no doubt would, make others who might look to the pretender think more carefully before showing their hand; the kind of hesitation that Henry would be relying on to prevent Richard's success. On 24 January 1495, while Sir William's fate hung in the balance, Richard was at Malines putting his signature to a remarkable document that serves both to demonstrate the desperate weakness in the young man's cause and the hay others were willing to make at his expense. Alternatively, the document is tantamount to a will, prepared before a single young man with no heir launched an invasion of England that might win him a crown or cost him his life. The document begins with a list of the illustrious titles Richard claimed for himself:

> We, Richard, by the grace of God, King of England and France, Duke of York, Lord of Ireland and Prince of Wales, only son of the King Edward IV, and legitimate heir of the Kingdoms, duchies, Lordships and Principalities mentioned; to all who will see or hear these letter, greeting.

It is worthy of note once more, since Maximilian was a party to the creation of this document, that complicity in the claim by a commoner to be royalty would have been considered beneath a prince, even to harm an enemy, since in doing so, he necessarily tarnished the burnished glow of his own golden exaltedness. Kings were appointed by God. Therein lay their power and mystique, and few, if any, kings would willingly diminish that notion simply to get one over on a distant foe.

Like his letter to Isabella of Castile, there is a great deal of morose self-pity running through the lines of the Latin letter, translated into French by Jean-Didier Chastelain in *L'Imposture de Perkin Warbeck*. The document continues by lamenting that human conditions are 'governed by the instability of fortune and exposed to her blows', but reflecting that 'one must retain confidence in Divine Clemency', 'which will end in removing errors of every kind and in giving merit to those to whom honour belongs'. The essence of what follows is the bequeathing of Richard's claim to the throne of England and France (here perhaps the latter is of most interest to Maximilian) and his other titles to Maximilian and his heirs in the event that Richard dies without a legitimate heir of his own. Such a measure is necessary, the document notes, because 'given the uncertainty of human destiny, it could be that Our fatal day arrives for Us before We are re-established in Our before-mentioned heritage'. If Richard should die still trying to recover what he named as rightfully his, then:

> Our most Serene Lord Maximilian, King of the Romans or his successors will be immediately enabled to reclaim, acquire and possess the Kingdoms

of England and France, the Duchy of York, the Lordship of Ireland and the Principality of Wales, with all the titles, dignities, rights and goods pertaining thereto.

Furthermore, the document is at great lengths to tie the wrists of the young man so that he cannot extricate himself from the agreement. 'This cession and transfer, or other appellation with which one may designate it, We have by a definite deposition incapable of any doubt whatever, promised it in perpetuity to Our Serene Lord Maximilian King of the Romans', with the only obligation given to Maximilian the very one he would most want, 'that he will never renounce the said gift, not violate nor contravene, but will guarantee the perpetual validity of it'. Richard could never undo his gift and Maximilian was bound to press the claim after the young man was gone. The Holy Roman Emperor would, in effect, be contractually bound to claim the crowns of England and France, both of which were currently at odds with his own authority, particularly in Flanders. The restrictions on Richard's ability to backtrack were further tightened at the end, causing him to stipulate that:

> We solemnly swear on the Holy Scriptures never to go back on the foregoing, but to observe it on the contrary in general as in particular, and above all never to ask Our most Holy Lord the Pope or his successors to be excused from Our oath, no matter for what reason, never to dispose of Our own will of these concessions, renouncing all rights, judicial on any pretext such as being a minor in age, constraint, respect or error.

One item within the closing sentence of the main part of the document has frequently been pointed to as proving that Richard was not truly Richard, Duke of York, second son of Edward IV. The fact that Richard would not be allowed to renege on his promise on the grounds that he was a minor has been suggested to mean that the young man signing and sealing this document was younger than the real Richard, Duke of York would have been. Richard, Duke of York, born on 17 August 1473, would have been 21 years old on 24 January 1495 and so would have no need to mitigate a minority that no longer applied to him. However, this item is only given as part of a list of potential methods Richard might have used to wriggle free from the promise he gave. Richard, Duke of York would only have been a few months past his twenty-first birthday, perhaps had a fresh, youthful look about him and Maximilian's lawyers were simply being careful. It seems unlikely that the Holy Roman Emperor would know the date of birth of the second son of a king who had died more than a decade earlier, before Maximilian had come to his own throne. Negating Richard's claim on this basis would also assume that the boy himself or his aunt Margaret were certain of his date of birth and precise age at a time when such things were poorly recorded and the young man had been separated from any close family who might have known it for a decade or more. Margaret had not known the boy well, seeing him probably only once before Edward IV's death and was unlikely to know his exact birthday. The mention of the possible defence of being a minor cannot sufficiently dispel the possibility that Richard was who he claimed to be, since he may have been unsure of his own precise age, having no one to give him such information, and Maximilian's lawyers, as lawyers will, erred on the side of caution when dealing with such a young man to ensure he could not one day protest that he had been less than twenty-one on the date the document was sealed.

The deed is signed 'Richard of England' in a hand that Sir Frederic Madden asserted in *Documents Relating to Perkin Warbeck, with Remarks on His History* in 1837 was both bold and identifiably English, a crucial point against the assertion that this was a boy born to a middle-class family from Tournai. Several things are more striking about this document, though. The need to prepare a will demonstrated that Richard was fully intending to try and win his crown in battle. However, it also shows the desperate position he was in, utterly reliant on Maximilian to prop up his floundering cause so that the Holy Roman Emperor could extract whatever terms he desired, including the handover of Richard's claim. Though isolated amidst those doubtless assuring him of his impending success, it may have seemed a throwaway promise that would amount to nothing once Richard was king and set about producing heirs.

The second aspect of the document worthy of note is the tone, which appears negative and somewhat miserable. As he had done to Isabella, Richard again bemoans the fortunes that have seen him cast away from home and his inheritance as if seeking pity. It is hardly an attitude or demeanour to inspire or rouse men to lay down their lives. Contrast

Richard's attitude to public documents by Edward IV, Richard III and Henry VII and his tone is almost pathetic. Richard III had lambasted Henry Tudor in a proclamation issued before his invasion as a traitor who meant to wreak havoc in England so that:

> for this and other inestimable dangers to be avoided, and so that the king's rebels, traitors, and enemies may be utterly put off their malicious and false purpose if they enforce to land, the king our sovereign lord wills, charges, and commands each and every native and true subject of this his realm, like good and true Englishmen, to endeavour with all their powers to see to their own defence and that of their wives, children, goods, and inheritance against the said malicious purposes and conspiracies, which the ancient enemies have made with the king's rebels and traitors for the final destruction of this land.

Henry Tudor himself had landed in Milford Haven as king, not as one trying to press a claim, but as the already-appointed, rightful King of England, issuing proclamations and commands as though he already wore the crown. In comparison, Richard's brand of morose surrender to the winds of fortune is hardly stirring, and this would prove a vital flaw in the young man's make-up, perhaps exacerbated by a lack of good, experienced advice. Men would not risk treason against the reigning king for a young man who blamed fickle luck for his situation and pitied himself his losses. Richard's only hope was to thunder into England as the son of the mighty warrior-king Edward IV, but not all sons are like their father.

This document is significant too for its longer-term impact, though it is often forgotten in what was to follow. It may have been the final nail in the coffin of Richard's historical reputation. Margaret's hand can certainly be seen at work, weaving through this deed as it did through all the threats to Henry VII until her death. Richard probably represented her last real hope of a Yorkist restoration as the only heir left in her hands. If he failed, then she could only continue her avowed determination to remove Henry VII by further inveigling her relations by marriage, the Hapsburgs, whilst she still had some influence over them, Richard and the course of events. This she did by dangling the inviting prize of two rich crowns before the perennially impoverished Maximilian. Why, then, did Maximilian never press the claim he was so clearly entitled to after Richard's death? The only reason he would be unable to do so is if Richard had a legitimate heir at his death. This consideration may prove important later, but the document might also explain why the imposture of Perkin Warbeck was so readily accepted, not just amongst Tudor writers, but by the wider Yorkist cause. If any future White Rose claimant, including those de la Pole brothers of the Earl of Lincoln who would go on to haunt Henry VII and Henry VIII for decades, had acknowledged that Perkin had really been Richard, Duke of York, they would have undermined their own cause, because the Yorkist claim would then pass either to Richard's heir or to Maximilian and his heirs. Future Yorkist threats to the Tudor regime, as well as the Tudor monarchs themselves, need Richard to be a fake, an imposter. In this one thing, they were united and it was this document that probably consigned Richard to the oblivion of an exposed imposter, even amongst those who would take up the same cause of Yorkist restoration, because to acknowledge him was to gift the claim he possessed to another.

As spring warmed the air on both sides of the Channel, Maximilian was preparing to travel back home for the convening of the Diet of Worms that would lay the ground for a root and branch reform of his empire. On 5 May, the *Calendar of State Papers of Venice* record a message from the ambassadors Zacharia Contarini and Benetto Trevisano passing on news that they had met with Lord Philibert, one of Maximilian's diplomats, on their way to the Emperor's court who had 'told them that the Duke of York, son of the late King Edward, had taken the field against the King of England under the favour of the Archduke, and that the King of the Romans was nowise concerned therein', suggesting that Maximilian was already distancing himself from Richard's attempt, which was apparently getting underway, though he was perhaps leaving the endeavour to his son, Archduke Philip, who would soon be turning 17. Maximilian's removal from the scene did not, as will be seen, diminish his direct interest in Richard's adventures, but the emperor had other matters that were proving more pressing. On 31 March the Holy League, also known as the League of Venice, had been proclaimed, creating an unprecedented union between the Pope, Maximilian, Ferdinand of Aragon (primarily in his capacity as King of Sicily), the Duke of Milan and the Republic of Venice to oppose the aggression of Charles VIII into northern Italy. Charles was already in Naples and met with the League's forces on 6 July at the Battle of Fornovo as the League tried to cut off Charles' route back to France and the French king tried to beat the closing of the trap. Maximilian had a good reason to distance himself personally from Richard's cause. England was being courted as a potential member of the League to increase its weight and authority.

The two Venetian ambassadors wrote to the Doge of Venice again on 9 June from Maximilian's court at Worms to convey the emperor's understanding and sympathy at the expense Venice was incurring in furthering the efforts of the League, which also stated its aim as the resistance of Ottoman expansion. The emperor was, the ambassadors wrote, incurring 'very heavy disbursements, owing to the movements both of the Duke of Guelders and of Robert de la Marck, about whom he hears this very day that they have burnt certain villages of his in the duchy of Luxemburg'. They also wrote that Maximilian offered news 'of the proceedings of the Duke of York, who laid claim to the crown of England, and is now attacking the island with 1,500 men, independently of mariners', adding that Maximilian 'means to send him a reinforcement of 800 men' and that Richard had a further ally in the Scots, whose ambassadors in Worms 'tell him they hope for certain victory'. Less than a week later, on 14 June, they wrote again and Richard's favour amongst the Scots ambassadors was again mentioned, the ambassadors noting that 'they seem to be requesting Maximilian to league with Scotland against England, promising to favour the Duke of York, hoping thus to recover Berwick and certain other places belonging to their King, which have been held by England for many years', adding that the Scottish sought a marriage between their king, James IV, and Maximilian's daughter Margaret.

Back in Flanders, the fleet of fifteen ships was prepared and, though it may not have been filled with as many men as the Yorkists might have hoped for, it sailed in early July for England. On 3 July 1495, the small fleet lay anchor off Deal in Kent, but something seems to have struck Richard with fear. Hall records that the people of Kent:

> hearynge that this feyned duke was come, and had heard that he was but a painted ymage, doubtyng a space what to do, whether to helpe him or to resist his power, at the last remebryng what evell chaunces their forefathers had, and how smal a profite such as have rebelled have gained, thought it neither expedient nor profitable for theim to aide & assyst hym.

Hall probably drew on André's account of the attempted landing, though the blind poet believed 'the Kentish folk with one accord determined to resist the royal foes' with less vacillation than Hall ascribes to them. Both accounts explain that a few hundred of Richard's men made land and the Kentish men tried to entice Richard himself ashore with warm words of encouragement, but that some nagging doubt counselled the young man to caution and he remained aboard his ship.

When it became clear that Richard would not leave his ship, the men of Kent attacked his forces and killed, according to Hall, 150 men, capturing a further eighty and handing them over to Sir John Peachey. They were taken 'railed in ropes likes horses drawn in a cart' and hanged, their corpses displayed along the coastline as a deterrent to others. André has a greater number captured, recalling that 'they were bound with ropes in a row like thieves – except for the wounded, who were carried on carts – and they entered London to the great anticipation of all. After several days, about four hundred lost their lives; some lost their head, others died by the noose.' Richard's ship sailed away from the debacle at Deal and made for Ireland. Henry, who had left on progress to visit his mother, received word of the failed attempt and later in the year sent Sir Richard Guildford into Kent to thank the county for its loyalty. If Richard sought some comfort in this setback, he may have seen a parallel with Henry VII's own attempt to land in England in 1483, which had seen him avoid coming ashore to a jubilant welcome, caution that had probably saved his life. If Richard felt reassured by this notion, the same parallel can only have further heightened Henry's own fear.

Venetian ambassadors continued to report news arriving at Maximilian's court about the invasion. On 11 July, the Bishop of Brixen, Maximilian's ambassador to Venice, had passed on news that the emperor had been delayed in reaching Worms by continuing problems in Guelders and the Low Countries and also by the expense incurred in 'having to dispatch the Prince of York, the new King of England, for the defence of his right', assuring the Doge that once he had won his kingdom, Richard would lead England into the League. The Venetian ambassadors at Worms, Contarini and Trevisano, conveyed news that had reached Worms on 17 July that Richard's invasion had been successful, reporting that 'from his counsellors at Mechlin, the residence of his son the Archduke Philip, he has received intelligence that they are of opinion that the Duke of York, who some while ago went over to Ireland, has reached England, and been received by some of his adherents, whereat his Majesty rejoiced greatly'. The news of a correction was reported by the same ambassadors six days later on 23 July, with news that:

> the Duke of York, the kinsman of his Highness, had arrived with his fleet in the neighbourhood of London, and that, not having found the population well disposed towards him at the spot where he was most anxious to land and attack the hostile army, he had removed to another part of the island; though he nevertheless gave hopes that his affairs would prosper.

European politics began to overtake Richard's cause, whilst at the same time exposing the sustained fear of him in England, by mid-August 1495. Henry VII played a trump card to sow division amongst the leaders of Europe that he hoped would force the emperor to abandon his public and financial support for the pretender. The Venetian ambassadors reported that:

> Dom. Angelo of Florence, ambassador from Ludovic Sforza Duke of Milan to his Cæsarean Majesty, had shown them a paragraph in letters from his Duke, to the effect that he had received a notification from his ambassadors in Spain, purporting that the King of England wishes to be included in the League. The Duke therefore desires Dom. Angelo, in unison with the Spanish ambassadors at Maximilian's court, and with Contarini and Trevisano, to urge his Cæsarean Majesty to consent to this, adding that, should his Majesty refuse on account of the Duke of York, be he told that the need of existing circumstances requires the admittance on behalf of his Majesty of the said King of England, and that the dispute between them be referred for arbitration to the sovereigns of Spain.

Henry had told those within the League that were closest to him that he wished to join, but was distracted by Richard's attempts on his throne, exacerbated by Maximilian's support. As the English king must have intended, those keen to secure England's assistance began to nudge Maximilian away from his open support of Henry's rival. Henry was swiftly willing to abandon his previous cordiality with Charles VIII as an expedient to rid himself of this present threat.

In the absence of orders from Venice, the ambassadors wrote that they were, for the moment, leaving the matter in the hands of the Spanish and Milanese ambassadors who did have instructions from their masters, though they offered the news that:

> From the statement made by Dom. Angelo of Florence, understand that the King of the Romans gives him and the Spanish ambassadors fair words, Dom. Angelo being of opinion that he is awaiting the result of the Duke of York's expedition, which will be known in a few days; as, should he succeed in his attack on England, Maximilian would admit him as they have already written; whilst on the other hand, should the Duke be worsted, the present King will be accepted in his stead.

It seems that the pressure was beginning to bear fruit but that Maximilian was not so fickle as to drop immediately a venture into which he had poured much money and effort. Of course, it could have remained the case that Maximilian firmly believed in Richard and his cause, even though he felt the weight of mounting diplomatic pressure. On 5 September, the Venetians again wrote to their master to explain that a Neapolitan ambassador had shown Maximilian a letter reputed to be from the King of England stating that 'the Duke of York was in Ireland with but a few troops, and that the King had made great preparations, meaning to send in pursuit of him, so that they hoped speedily to get possession of him', clearly hoping to further convince Maximilian that the revolt was over and no longer warranted his support. The report also contained news that can hardly have been well received by Maximilian; the French were sending emissaries to try and maintain the good relations between England and France and Henry VII had written that 'in England the King of the Romans was held in no account.' The Venetians simply noted that 'His Majesty listened without making reply.'

Richard's depleted fleet had made its way along the south coast, turning north to make for Ireland and what he must have hoped would be another warm reception, but the gilt was beginning to peel from this shining adventurer. Sir Edward Poynings, one of Henry VII's most trusted and able knights, had been appointed Lord Deputy Lieutenant of Ireland on

13 September 1494 for the express purpose of purging Yorkist support from that nation in the name of Prince Henry, still far too young to be involved in the execution of the post of Lord Lieutenant he held. During their visit to England after the Lambert Simnel Affair it is likely that the Irish lords had understood clearly enough that their cards were being firmly marked. Even Kildare, who had made many smile at court and won over the king must have known how close to the wind he was sailing. Ireland was in no mood to welcome the rebel leader of an already failed invasion. Although James FitzGerald, Earl of Desmond received Richard and offered him support, the remaining Anglo-Irish nobility kept a safe distance and there was no popular hailing of a newly arrived son of York this time. The Earls of Desmond were a cadet branch of the Geraldine family who were also Earls of Kildare and it is possible that Desmond acted on the instruction of Gerald FitzGerald, Earl of Kildare, but it was hardly the reception that Richard must have hoped for.

Richard's small fleet was bolstered a little when a Scottish ship, the *Keheout*, which might have an equivalent English name of the *Spy*, arrived, apparently as a gift from King James IV of Scotland. An English ship named the *Christopher of Plymouth* was captured to further strengthen Richard's force and, with Desmond's help, he set about laying siege to Waterford, significantly the only town to have held out against the Yorkist forces in 1487. Was there perhaps some revenge for his older brother to be had there? It was an odd course of action, to attack the most hostile town rather than to try to charm the more supportive Irish lords to his cause and it did not go well. The siege began on 23 July and Sir Edward Poynings was quick to gather an army and march to the town's assistance. The citizens of Waterford were doing a sterling job in their own cause, firing cannon from Reginald's Tower and destroying one of Richard's ships. When three more ships were captured by the Irish, Richard was forced to give up and lift the siege on 3 August after just eleven days. It was a second failure in two attempts on this voyage and confidence must have been ebbing away from his small force, not least in the lack of luck and military competence their leader was demonstrating.

The news worsened further for Richard as Henry's attempts to cut him off from the support that had brought him this far picked up pace. Ireland was already closed to Richard and when Archduke Philip, Maximilian's son in whose name the emperor had ruled Flanders during Philip's minority, came of age, Henry was swift to send an embassy in response to Philip's overtures of peace. England had imposed trade embargos on Flanders for their support of Richard that were deeply damaging to the merchants crucial to the region's success. The English ambassadors included Richard Fox, then Bishop of Durham, Viscount Welles and Sir John Kendall, the Grand Prior of England of the Order of St John. The Order had its headquarters at Clerkenwell Priory, enjoying wealth and influence in political circles. Sir John was a noted soldier and would soon take a front row seat in the problem of Richard of England. For now, though, he was clearly a trusted diplomat tasked with finding peace between England and Flanders. A deal was sealed on 24 February 1496 that would lift the embargoes subject to an agreement from both sides not to aid the other's enemies. Flanders, now firmly under Philip's direct rule, and Margaret with it, was cut off from Richard as the diplomatic net tightened.

Broader considerations across Europe also continued to eat away at Richard's support. On 22 August 1495, Ferdinand and Isabella wrote from Spain to their ambassador in England, Roderigo de Puebla, on several matters, including the failure to receive letters he claimed to have sent. Henry clearly still wanted to be admitted to the Holy League, and although Ferdinand and Isabella thought that impossible at present because the King of France was 'before the gates of Rome', they included a copy of the treaty establishing the League, with some hand-written notes in the margins regarding Henry's admission to the League and advising him that nothing more than a letter to the Pope expressing his adherence to the aims of the League was required. The Spanish monarchs suggested that because the League aimed 'to preserve the patrimony of the Church and the dominions of the confederates', 'Henry will therefore gain much by entering it, for he will thereby tie the hands of the King of the Romans, so that he will no longer be able to assist the person who calls himself Duke of York, or any other enemy of his'.

They continued to assert that Maximilian 'is inclined to be reconciled to Henry, and to turn him out', the *him* presumably being Richard, who was now outside any territory controlled by Maximilian or his son anyway. Ferdinand and Isabella assured de Puebla that they had instructed their ambassadors at Maximilian's court to apply all the pressure they could to bring about the end of the breach between England and the Empire, since this appeared 'a favourable moment for the reconciliation of Henry with the King of the Romans, now that the latter has got rid of the so-called Duke of York, that being a thing which Henry seems to have desired'. On the subject of the pretender to Henry's throne, they told de Puebla, presumably meaning the sentiment to be passed on to Henry, that they:

> Are very glad to hear that the person who styles himself Duke of York had not invaded England, but had gone away. Henry is more at liberty now to do what it becomes him to do, and the so-called Duke of York seems to have turned out to be an impostor.

The word translated here, as imposter, was *burla* in the original Spanish, a word meaning joke or jest, and taken in this context to mean that Richard was really an imposter and not just a pretender. As negotiations to marry one of their daughters to Henry's son, Prince Arthur, continued, the Spanish had a vested interest in the King of England's security and stability that was at least an undertow in their policy toward Richard, but it demonstrates that broader concerns than simply his true identity motivated leaders across Europe both in their support for and their distancing from his cause.

Richard of England's options, like his allies, were diminishing quickly as his own failure to win a swift and decisive victory, along with wider European concerns beyond the head upon which the crown of England rested, caused a chill to run through the warm welcome he had previously enjoyed across the courts of the continent. If not earlier, it was perhaps here that an imposter might cut his losses and slip into the shadows of anonymity. The Victorian historian James Gairdner believed that the failure and lack of personal effort at Deal served to prove that Richard was no true Plantagenet, berating the 'contemptible abandonment of his men', but this is insufficient proof. Edward II and Richard II had not been personally brave soldiers, but both were the sons of warriors of legendary status that equal, if not surpass, Richard's supposed father, Edward IV. He seems a more cautious, suspicious man, not unlike Henry VII. Two years after the failure of Henry's 1483 invasion, he had returned, armed not only with French men and money, but a strong degree of luck. Richard did not give up after his setbacks in Deal and Ireland, and that perhaps serves to negate Gairdner's damning verdict. After three years, none would have blamed the man deprived of all the support he had once garnered in Ireland, France, Flanders, the Holy Roman Empire and even England for giving up on an imposture, cutting his losses and walking away with his life. That was not the course Richard took. It may be suggested that he had come to believe his own lies by this point, but to pursue a cause beyond the point of no apparent hope suggests not only a degree of personal bravery not usually ascribed to Richard, but also a conviction that could not be shaken. A conviction in his birth right, perhaps.

Besides, he was not completely cast into darkness after the people of Waterford repulsed his attack. A bright star shone from the north, and Richard sailed towards its source. The light came from the aggressive, ambitious court of King James IV of Scotland and it would mark a new chapter in the exploits of Richard of England.

9

A New Believer

He is of noble stature, neither tall nor short, and as handsome in complexion and shape as a man can be. His address is very agreeable. He speaks
Latin very well; French, German, Flemish, Italian and Spanish … besides
the language of the savages who live in some parts of Scotland on the
islands. He fears God and observes all the precepts of the Church.

Pedro de Ayala's description of King James IV from the
Calendar of State Papers of Spain

Scotland and England were inveterate enemies. Brief periods of cordiality punctuated centuries of bitter border skirmishing. James III had been
killed on 11 June 1488 at the Battle of Sauchieburn, fighting a group of
rebel nobles who opposed his frequently desperate attempts to secure a
peace with England. The rebels, led by the Earls of Angus and Argyll, had
taken custody of James III's eldest son and namesake, the 15-year-old James,
whose father had begun favouring his second son, creating him Duke of
Ross. Prince James may have been a reluctant figurehead for the rebellion
and it seems likely he had not wanted his father's death, though the favour
shown to his younger brother must have rankled. Becoming king on his
father's death, James IV became committed to reigniting war with England.
Such a popular policy proved as difficult to bring to a successful conclusion as it had always been and by 1492 James had been compelled to sign
the Treaty of Coldstream with Henry VII that ran until 30 April 1494. On
25 June 1493, negotiations had begun for a new treaty to last seven years,

which was concluded in July, at which point Henry paid James 1,000 marks in compensation for past injuries. If Henry felt he had secured his northern border, he had underestimated the King of Scotland's commitment to a policy of war.

When Pedro de Ayala, the Spanish ambassador to James IV's court, wrote a description of the Scottish king for his masters, it overflowed with superlatives and effusive praise. James was, he wrote, a handsome and well-built man, fluent in several languages and a pious, God-fearing man. The ambassador continued that James 'gives alms liberally, but is a severe judge, especially in the case of murderers', insisting that he was 'courageous even more so than a King should be', as de Ayala himself could bear witness to and leading to a criticism that James 'is not a good Captain, because he begins to fight before he has given his orders', conjuring images of the king thundering off as his men stand about uncertain what they should be doing, and eventually just following their enthusiastic commander's lead. The ambassador wrote that James had justified his tactic of leading from the front by explaining that 'his subjects serve him with their persons and their goods, in just and unjust quarrels, exactly as he likes, and that therefore he does not think it right to begin any warlike undertaking without being himself the first in danger'. A keen hunter, de Ayala enthuses further 'I tell your Highness that God has worked a miracle in him, for I have never seen a man so temperate in eating and drinking, out of Spain.'

> He lends a willing ear to counsellors, and decides nothing without asking them; but in great matters he acts according to his own judgment, and in my opinion he generally makes the right decision. I recognise him perfectly in the conclusion of the last peace, which was made against the wishes of the majority in his kingdom.

In all, de Ayala found James a near perfect example of a king, concluding his description by assuring his masters 'I can say with truth that he esteems himself as much as though he were Lord of the World. He loves war so much that I fear, judging by the provocation he receives, the peace will not last long.' The ambassador was astute in his measuring of the Scottish king.

de Ayala would later suggest that Ferdinand and Isabella seek a marriage for one of their daughters to James, advising 'he would always be a faithful ally, near at hand and ready to assist ... the kingdom is very old and very noble, and the King possesses great virtues and no defects worth mentioning'. The ambassador was less enamoured of James' people. 'They spend all their time in wars, and when there is no war they fight with each other. The Scotch are not industrious, and the people are poor', complaining also that they 'are vain and ostentatious by nature'. He did concede that the people had improved somewhat under James' rule, continuing that:

> since the present King succeeded to the throne they do not dare to quarrel so much with one another as formerly, especially since he came of age. They have learnt by experience that he executes the law without respect to rich or poor. I am told that Scotland has improved so much during his reign that it is worth three times more now than formerly, on account of foreigners having come into the country and taught them how to live.

It was to this kingdom and its king that Richard pinned what was perhaps his last hope. When he landed on the west coast, James sped across the country to meet him and the two came face to face on 20 November 1495. James' motives are as difficult to discern for certain as those of other rulers who had supported Richard. As de Ayala had noted, it was hardly a secret that James wanted war with England and this young man, washing up on his shores in desperation, provided the perfect vehicle to achieve that aim. Richard represented the greatest threat to the English king and so the perfect weapon for James. The lure for Richard was easy to see too. He had a ready ally in James at the moment when all others seemed to be setting him aside in the face of Henry's clever charm offensive. As with other rulers, it is important to understand James' motives but not to assume that they were simple or one-dimensional. He had much to gain from promoting Richard's cause, but much to lose by championing a commoner to take a king's throne and by adopting a lost cause. If James was, as de Ayala asserted, a harsh judge and a God-fearing king then he seems unlikely to falsely recognise an imposter, though it is questionable whether he could identify Richard one way or the other based on looks alone. There were the three physical marks that Richard had previously mentioned, but importantly, the young man held his own for a prolonged period of time at the king's court, never raising suspicion for a lack of manners, culture or regal bearing. It is unlikely, though possible, that James either knew Richard was a fraud or didn't care whether he was genuine or not, but there are signs that James may well have believed Richard was the genuine Duke of York.

As early as 6 November 1495 the *Accounts of the Lord Treasurer of Scotland* begin to show a steady stream of expenses incurred in relation to Richard's arrival. Before the king met the newcomer, arrangements were being made to set the scene, with arras work being transported from Edinburgh and immediately after their first meeting, there is a record dated 27 November of 'Expenss maid apon Prince Richard of En[gland] and his servitoris fra his cumin in Scotland'. Polydore Vergil, Edward Hall and others place a speech into Richard's mouth on his meeting with James in which he explains his wanderings around Europe, adding that murderers appointed by his uncle Richard III had killed his brother but taken pity on him before telling the king both boys had been murdered. This is the application of a later official story backward in time to increase its air of authenticity, since none of the chroniclers of the next century are likely to have had access to Richard's words on that day, though it seems likely that James' court was enwrapped by Richard's retelling of his story in the hope that it would ingratiate him with a new ally.

Perhaps the surest sign that James believed he was dealing with a true prince came in January 1496. It seems that Richard was introduced to Lady Catherine Gordon soon after his arrival in Scotland. Catherine was of fine Scottish lineage, though the precise nature of that descent is unclear. Her father was George Gordon, Earl of Huntly, by all accounts a terrifying man who, from his powerbase at Strathbogie Castle in the Grampions, was second only to the king in authority across Scotland. He was a key member of James' Privy Council and, at around sixty, had made the successful transition between James III's rule and that of his son. It is possible that Catherine was a daughter of Huntly's second marriage to Princess Annabella of Scotland, herself the youngest daughter of James I and his queen Joan Beaufort, providing a crucial connection to the Lancastrian bloodline for Richard and making her a cousin to James IV. There is also a strong suspicion that Catherine was the second daughter of Huntly's third marriage to Elizabeth Hay, which would remove the close tie to James and the House of Lancaster, but leave her still the daughter of one of the most powerful men in Scotland. One thing seems beyond doubt: Catherine Gordon was considered a beautiful young woman of a similar age to Richard. André described her as of 'modest and graceful look and singularly beautiful' and Henry VII seems to have become smitten with her when the threat she joined herself to was eliminated. When Richard reached Edinburgh, he was installed at the Black Friars near to the Palace of Holyroodhouse and was swiftly betrothed to the beautiful Catherine.

It is likely that Richard and Catherine were married in mid-January 1496 and that a tourney on 13 January was held to celebrate the marriage. The *Accounts of the Lord Treasurer of Scotland* record expenses incurred for gifts to Richard for the tournament of 'a pair of hose' of 'risillis blak' costing 35 shillings, lining and points at 5 shillings, 'half an elne of purpour dammas to begare the sammyn' at 20 shillings, a cassock 'against the tournay' and a 'pair of arming hose' as well as 'xiiii ellis of white dammas to be the Princeis spousing gowne'. A letter lies amongst the *Calendar of State Papers of Spain* written by Richard, probably in his own hand, to Lady Catherine before their marriage, which drips with the kind of courtly love that might be expected of a noble prince to his lady:

Most noble lady, it is not without reason that all turn their eyes to you; that all admire, love, and obey you. For they see your two-fold virtues by which you are so much distinguished above all other mortals. Whilst, on the one hand, they admire your riches and immutable prosperity, which secure to you the nobility of your lineage and the loftiness of your rank, they are, on the other hand, struck by your rather divine than human beauty, and believe that you are not born in our days, but descended from Heaven.

All look at your face, so bright and serene that it gives splendour to the cloudy sky; all look at your eyes as brilliant as stars, which make all pain to be forgotten, and turn despair into delight; all look at your neck, which outshines pearls; all look at your fine forehead, your purple light of youth, your fair hair; in one word, at the splendid perfection of your person – and looking at, they cannot choose but admire you; admiring, they cannot choose but love you; loving, they cannot choose but obey you.

I shall, perhaps, be the happiest of all your admirers, and the happiest man on earth, since I have reason to hope you will think me worthy of your love. If I represent to my mind all your perfections, I am not only compelled to love, to adore, and to worship you, but love makes me your slave. Whether waking or sleeping, I cannot find rest or happiness except in your affection. All my hopes rest in you, and in you alone.

Most noble lady, my soul, look mercifully down upon me your slave, who has ever been devoted to you from the first hour he saw you. Love is not an earthly thing, it is heaven born. Do not think it below yourself to obey love's dictates. Not only kings, but also gods and goddesses have bent their necks beneath its yoke.

I beseech you, most noble lady, to accept for ever one who in all things will cheerfully do your will as long as his days shall last. Farewell, my soul and my consolation. You, the brightest ornament of Scotland, farewell, farewell.

It was a heady romance indeed and possibly a true love match between a woman looking for her knight in shining armour and a world-weary adventurer seeking a throne, but perhaps more than that, a home. Richard had found a ready friend in James, a man of similar mind willing to hear his plans and give substance to his desires. He had a wife, too. After so many years of travelling, hoping, daring and unfulfilled promise, Richard had something akin to a normal life. It is worth noting also that Catherine's father, the belligerent Earl of Huntly who harboured a strong sense of his own powerful position, offered no recorded objection to one of his daughters being given in marriage to a commoner posing as a prince. There is at least the suggestion in this lack of a protest that Richard was accepted in Scotland as the true son of Edward IV. Of course, he was also James' pass to the war with England he so desired.

At the beginning of January 1496, a letter within the *Calendar of State Papers of Venice* records the observation that Maximilian had wanted peace with Henry due to the ancient ties between the Kings of England and Dukes of Burgundy until Henry had made peace with France. Now, 'owing to the strong ties of confederation and relationship existing between him and the Sovereigns of Castile, and at the request of the Pope and other confederates', Maximilian had 'consented to receive the King of England into the League'. Henry apparently responded to the offer by refusing to join the Holy League, stating that 'not having yet seen the articles of the League, he could not determine to join it', despite Ferdinand and Isabella having sent him a copy of the treaty in earlier despatches. The king also observed that 'as peace had been made between the King of France and the Dukes of Venice and Milan, he considered the League broken and dissolved'. This response from Henry suggests that his professed desire to join the Holy League had been a ruse to sap support from Richard's cause and that now, considering it to have worked as well as it could, Henry abandoned the pretence and kept his hands free in his foreign dealings.

The desire on other sides to bring England within the League seems to have been genuine and unaware of Henry's deeper game. An earlier entry in the *Calendar of State Papers of Venice* details the lengthy discussions still taking place at Maximilian's court in early January. The emperor had insisted that:

> having no league or relationship soever with the King of England, the Duke of York, whom he firmly believes to be the son of King Edward, came to him; and that he considered it his duty not to abandon the Duke, nor to fail affording him all just and fitting favour.

By this point, Maximilian seems to have had little to gain from continuing to support Richard, demonstrated by the same despatch, which records that 'should the King of England approve, the King of the Romans offered to negotiate a 10-year truce or peace between him and the said Duke of York', which clause the Spanish ambassadors warned 'would be tantamount to telling him that he did not choose to admit his King into the League'. They advised the removal of all references to Richard because 'all the paragraphs alluding to the Duke of York would only irritate the King of England'. The Venetian ambassador was asked for his opinion and agreed with the Spanish representatives, adding that:

> during the past months the Sovereigns of Spain had given the Signory to understand that it would be very desirable the King of the Romans should drop the affairs of the Duke of York, as this was not the moment for disturbing the kingdom of England, the admission of whose King into the confederation would be advantageous; as he on one side, the King of the Romans on the other, and Spain in her own quarter might simultaneously invade France, to the advantage of the confederates.

Milanese and Neapolitan ambassadors concurred with their colleagues from Venice and Spain. Ludovic Bruno withdrew to take instructions from the emperor and returned to the ambassadors with their answer. Maximilian was:

content to cancel all the paragraphs relating to the Duke of York, but insisted that the obligation on the part of the King of England to attack France should stand; not so much from any hope of its being observed, but because, unless inserted, the King of England would have obtained a promise from the King of the Romans not to favour the Duke of York; the League nevertheless deriving no advantage thence.

The Spanish ambassadors pressed harder, suggesting that Henry would still not be interested in joining the League if new requirements to attack France were included, but offered that Ferdinand and Isabella would vouch for Henry to enter, since they strongly desired it and considered it enough of an advantage that, once within the League, Henry would not be allied to France and so would not provide Charles with troops when the other members attacked. Ludovic Bruno returned with something of a capitulation. Maximilian agreed to act as the ambassadors advised. He gave the English envoy, Lord Egremont, a gold cup and 100 florins to take home with the news of the emperor's agreement to drop clauses relating to Richard from England's treaty to join the League. It was another hammer blow to Richard's cause that was completely outside his control. Henry knew exactly what he was doing and dangling his promise to join the League was working to apply pressure on those still supporting Richard, even though, as we have already seen, he had no real intention of allowing himself to be restricted in his policy by joining such a group. What is also clear is that Maximilian was clinging to his belief in Richard's legitimacy and that only the combined pressure of all his allies forced him to reluctantly drop clauses that sought to protect the pretender. It is unlikely that this was a negotiating strategy alone, since in the end he gave it up for no gain, but it was clear that now, even the Holy Roman Emperor could be dissected from the cause of Richard of England.

The continued adherence of Maximilian to the pretender was still clear, despite this exchange and the pressure being brought to bear. The emperor had dropped the clauses he had wanted, but not Richard himself. On 19 February, the *Calendar of State Papers of Venice* record a report from Zacharia Contarini that he had explained to the emperor the doge's plan to gather embassies from all members of the League to travel to England and try to convince Henry to join them. Henry's careful work was making England a desirable ally across Europe, increasing England's, and his own, prestige. Contarini informed the doge that Maximilian 'had recently received letters from the Duke of York informing him that his affairs were prospering, and that, through the disturbances imminent in England, he hoped for victory'. Maximilian argued that if Richard were to win the crown, he would join the League in attacking France immediately, without the need to pander to Henry. The emperor therefore determined to wait for the outcome of Richard's next action. Contarini wrote that Maximilian felt that 'as the Duke had embarked in the undertaking at his persuasion, and placed hope in him' the emperor would be disappointed 'if, through the negotiation for bringing Henry VII into the League, the Duke of York's success should be impeded', to which the ambassador had made two points. First, he believed Henry could be convinced to join the League with an obligation to attack France, an alteration from previous advice to drop this clause which reflects the view that it would be easier to draw Henry into a war than convince him to negotiate about Richard or tolerate his continued threat. Secondly, Contarini added that the Spanish monarchs feared failure to secure England's membership of the League would drive Henry into closer alliance with France before reminding Maximilian 'he would not omit repeating what the Sovereigns of Spain intimated, namely, that it would be advantageous that the King of the Romans should lay aside the affairs of the Duke of York, as this was not the moment for disturbing England'. Maximilian took a firmer stance than previously by replying that 'he would await advices from Mons. de Beure and his other ambassadors now in England concerning the affairs of the Duke of York, which would reach him in a few days, and that he would then decide'.

Maximilian's support was constant, and he was clearly still receiving updates from Richard, but he was now firmly detached from any effort to invade England and, from the other side of Europe, unable to provide direct support even if he had wanted to. Richard was no less watched, though with different motives, from within the halls of Henry's palaces. On 5 March 1496, instructions were written for a third embassy to Charles VIII in France by Clarenceux, King of Arms, recorded by Madden in *Documents Relating to Perkin Warbeck*. The official purpose of the trip was to suggest a meeting between the two kings, perhaps not least to galvanise the fear of an alliance already running wild through the League. There was talk of a marriage between the Dauphin and Henry's daughter Margaret, talk of money that Henry had loaned to Charles and Henry also sent congratulations on the pregnancy of Charles' wife, suggesting that since his own queen was also pregnant, if one of them had a boy and one a girl, the two should be betrothed. There is no record of Elizabeth of York being pregnant at this time, so unless Henry referred to an unrecorded pregnancy that did not reach full term, he was playing games again to maintain his relationship with France whilst also courting her enemies. Clarenceux's instructions again contained a separate, confidential reference to Richard, currently in Scotland.

> Item, if it should happen that the French King, or any great personages of his Council, should make any question or inquiry, how the King and the king of Scotland accord, seeing that the latter supports and entertains the garçon in his kingdom, or in similar words, and in case they do not speak on the subject, the said Richmond is to endeavour by all proper means to give occasion to such remarks, – he may reply, that concerning this affair, the King cares nothing about it, and that it is the least of all his troubles. For the said king of Scotland is unable to injure him in any manner whatever, except, perhaps, in making him spend his money in vain.

Henry clearly gives Clarenceux, who is also Richmond Herald, authority to not only answer questions raised, but, if the matter is not raised by Charles or any of his advisors, to discreetly raise the matter himself to create an opportunity to assure Charles that Henry feared nothing from either Richard or James. There is again the odour of protesting too much about Henry's bluff confidence and his need to have the matter raised betrays that it was far from being of no concern to him.

Clarenceux had an additional secret task that required him to contact the Cardinal of St Malo, one of Charles' most confidential advisors, for two purposes. The first was to advise the Cardinal that Henry was certain that James would make some attempt to invade England during the year, but that 'en riens ne le craint'; Henry 'in no way fears him'. The lie is immediately given to this claim by Clarenceux's second charge: to consult with the Cardinal about a message Henry had received from Sir Charles Somerset, recently on embassy to France, that several French nobles had offered, if Charles would approve, to take John Stewart, Duke of Albany, a first cousin of James IV who was presently in France, to sea and try to replace James with the duke if the king proceeded with any plan to invade England. Clearly this appealed to Henry and he hoped to be able to confirm the offer, suggesting again that he was not as unconcerned as he tried to appear.

More news reached Henry to add to his worries. On 14 March, a deposition was given at Rouen by Bernard de Vignolles, a servant of Sir John Kendall, the Grand Prior of the Order of St John. The document reached Henry and was endorsed in the king's own hand 'La confession de Bernart de Vignolles' and retained amongst his official papers. The story de Vignolles told, long and rambling as it was, must have seemed at the same time both fantastical and deeply worrying. The crux of the plot de Vignolles sought to expose was that 'the said Prior of St John and sir John Tonge, and Archdeacon Hussey ... sought ways and means of procuring the death of the King of England.' It was claimed that the three men had tried to arrange the king's death whilst in Rome using an astrologer. When this failed to produce any sign of working, de Vignolles was sent to Rome to kill the man, but instead encountered another astrologer who offered him a foul poison which, he claimed, could be spread around a door frame and would cause the next person to walk through the door to kill whoever was inside. de Vignolles panicked and got rid of the poison, replacing it with earth and soot. After delivering the fake concoction to Kendall, the Prior kept trying to force de Vignolles to leave England, but six months of illness prevented his departure. This might have been far-fetched nonsense, though belief in the occult ran strong. Of far more interest was the other allegation levelled at the Prior by de Vignolles.

Bernard claimed that he had seen and read letters to the Prior from another member of the order discussing 'The Merchant of the Ruby', a code name for Richard. The letters described how the merchant had been unable to sell his wares for the right price in Flanders so was intending to offer them to the Holy Roman Emperor, meaning that Richard was having difficulty raising the funds he needed for his invasion. Furthermore, de Vignolles asserted that he had been present at Sir Thomas Tyrell's manor at Avon Tyrell, Hampshire, which Sir John had frequently visited, during a conversation between the two men about the pretender. This Thomas Tyrell is likely to be the brother of Sir James, though James had a son named Thomas also. The conversation allegedly began with Sir John recalling that he had heard of Edward IV staying at Avon Tyrell on several occasions, to which Sir Thomas had replied that he hoped King Edward's son would one day 'make good cheer' there as his father had. Sir John's home at

Clerkenwell, the headquarters of the Order in England, was raided and his correspondence seized, but no evidence against him was found. The Grand Prior had visited Rome in December 1484 on behalf of Richard III and whilst it is impossible to prove, it cannot be ruled out that this was part of the investigations into relegitimising Edward IV's sons after the death of Richard III's only heir, which would mean that Sir John knew the boys were alive at the end of 1484 and that he may have understood Richard to be the genuine Duke of York. Although a pardon was issued to him on 1 July 1496, he remained on Henry's council and de Vignolles remained in Sir John's service, apparently never being unmasked as the source of the accusations against his master.

The most worrying part for Henry must have been not only that this was another of his inner circle implicated in plots that favoured the pretender, coming only just over a year after Sir William Stanley's execution, but that Richard was being spoken of within the halls of English manors as the true son of Edward IV. For a man whose life had made him acutely suspicious and supremely cautious, it must have made him anxious to wonder just how many others whispered against him before fireplaces in their halls whilst smiling to him at court. On 2 April, Zacharia Contarini reported to the Doge of Venice from Maximilian's court that the Spanish ambassadors had received word from England that:

> the English ambassadors accredited to the King of the Romans were about to set out, the object of their mission being to learn thoroughly the opinion of the King of the Romans relating to the Duke of York's business, concerning which they think the King of England will make stipulations before joining the League.

Henry now dropped his pretences and apparently planned to openly confront Maximilian about his continued support of Richard, holding England's entry to the League, which all its members desired, over the emperor's head like the Sword of Damocles, which Henry must have increasingly felt hovering above his own throne.

The *Calendar of State Papers of Venice* continue to demonstrate Maximilian's grasp of the situation, as Contarini reported on 5 April that he had informed the emperor of an embassy sent from Venice to England to try and entice Henry to join the League once more, adding that the Pope had sent a similar emissary too. Maximilian was urged to join the effort, but the reply that came from his representative, Ludovico Bruno, was that:

> From the King of England neither good nor evil could be hoped for, as the demonstration made by him of being on good terms with the League, and especially with the King of the Romans, proceeded solely from fear of the King of the Romans favouring the Duke of York, which same fear is entertained by the King of England with regard to the King of France.

In Maximilian's opinion, Henry 'will therefore endeavour to remain neutral'. Even if the others were still tripping over themselves in desperation to lure Henry into the League, Maximilian, a man widely judged a fool and a failure, had seen right through Henry's schemes. Maximilian told Contarini that the fear of the Duke of York should be used to force Henry to join rather than pleading with him. It was fear of Richard's cause that would force Henry to attack France with the rest of the League so that he might rely on their protection against the threat. Maximilian was calling Henry's bluff. The emperor had sent word to the Spanish ambassadors in England to offer Henry entry to the League 'according to the form of the clauses, with the condition to attack the King of France', since Maximilian himself would not offer such terms 'because it did not become him to seek it himself, by reason of the understanding and articles agreed to between him and the Duke of York'. Although Maximilian was still being forced to distance himself from Richard's cause, there is still no reference to him as anything other than the Duke of York, Edward IV's true son.

In contrast to Maximilian's stoic defiance, the Spanish monarchs and the King of France were increasingly desperate to try and win Henry over, both offering to produce the imposter's parents or provide witnesses who could testify that he was not Edward IV's son. One of the results of this anxious push to woo Henry was the Setubal Testimonies, gathered on 25 April 1496 at Setubal in Portugal by Don Alonso de Silva, Knight-Commander of Calatrava and recorded by Fernan Peres Mexia. The Testimonies were a concerted effort to gather a coherent understanding of who Richard really was and how he came to be troubling the King of England. Portugal was one of England's longest-standing allies and the Anglo-Portuguese Treaty of 1373 between Edward III of England and King Ferdinand and Queen Eleanor of Portugal is the oldest treaty in the world still active today, providing for mutual friendship and support between the nations and last called upon in 1943 when Portugal leased England a naval and air base in the Azores. Portugal was far from a neutral or disinterested party in these affairs. The first evidence offered came from Rui de Sousa:

> First to be interrogated and questioned was Rui de Sousa, knight of the household of our Lord King of Portugal. In my presence, Don Alonso asked the said Rui de Sousa if he had known the Duke of York, son of King Edward, when he was in England. To which he answered that he had seen him and that he was a very noble little boy and that he had seen him singing with his mother and one of his sisters and that he sang very well and that he was very pretty and the most beautiful creature he had ever seen, and he also saw him playing very well at sticks and with a two-handed sword. And then he heard it said that they had put him and his brother too, the Prince of Wales, in a fortress where a body of water passed by, and that they bled them, and they died from the forced bleeding.
>
> Then Alonso asked the said Rui de Sousa who the person was who now called himself the Duke of York; Rui de Sousa said that a youth had come to Portugal with the wife of Duarte Brandon, a Portuguese knight, and he had seen him walking in the Court of Portugal behind a fidalgo [gentleman] who was called Pero Vaz da Cunha, who treated him as his page, and when they had the celebrations for the Lord Prince of Portugal, [Pero Vaz] dressed him up, and he saw him in a doublet of brocade and a long gown of silk. And after that he knew nothing more until now, when he'd heard what people were saying about him. Don Alonso then asked him if he resembled in his person the Duke of York he had seen in England; he said no, because the other one was very beautiful.

Rui de Sousa clearly offers a version of the pretender's story that denies he is the Duke of York, since de Sousa had seen Richard, Duke of York and Richard of England and was certain that they were not the same person because they did not look alike – or at least, one was more beautiful than the other. The latest that de Sousa could have seen Richard, Duke of York was in early 1483 when he was 9. Most versions have the pretender arriving in Portugal in 1487, at least four years after de Sousa had last seen the duke. It is not unreasonable to suspect that a boy would have changed significantly between the ages of 9 and 13, nor that he may have picked up scars or marks during a perilous time in hiding either during Richard III's reign or at the beginning of Henry VII's, when his identity would have made him a marked man. Certainly, it is reasonable that he might have become less 'beautiful'.

The next person to be questioned was Duarte Brandon, known in England as Sir Edward Brampton. Brampton's story is the stuff of sweeping, swashbuckling fiction, perhaps embellished in parts by himself, but otherwise a true story of the extraordinary. Brampton was born to a Jewish family in Portugal as Duarte Brandao. He travelled to England in 1468 where he stayed at the Domous Conversom, a home provided for Jews who converted to Christianity in London where those converting would traditionally take the king as a godfather and frequently adopt his name. Initially, Duarte was known as Edward Brandon but seems to have re-emerged after the return of Edward IV from exile in 1471 as Edward Brampton. Brampton was fond of citing the king as his godfather and appears to have fought for Edward IV, even befriending the king, if his stories were not too far exaggerated. Brandon became the first former Jew to be knighted in England by Richard III, fought against Buckingham's Rebellion in October 1483, recovered a portion of the fleet taken to sea by Sir Edward Woodville and in August 1484 received an annuity of £100 along with estates in London and Northamptonshire from the king. The timing of these gifts may become significant later, but when Richard III was defeated, Brampton fled to Flanders and then returned to Portugal, where he rose in the service of John II and then Manuel I, aided by his strong knowledge of and experience in England. We are not yet done with the story of Sir Edward Brampton, but in 1496 at Setubal, he offered the following testimony:

> Then in my presence and that of the witnesses Don Alonso, Knight. Commander of the Order of Calatrava, asked Duarte Brandon Portuguese who was brought up in England in the household of King Edward, if he knew who this person was whom they now called the Duke. He said it was the worst evil in the world that he and his brother the Prince of Wales had been killed, and the one who they now said [was him] was a youth from a city called Tournai and his father was a boatman who was called Bernal Uberque and he lived below the St Jean bridge and [the boy] was called Piris. And his father had placed him in the said city of Tournai with an organist to teach him the craft for a certain number of years, and the boy had run away. And the boy came to a place called Middelburg

where his [Brandon's] wife had fled from the plague that was in Bruges. In Middelburg he found a position with a craftsman who lived opposite the place where his wife was staying. The craftsman sold needles and purses, and the boy got to know some of the French boys who were in his wife's service. And when the said Duarte Brandon sent for his wife to take her into Portugal, [the youth] found out and told her boys that he wanted to go with them to Portugal and that he would live with the son of Duarte Brandon. So he went on board ship with [Brandon's] wife and came with her to Lisbon. And his wife asked him [Brandon] if he wanted to take him for the household and he answered no, that he had other French boys in service and didn't want any more, but he would place him with a fidalgo. And he gave him to Pero Vaz da Cunha. And he, in the season, attended the celebrations of the Lord Prince of Portugal and clothed [the youth] in a doublet with sleeves of brocade and a gown of silk and other things, and he was with him at the celebrations and in them.

A few days after that one of [Brandon's] boys was being sent in a ship to Flanders and the said boy told him that he wanted to go with him; he wasn't staying in that country since Duarte Brandon did not want to take him in as his son, but when he had agreed to go with Brandon's boy the ship sailed and he was left behind. Then he came across another ship that was ready to leave, and asked where it was going. They told him, to Flanders; he asked them if they would take him; they said yes, but they had to go to Ireland first; he said it didn't bother him. So he folded up all his clothes and put on other old ones and boarded the ship, and he went with them. And when he arrived in Ireland and disembarked as they told him, he had taken off his jacket and dressed himself in that doublet with the sleeves of brocade and the robe of silk. And since those are wild people they ran after him because of that little bit of brocade, and some started to say that he was one of those of Lancaster and others that he was King Edward's son, and so people started to join him until little by little matters got as they are now.

Brampton's story dovetailed nicely with that provided by Rui de Sousa, offering an heir of authenticity. If Brampton believed it was the 'worst evil in the world' that the Princes in the Tower had been killed, his actions during and after Richard III's reign suggest he had not, at least then, blamed Richard III for such a dastardly act. The boy is again held to be a fraud, a son of Bernal Uberque of Tournai and named Piris. Brampton's boy had been something of an adventurer, leaving home for Portugal and then catching a ship bound for Flanders via Ireland, where the 'wild people' were so impressed by his fine clothes that they assumed he must be royalty and began him on the course he had followed ever since. Within a short space of time, this boy from Tournai, on the River Scheldt in what is now Belgium, was able to pass himself off convincingly as an English prince around the courts of Europe. Such a feat seems unlikely. Why would Brampton lie? To cover up his own part in the truth, perhaps, or because the boy had abandoned his anonymity against Brampton's advice? Sir Edward will feature again later in Richard of England's story, but Don Alonso would provide testimony from one more source:

And on the 28th of the said month, in my presence and that of the witnesses recorded below, Alonso de Silva questioned and interrogated Tanjar, a herald of the Lord King of Portugal, asking whether he knew who the person was who now called himself the Duke of York. The herald said he had known him here in Portugal and that he had seen him living with a fidalgo called Pero Vaz da Cunha, and that he had never taken him for a local because it was plain to see that he was a foreigner. And he knew that he had come with the wife of Duarte Brandon. When that herald was going into Flanders once, he was in Tournai (of which he was a native) and he was in the house of one of his relations where he was staying, when the boy's father turned up. Since people had told him that [the herald] had come from Portugal and had seen his son there, he asked him [if he had]. The herald said he didn't know him. Then he asked: 'Who did he go?' The father said he went with the wife of Duarte Brandon, in a ship with her notary.

The herald said that he had seen a youth arrive over there in Portugal, the one who had since gone to Ireland, and that they had raised him up as a king, saying he was the son of King Edward. The father said: 'That's my son.' 'What distinguishing marks did he have?' asked the herald. The father said he had a mark on his face under his eye, and he was a bit of a fool, and he had an upper lip that was raised up a bit and thin legs, and that when he left there he was fourteen going on fifteen. The herald said that he had all those marks.

Then his father, weeping, said, 'That is my son, who got him mixed up in this, ah me, they will kill him.' For his father had no other [son], and by that mark that he had on his face and another that he had on his breast they said that he was the Duke of York.

And his father is a boatman, the master of a boat that comes and goes between Flanders and other places by river and he is rich and he is called John Osbeque, and the boy is Piris, which is Pedro in Flemish.

The herald Tanjar provided evidence of a conversation with the boy's father whilst on a visit to Tournai. There is an explanation offered for the three markings that Richard had repeatedly asserted would identify him as the true Duke of York and they are listed as a mark under his eye, perhaps the one suggested in the pencil sketch completed in Flanders, a raised upper lip and thin legs. The alleged father stated that these markings belonged to his only son who had gone to Portugal with Sir Edward Brampton's wife at the age of 14. Tanjar provides the name John Osbeque for the father, which is significantly different from Edward Brampton's Bernal Uberque, though the boy is again named as Piris, a Flemish version of the Portuguese Pedro, which is Anglicised to Peter. The Setubal Testimonies demonstrate clearly the lengths that European powers were willing to go to in order to aid Henry VII. It is important to question whether their true quest was for the truth or an explanation that Henry could use, especially since it is striking that an enquiry designed to provide Henry with ammunition offers three accounts that are similar, but not the same, giving different names for the boy's father, the herald's account sounding a little too convenient with the father tracking down a Portuguese herald for news of a boy somewhere in his country and offering three physical signs to prove he was the boy from Tournai which probably mirrored the three Richard had been using to try and establish that he was really the son of Edward IV. Furthermore, the father's assertion that the boy was 'a bit of a fool', possibly meant to explain how he had been tricked into pretending to be the Duke of York, cannot be true, since other rulers were sufficiently convinced to support him and to never question his manners, appearance or intelligence. The official story was, slowly, beginning to take a more solid form which it would appear to lose again soon.

At the other side of Europe, Henry's efforts continued with a smooth grace that belied his increasing fear. The *Calendar of State Papers of Venice* record Zacharia Contarini writing from Augsburg on 20 May 1496 to update the Doge and Senate on progress with negotiations to convince England to join the League. Contarini had spoken with the English ambassador, who explained:

> the King of England, having been requested by the Pope, the King of the Romans, Spain, Venice, and Milan, to join the Holy League, was well disposed so to do, but that, being now at enmity with the Kings of Scotland and of Denmark, and entertaining suspicion of the Duke of York and of other rebels in Ireland, he does not see how he can wage offensive war against the King of France, or even furnish the subsidies required by the clauses for a defensive war, both on account of his being at so great a distance from the confederates and by reason of the enmity and suspicions aforesaid.

Henry was replaying the same message: I'd love to join, but I'm prevented by this pesky troublemaker. The hope was clearly that the League's other members would bring about a swift resolution to the problem.

Contarini's letter of 20 May goes on to report that the English ambassador, Sir Christopher Urswick, was summoned before Maximilian and asked directly whether England would join the League and attack France. Urswick's response was a perfect political evasion, mirroring what he had already intimated to Contarini earlier, explaining 'when urged to levy war and invade France, he stated he was not aware that any of the allies had proceeded to such an act save the Sovereigns of Spain, nor was it just that his King, being the last to join the confederation, should be amongst the first to invade', adding that he would expect full details of troop numbers to be supplied, an invasion plan, details of timescales and how any territory captured was to be shared. Urswick ended by saying that he could not agree to anything more without instructions from his king, but that he was happy to write to Henry to request such orders. At this point, Urswick was dismissed and Contarini reports Maximilian's speech to the remaining ambassadors directly:

> Should you approve, we will dismiss this ambassador, and send our own ambassadors immediately after him to negotiate this affair with the representatives of the other confederates, and also to negotiate some form

of agreement between him, the King of Scotland, the Duke of York and others his enemies, provided he bind himself to attack the King of France.

The ambassadors counselled Maximilian that it would be quicker to allow Urswick to write home for instructions, but that if the Englishman wished to leave, commissioners already in England should be tasked with continuing the negotiations rather than new ambassadors being sent by the emperor. It seems Maximilian was not trusted to restrain himself from pouring fuel on the fire of Henry's fears, particularly since the emperor had suggested that doing precisely that was the best way to stir the King of England into action. Contarini explains their reasoning clearly enough. First, Maximilian's own ambassadors 'assented with some little difficulty, on account of the Duke of York; and, secondly, because the missions of the King of the Romans were wont to be more tardy than the need required'.

Maximilian appears not to have taken offence at the frankness of the admonition but insisted that Urswick had to leave, having, Maximilian was certain, been compromised by the French so that he gave falsely negative reports of the emperor to Henry VII, this being the cause of the peace between England and France. Maximilian agreed not to send his own embassy but to leave the matter to the Spanish ambassadors already in England, adding his own belief that 'until the King of England was safe from the Duke of York, and from those who favour the latter, he would never attack the King of France nor give subsidy to the confederation; and he therefore thought it advisable to promise that immediately on the King of England joining the League, the confederates would send their ambassadors to arrange these differences'. Contarini wrote again on 14 June to Venice that Maximilian had learned that Henry had sent an embassy to France which Sir Christopher Urswick had singularly failed to inform the emperor of, causing the emperor's representative, Erasmo Brascha, to repeat Maximilian's belief that 'by reason of the King of England's suspicion of the Duke of York, he will endeavour to be on good terms with everybody, and on no account quarrel with the King of France.'

It should not be considered incidental that during Contarini's entire correspondence on this subject, he never fails to refer to Richard as 'the Duke of York', never qualifying it with reference to an imposture, the name Perkin Warbeck or using Henry's dismissive *garçon*. Official Venetian State Papers do not refer to Richard as a fraud, only an impediment to

Henry's membership of the League. Receipt of a letter is also recorded within the *Calendar of State Papers of Venice* dated 15 June 1496 from Piero Contarini (perhaps a relation of Zacharia) and Luca Valaresso, the Venetian ambassadors in England, which record that as the year progressed 'King Henry was in dread of being expelled from the kingdom by his nephew, the Duke of York, then in Scotland, whose King meant to assist him, and had given him a niece of his in marriage.' Whilst Henry laughed of the *garçon* in his public despatches, it seems he was less able to hide his mounting fears in person. As it turns out, Henry had good reason to know the extent of the threat.

In Scotland, Patrick Hepburn, Earl of Bothwell was proving an eager and productive spy for the King of England. Within *Original Letters Illustrative of English History, Vol. I* is a long letter sent from the Earl as part of his intelligence gathering on Henry's behalf. Bothwell told Henry that 'I ondirstand without dout this instant xv day of September the King, with all the hailed peple of his realm he can mak, wilbe at Ellam kyrk within x myll of the marchis of England, and Perkin and his company with hym.' According to Bothwell, James planned to launch his invasion on 17 September with around 1,400 men, two ships and a small contingent supplied by Margaret from Flanders. Bothwell also refers to a scheme put to him by the English ambassador at James' court, Wyot, in which Richard should be seized from his tent at night, assuring Henry:

> I have been busy about it, and my Lord of Buchan takes upon him the fulfilling of it, gif it be possible; and thinks best now: in this lang night within his tent to enterprise the matter; for he has no watch but the King's appointed to be about him; and they have ordanit the Englishman and strangers to be at another quarter lugit [lodged] but a few about him.

Henry could only hope that Bothwell might be able to snatch Richard, but he now had to prepare for an invasion due to begin on 17 September 1496.

A proclamation issued by Richard just before launching his invasion from Scotland is recorded in Chastelain's *L'Imposture de Perkin Warbeck* and opens 'Richard, by the Grace of God, King of England, Lord of Ireland, Prince of Wales: To all those who will hear, see or read our present letters, greeting.' The proclamation continues at length to explain that Richard was now equipped to claim his right to the crown of England by force, reassuring those in England 'far be it from us to intend their hurt or damage, or to make war upon them, otherwise than to deliver ourself and them from tyranny and oppression'. Henry VII is labelled 'our mortal enemy, Henry Tudor, a false usurper of the crown of England' who had 'by all foul and wicked means sought to betray us and bereave us of our life'. Richard claimed he would fight not only for his own right, which he might overlook, but for that which he could not forget, the freedom of his people, since 'this Tudor, who boasteth himself to have overthrown a tyrant, hath, ever since his first entrance into his usurped reign, put little in practice but tyranny and the feats thereof.' The proclamation was designed to be a rousing condemnation of Henry's rule, which it had to be if it was going to achieve its aim of drumming up support for Richard in England.

The next paragraph begins with an intriguing reference to Richard III, which is notable for the complete lack of an accusation against him for the murder of Edward V, since Richard was claiming to have survived as the 'younger son and now surviving heir male of the noble and victorious Edward the Fourth'. Had Richard learned, or known all along, that his elder brother had not perished in the Tower but had invaded England in 1487, assuming that he met his death at Stoke Field or shortly afterwards? Either way, Henry was never going to comment on the matter, let alone produce a royal prisoner who would cause him untold problems. Richard wrote that 'King Richard, our unnatural uncle, although desire of rule did blind him, yet in his other actions, like a true Plantagenet, was noble, and loved the honour of the realm and the contentment and comfort of his nobles and people.' Richard III is called an 'unnatural uncle', which can only really be a reference to an accusation of having murdered Edward V, which was already part of Richard's story anyway. The reason for offering so glowing a report of his uncle becomes clear in the following sentence when Henry VII is compared unfavourably to Richard III. Having bestowed Richard III with some redeeming features, Henry, for the sake of propaganda, is made a worse king with no redeeming features at all:

> But this our mortal enemy, agreeable to the meanness of his birth, hath trodden under foot the honour of this nation, selling our best confederates for money, and making merchandise of the blood, estates, and fortunes of our peers and subjects by feigned wars and dishonourable peace, only to enrich his coffers.

Some of this may have rung true with Henry's subjects, but it is a standard tactic prior to an attack, not dissimilar to several others throughout the Wars of the Roses. Little can really be taken from the reference to Richard III since it is really a set-up line for the blistering attack on Henry. If Richard was bad, Henry is worse.

The proclamation goes on to detail Henry's tyranny, his poor treatment of the Earl of Warwick and the forced marriages of Warwick's sister and Princess Elizabeth, the latter to the king himself, complaining that many nobles were forced to purchase their freedom from Henry and that evil, low-born men surrounded the king to be 'the principal finders, occasioners, and counsellors of the misrule and mischief now reigning in England'. All of these things Richard promised to correct, seeking support from every quarter by also offering pardons to all and announcing his intention to 'unyoke our people from all heavy burdens and endurances, and confirm our cities, boroughs and towns in their charters and freedoms', giving 'our subjects cause to think that the blessed and debonair government of our noble father King Edward, in his last times, is in us revived'. Richard offered a reward of one thousand pounds and an annuity of a hundred marks to any man who would capture or kill Henry 'to stay much effusion of blood', which Richard wished to avoid if at all possible.

In the final paragraph, Richard notes that 'God hath moved the heart of our dearest cousin, the King of Scotland, to aid us in person in this our righteous quarrel', but insists that James has extracted no promise of land, money or anything else in return for his assistance and has promised to withdraw from England as soon as Richard has the upper hand over his enemy, 'contenting himself only with the glory of so honourable an enterprise, and our true and faithful love and amity'. This last assurance seems unlikely; James would surely want something for his troubles and investment, but invading England with a Scottish army was sure to instil more fear than sympathy for Richard's cause and the detrimental effect of that needed to be mitigated. As a piece of propaganda, this was standard fare. It can offer little to confirm Richard's true identity too, since he would hardly cast any doubt upon his own cause by entertaining the suggestion that he was an imposter. The only real clue lies once more in the reference to James as 'our dearest cousin'. For a king to allow someone he knew to be a commoner to address him in such a way was to the detriment of his own majesty and was never something a monarch did lightly. Either James firmly believed Richard was the Duke of York, or he was so desperate for a fight with England that he bit his tongue at the imposture. It is almost impossible to tell which might be true, but James' treatment of this young man over previous years and since his arrival in Scotland certainly suggested his belief in Richard's authenticity.

The *Accounts of the Lord Treasurer of Scotland* record gifts to the Duke of York in the build up to the date set for the invasion. On 10 September, he dispersed 'two hundred of gold party to the Duke of York's banner' and on 14 September gave 14*s* for the duke's offering. Around the same time, James gave a gift of £36 into the duke's purse. When 17 September arrived, James, Richard and their army crossed the Tweed and began to press south into England. Scottish historian Tytler and Francis Bacon agree that when support for Richard did not materialise, the Scots quickly fell to burning, raping and pillaging as James turned his cannons on the stone towers in which the poor took refuge in their terror. This was precisely what the English would always fear about a Scottish army coming south and perhaps exactly what James had wanted all along. The sources are scarce, but Tytler and Bacon reported that Richard pleaded with James to stop attacking those who had done no wrong only for James to retort angrily that the people had not come to Richard's side, so deserved what they were getting. Doubtless his men were enjoying delivering these just desserts too. At this, Richard, turned his horse and rode back across the border into Scotland, telling James he would rather give up his crown than see such injustice. Once more, the lack of martial prowess and perhaps stomach for the sights of war have been levelled at Richard after this episode to suggest that he cannot have been a true Plantagenet, but that argument does not hold water, as we have previously seen. If Richard were really an imposter, he might have cut his losses and lived as an exile in Scotland now, married to a fine noble lady. Having mustered and launched an invasion, it seems unlikely that an imposter would surrender such an opportunity for the sake of a few common people, having spent years crafting it, unless he can truly be charged with cowardice in the face of what might befall him if he met Henry's army.

By 21 September, Richard was back at Coldstream, where he is recorded as receiving £74 8*s* at the king's command 'when the Duke of York came home'. James had not abandoned his friend, or his identity, in anger at the abortive invasion. It must have been clear, though, that Richard was not going to acquiesce to the kind of vicious campaign James either wanted or believed was necessary to remove Henry. Richard's hope in his proclamation that someone might seize or kill the king to avoid fighting might have stemmed as much from his own distaste for or fear of fighting as from a genuine chivalric call to avoid the effusion of Christian blood. Does this aversion make him an imposter? It must be remembered that Richard, Duke of York had been 9 years of age when his father died and had been living in his mother's household with his sisters. He had not yet embarked on any kind of knightly training that would harden nobles into their teens against the sights of battle and fear of hurt. A commoner would not have received such training, but neither would Richard, Duke of York, after his life became more unsettled, first by his uncle's accession and then the advent of Henry VII's reign when he was 11 that might have left him a disconnected wanderer as Richard would later claim. Sadly, the lack of martial ability is little assistance in trying to discern Richard's true identity.

Henry's efforts abroad to defeat Richard's threat continued to bear fruit. The *Calendar of State Papers of Spain* records the marriage treaty finalised in London on 1 October 1496 that would see Prince Arthur married to Ferdinand and Isabella's daughter Catherine of Aragon. Amidst the terms is no direct reference to Richard or any other Yorkist heirs but it is believed that the Spanish monarchs had been unhappy about arranging the union, and had no intention of sending their daughter to England, whilst Henry faced domestic threats to his crown. The conclusion of the negotiations may have hung upon the outcome of Richard's invasion, now no longer an immediate threat. The wedding was to be contracted when Arthur 'shall have completed his fourteenth year of age', at which point Catherine would travel to England. This would give Henry until 1501 to see that the threats were completely removed and the treaty may have been concluded in order to assist in projecting Henry's security and acceptance amongst other European rulers, though it would seem to have still depended on satisfying Ferdinand and Isabella that England was a safe home for their daughter and the English crown would pass smoothly to Arthur.

In October 1496, after more than a year of vacillating and wrangling, Henry signed up to the Holy League. He had been under pressure from all quarters, including the Pope, to join the League but had provided excuse after excuse for not doing so. The marriage treaty with Spain may have been dependent on England's accession to the League, but Richard's failed invasion and the threats Maximilian wished to bring to bear may have forced Henry's hand and left him unable to put off a decision any longer. On 13 November, Luca Valaresso, one of the ambassadors from Venice to England tasked with encouraging Henry to join the League, returned to Venice and continued to report a darker picture than Henry was painting. The *Calendar of State Papers of Venice* note his opinion that:

> Owing to the war between England and Scotland near at hand the island was in a disturbed state, and it had been reported lately that the English and Scotch fought a battle in which 15,000 men were killed; and the cause of the war was that the Duke of York had taken [for wife] a kinswoman of the King of Scotland, and meant to invade and seize the kingdom of England, as he was the son of King Edward.

The scale of the fighting is likely to be exaggerated, but Valaresso maintained that England was unsettled and, most notably, continued to refer to Richard as the Duke of York, 'the son of King Edward'.

10

The Wrong Place
at the Right Time

He wanted to attack the King of Scotland for the overthrow of the Duke of York, and under pretence of this he amassed much money, and the people complained of paying; and it was said that the King had placed all his property in a tower nearest the coast, that he might escape if necessary.

Calendar of State Papers of Venice regarding Henry VII's preparations to fight Richard

When Parliament gathered at Westminster on 16 January 1497, its primary function was to vote through heavy taxation to allow Henry VII to raise funds for a war against Scotland that would provide him the opportunity to be rid of Richard once and for all. The Council had estimated that a huge £120,000 was required to fund the expedition but Parliament was in no mood to simply agree to such a crushing weight. Two taxes of a tenth and a fifteenth were approved to be collected at the end of May and in early November, but the condition was applied that if no army was put into the field or a truce was made, the second tenth and fifteenth would be cancelled. Both taxes would not raise anywhere near the sum Henry and his Council wanted. *Rymer's Foedera* contains a commission sent by Henry on 13 February 1497 to Sir Thomas Dacre, Lieutenant of the West March, ordering him to muster an army 'since our enemy of Scotland, with a great array of our rebels and traitors, has hostilely invaded our Kingdom of England, and cruelly slain our subjects, neither sparing age nor sex, and has burned and destroyed without remorse castles, fartalices and towers, and intends further mischief'. The tone is one of frustrated annoyance and shows that the king still saw a likely threat from across the border, though Henry would have been further outraged had he known that Lord Dacre had secretly offered his support to Richard, only to fail to rise when the Scottish army came south.

Henry's problems came more quickly from the south-west than the north as Cornishmen refused to pay the tax granted by Parliament on the grounds that they did not see why they should have to fund a war so far away from their homes. There were reports that the leaders of the Cornish uprising sent messages to Richard in Scotland asking him to come and lead them against Henry, but the revolt was over before Richard could make his move. As the Cornishmen mobilised, led by a lawyer, Thomas Flammock and a blacksmith named Michael Joseph, or Michael An Gof, James Tuchet, Lord Audley met them in Somerset and took control of the swelling group of angry men. When they arrived in Taunton, the provost, who was responsible for overseeing the collection of the tax, was killed and the mob moved on to Wells, Winchester and Salisbury on their march east. As they closed in, Henry received news that Charles VIII was fuming at Henry's agreement to join the Holy League against him and had offered James £100,000 for Richard. Scotland was poised to fall upon him from the north and Flanders was hardly a firm friend.

The queen and her children, including Prince Henry, Duke of York, now aged nearly 6, took refuge in the Tower as a force numbered varyingly by contemporary sources between 16,000 and 40,000 neared London and set up camp just outside the City. Prince Arthur was at Ludlow, but Prince Henry, his sisters and his mother were to be subjected to the terror of a looming attack on their position. Henry had been raising an army of his own with the assistance of his Chamberlain, Lord Daubeney, and may have gathered as many as 25,000 men at Lambeth. On 17 June, the two forces clashed at Dartford and on Deptford Bridge, the king's forces crushing the poorly organised and provisioned rebels. Cornish casualties numbered around 2,000 whereas the royal army lost only about 300. Henry re-entered the capital to a rapturous welcome, liberating his family from the Tower and returning them to the comfort of his palace at Sheen after overseeing the executions of the rebel leaders. On 27 June, Lord Audley was drawn from Tower Hill to Newgate, his coat of arms reversed as a sign of his treason and dishonour, and beheaded. Flammock and Michael An Gof were hanged, drawn and quartered, their dismembered bodies returned to Cornwall to be displayed.

By 1 July, Henry was at Sheen with his family. Only a few days later, on 6 July, Richard and his wife Catherine Gordon left Scotland, perhaps intending to make for Cornwall, unaware that the uprising had already failed. The last payment in the Scottish accounts made to Richard by James was a gift of £112 on 27 June. James had not abandoned Richard, though, and the plan may well have been to open up another front in the fight against Henry, with Richard leading the men out of the west, leaving James and his Scottish army free to invade from the north again without Richard's critical eye hampering their cause. Although he conflated events, Gutierre Gómez de Fuensalida, a Spanish Ambassador to Germany, Flanders and England between 1490 and 1507, wrote to Ferdinand and Isabella:

> … it is certain that there is nobody in England who does not marvel at what they have seen: for at a time when the whole Kingdom was against the King, and when Perequin had entered the country calling himself King, and the King of Scotland was coming in by another way, and the whole country was in rebellion, and the men of Cornwall were giving battle at a short distance from London; when, had the King lost the battle he would have been finished off and beheaded; that at that very moment a marriage should have been arranged on conditions disadvantageous to your Highness, filled everyone with amazement.

There is a strong note of chastisement that the monarchs would risk one of their daughters in so dangerous and precarious a place, though it is possible that the marriage agreement was meant to strengthen Henry against these very threats. The Infanta was not due to leave Spain for a few years more.

Henry tried to open negotiations with James, appointing Richard Fox, Bishop of Durham to try and reach agreement with the Scots on 4 July 1497, apparently in response to a second incursion over the border during which James had laid siege to Norham Castle before the approach of the Earl of Surrey caused him to retreat again. Surrey had pursued James, attacking four castles and getting within a mile of James' position. The King of Scotland sent the earl a challenge to single combat to decide the ownership of Berwick, which James might well have won, but Surrey diplomatically pointed out that he would not be permitted to kill a king, though the king would be entitled to kill him, making the fight somewhat unfair. The day after receiving his commission, secret instructions were given to Fox at Sheen, recorded in the *Cotton MSS*, which insist that the handover of Richard was a red line in the negotiations:

> And therefore, you shall demand and require on our behalf of our said Cosen, that he deliver unto us Perkin Warbeck, the wch deliverance of him we desire not for anie estimation that wee take of him, but because our said Cosen received him within his land, & favourably hath entreated him & divers others of our Rebells, during the peace concluded be twixt us both, & over that, having him in his companie, entred in puissance within our land, the which was the cause & ground of breache of the said peace, & less therefore may wee not do with our honor, then to have the deliverance of him, though the deliverance or having of him is of noe price or value.

There is once more the air of panic as Henry tried to present a calm front to the threat he clearly felt. The king desperately wanted custody of Richard, even though Henry claimed he was of no value or consequence. Both cannot be true. There is no admonition to James for holding up an imposter as a true prince, only the observation that James had supported Richard, who Henry wanted referred to as Perkin Warbeck. The insistence on this clause was immediately undone as the instructions continued 'if our said Cosen shall not be agreeable to the deliverance of the said Perkin unto us, as is before rehersed, the which as wee thinke (sith he is not the person that he surmised him to be, when hee obtained his sauft-conduct of our said Cosen, as it is well knowne through all these parts of the world)' then another form of peace was to be agreed on similar terms to that previously in place. It seems that as keen as Henry was to get his hands on the pretender, he needed to stave off another Scottish invasion more as other threats demanded his attention. The instruction concluded by reaffirming that Fox 'shall by all wise meanes to you possible, endeavor your self to have the said Perkin deliuered unto us … the which to obtaine and have, should bee to the conservation of our honnor, and most to our desire and pleasure'. Henry could not quite shake the need to have control of Richard.

Richard and Catherine's ship docked in Cork on 26 July and the couple arrived at Waterford on 1 August. Henry's sharp and diligent spies sent word to the king, who received their intelligence at Woodstock on 6 August and immediately replied, offering 1,000 marks to any man who captured Richard. The nineteenth-century historian Gairdner claims that the captain of Richard's ship had refused to land in England because his was not a war ship, but also because Catherine and her *children* were aboard, citing André as his source for this detail that would prove elusive but potentially crucial later on. De Puebla wrote to Ferdinand and Isabella on 28 August that Richard's ship had been intercepted and the 1,000-mark reward offered if he was given up, but the 'obstinate Biscayans, however, swore in spite of all this, that they had never heard of such a man. Richard was all the time in the bows of the ship hidden.' Something about the young man clearly inspired loyalty even in the face of a huge sum of money.

On 7 September 1497, Richard landed at Whitesand Bay in Cornwall, near to Land's End. If he hoped for a rapturous welcome amongst men thirsty to march on Henry, he found a cowed county nursing sore injuries and licking open wounds. There was little appetite for more, but Richard needed to try and harness whatever mood of dissent still lingered there. Richard placed his wife and, if they did indeed have any, his child or children, within the security of St Michael's Mount before the *Chronicle of London* records that he marched to Bodmin 'where he was accompaned with iij or iiij m men of Rascayll and most parte naked men. And there proclaymed hym silf kyng Richard the iiij, and Second son unto kyng Edward the iiij.' The Chronicle had previously recorded that Richard had landed with around a hundred men, so he had quickly gathered 3,000–4,000 followers in his short march across Cornwall. It appeared the appetite for vengeance was still alive in Cornwall after all.

In this atmosphere, with the king beset all about by hostile forces, the *Calendar of State Papers of Venice* records an account from England that Henry had sent:

the Queen and his children to a castle on the coast, with enough treasure and valuables to aid their escape … He wanted to attack the King of Scotland for the overthrow of the Duke of York, and under pretence of this he amassed much money, and the people complained of paying; and it was said that the King had placed all his property in a tower nearest the coast, that he might escape if necessary.

The caution is utterly believable of Henry, whose precarious years as an exile, dodging constant attempts on his life and being protected only as a bargaining chip, must have made him fear the worst and plan against it. Never in his eleven years on the throne had he been in such peril, threatened by a landing in Cornwall, an invasion from Scotland, aggression from France and with no real friends in Flanders or the Holy Roman Empire. Queen Elizabeth and her younger children were in fact in East Anglia, on progress, when Richard began to march across Cornwall, but they would remain away from the capital and the dangers they had just faced as the last wave of Cornish rebels had pushed closer to London. It is not impossible that Henry began to prepare an escape route.

On 17 September, Richard and his force arrived at Exeter and when the city closed its gates, the pretender attacked the North and East gates. Exeter was defended by William Courtenay, Earl of Devon who was married to Catherine of York, a sister of the queen and therefore also of the Princes in the Tower. The earl does not appear to have felt compromised, though he would hardly have expressed such a feeling to his king later. The attackers lost around 200 men before withdrawing and then, according to the *Chronicle of London*, trying again the following morning. During the assault, the Earl of Devon was reportedly injured, though he wrote to Henry that 'when Perkin and his company had well assaid and felt our Gunns, they were faine to desire us to have licence to geder theire company togeder, and soe depart and leave your Citty', explaining that because Henry wished the pretender taken alive and because the city was in poor condition to properly defend itself, he had granted the rebels six hours' grace in which to withdraw on the condition that no man from Exeter joined them. If Devon was certain that Richard was a fraud, the king would surely have forgiven the earl if the threat had fallen in the assault. The other possibility is that Devon either knew Richard was his genuine brother-in-law or at least was not certain and pulled his punches for his wife's sake, later having to make things right with Henry whilst keeping his options open should the invasion succeed.

Two days after leaving Exeter, Richard arrived at Taunton. Chastelain gives him 7,000 to 8,000 men by this point, which, if correct, makes the threat he now posed very serious. The level of the threat can be seen in a letter Henry wrote to the Bishop of Bath and Wells, recorded within *Original Letters Illustrative of English History, Vol. I*, explaining first the recent action at Exeter and then detailing the force the king was raising to defend against the mounting threat. 'The Perkin and his company, if they came forward, shall find before them our Chamberlain, our Steward of Household, the Lord Saint Mourice, Sir John Cheney, and the Noblemen of Southwales and of our Counties of Gloster, Wiltshire, Hamshire, Somersett, and Dorcet; and at their backe the garrison of our said City of Excester.' Henry continued that 'wee with our hoast royall shall not be farre, with the mercy of our Lord, for the final conclusion of the matter.' The reference to 'The Perkin' is interesting and the etymology of such a name is hard to confidently establish. It has been asserted anecdotally that the word has a Welsh origin, meaning 'One', so 'The Perkin' would be 'The One', but there is no real evidence to support this interpretation. The family name Perkin appears to be an anglicised rendering of the Welsh family name Peregrine, which may derive from the Latin *peregrinus*, meaning pilgrim. This makes sense as a sort of code name given to the pretender within Henry's circles, referring to his life roaming the courts of Europe. Once in use, it perhaps stuck when it came time to apply a name to him and was absorbed as part of the story.

Two days after arriving at Taunton, Richard's nerve broke. He fled at dawn on 22 September with a few close associates to Beaulieu Abbey, a Cistercian monastery in the New Forest in the county of Hampshire whose medieval Latin name was Bellus Locus Regis: The beautiful place of the King. Richard sought sanctuary within the Abbey but by 5 October he was a prisoner of Henry's men and was returned to Taunton, where the king had arrived. Here, the confession of Perkin Warbeck was first given – or received – by the pretender. The pretender became an imposter, his name recorded in this confession as Piers Osbeck and the detail of his life and adventures given as follows:

> It is first to be known that I was born in the town of Turney in Flanders, and my father's name is John Osbeck, which said John Osbeck was controller of the said town of Turney, and my mother's name is Katherine de Faro. And one of my grandsires upon my father's side was named Diricke Osbecke, which died. After whose death my grandmother was married unto Peter Flamin, that was receiver of the forenamed town of Turney and dean of the boatmen that row upon the water or river called the Schelt. Any my grandsire upon my mother's side was Peter de Faro, which had in his keeping the keys of the gate of Saint John's

within the same town of Turney. Also I had an uncle called Master John Stalin, dwelling in the parish of Saint Pias within the same town which had married my father's sister whose name was Johne Jane with whom I dwelt a certain season. And after, I was led by my mother to Antwerp for to learn Flemish in a house of a cousin of mine, an officer of the said town called John Stienbeck, with whom I was the space of half a year. And after that I returned again to Turney by reason of wars that were in Flanders. And within a year following I was sent with a merchant of the said town of Turney named Berlo, to the mart of Antwerp where I fell sick, which sickness continued upon me five months. And then the said Berlo sent me to board in a skinner's house that dwelled beside the house of the English nation. And by him I was from thence carried to Barrow mart and I lodged at the 'Sign of the Old Man' where I abode for the space of two months. After this the said Berlo sent me with a merchant of Middlesborough to service for to learn the language, whose name was John Strew, with whom I dwelt from Christmas to Easter, and then I went into Portugal in company of Sir Edward Brampton's wife in a ship which was called the queen's ship. And when I was come thither, then was I put in service to a knight that dwelled in Lushborne, which was called Peter Vacz de Cogna, with whom I dwelt an whole year, which said knight had but one eye. And because I desired to see other countries I took licence of him and then I put myself in service with a Breton called Pregent Meno, who brought me with him into Ireland. Now when we were there arrived in the town of Cork, they of the town (because I was arrayed with some cloths of silk of my said master's) came unto me and threatened upon me that I should be the Duke of Clarence's son that was before time at Dublin.

But forasmuch as I denied it, there was brought unto me the holy evangelists and the cross, by the mayor of the town which was called John Llellewyn, and there in the presence of him and others I took mine oath (as the truth was) that I was not the foresaid duke's son, nor none of his blood. And after this came unto me an English man whose name was Stephen Poitron and one John Water, and laid to me, in swearing great oaths, that they knew well that I was King Richard's bastard son, to whom I answered with like oaths that I was not. Then they advised me not to be afeared but that I should take it upon me boldly, and if I would do so they would aid and assist me with all their power against the King of England,

and not only they, but they were well assured that the Earl of Desmond and Kildare should do the same.

For they forced not what part they took, so that they might be revenged on the King of England, and so against my will made me learn English and taught me what I should do and say. And after this they called me the Duke of York second son to King Edward the fourth because King Richard's bastard son was in the hands of the King of England. And upon this the said Water, Stephen Poitron, John Tiler, Hughbert Burgh with many others, as the aforesaid earls, entered into this false quarrel, and within short time others. The French King sent an ambassador into Ireland whose name was Loit Lucas and master Stephen Friham to advertise me to come into France. And thence I went into France and from thence into Flanders, and from Flanders into Ireland, and from Ireland into Scotland, and so into England.

Richard, or Piers, claims to be a native of Tournai, his parents being John Osbeck and Katherine de Faro, and provides some other detail about members of his extended family in Tournai. His story has him dotted around the region learning bits of different trades and a couple of languages before travelling to Portugal with the wife of Sir Edward Brampton, where the story becomes similar to that given by Brampton at the Setubal Testimonies; the boy entered the service of Peter Vacz de Cogna before leaving him to travel to Ireland with a Breton merchant named Pregent Meno. In Ireland, he was mistaken for George, Duke of Clarence's son, the Earl of Warwick still (to the best of Henry's knowledge) in the Tower. It is at this point that credibility is stretched that bit too far and Henry's hand begins to become more clear in the confession. The use of Warwick draws a strong parallel with the Lambert Simnel Affair and gives weight to the assertion that everyone knew the sons of Edward IV were dead, hence their determination to find a credible Warwick. The insertion too of a confusion over the identity of the boy should assume creates the impression of a definite imposture taking form and imbues the whole story with a little more of an air of truth.

Having sworn a holy oath that he was not Clarence's son, more men came to him and told him he must be an illegitimate son of Richard III. The attribution of these varying identities gives the whole scheme that followed an air of farce, and that was the point. The constant denial on Richard's part that he was any of the people they believed him to be can only be a bid for the same clemency that had saved Lambert Simnel's life. He was claiming to be little more than an innocent pawn. The assertion that they would help him against the King of England if 'I should take it upon me boldly' is at odds with the story thus far, since a boy from Tournai would hardly seek assistance against a king he had no known dealings with or connection to. Any lingering sense of credibility is surely driven out by the claim that these men 'against my will made me learn English and taught me what I should do and say'. Ignoring the picture of compulsion designed to allow leniency to the put-upon boy if Henry wished, the notion that in a short space of time a young man from Tournai could learn English so well, be so fluent and with such a polished accent, that he could almost immediately fool Anglo-Irish nobles, an English Duchess of Burgundy, the French king and all his court, the Holy Roman Emperor and the Scottish king, not to mention dissident English men who gathered around him, is simply preposterous. The imposition of a foreign identity on one who had so clearly demonstrated themselves to be convincingly English is either desperate or foolhardy.

The final decision to set him up as Richard, Duke of York is made and the rest of his story, largely widely known, is contracted to his visits to France, Flanders, Ireland, Scotland and then his present invasion of England. All, in his own words, a 'false quarrel'. The fact that this document must have been set down by Henry's men is significant. The question is whether it waited for Richard's capture before being set out, or had already been written in preparation for the capture of Henry's deadly rival. The need for a confession can be seen in Henry's desire to have Richard taken alive. The substance may have been provided by Sir Edward Brampton, who had entertained Henry's ambassadors in Portugal in 1489 so well that Henry had received a glowing report of the knight who was now seeking to become a diplomat at the Portuguese court. Is it possible that Brampton, who had been one of the men appointed to care for Richard after his initial removal from England mentioned in earlier accounts of his life, had also been the man who had abandoned Richard at the moment he attained an age to look after himself? If so, Brampton may have espied a route to influence in his native Portugal as the holder of valuable information. An apparently willing witness at the Setubal Testimonies, Brampton could have alerted Henry to the danger he might soon face as early as that 1489 embassy that he offered to entertain.

The involvement of Brampton in the story of Richard's early life is given more substance by André, who recorded Richard's assertion that:

I was brought up by a converted Jew of the name of Edward, and before my pretence of being the younger son of the celebrated King Edward, I was a servant in England. The Jew was my master. He was in the intimate circle of the King and his children.

Brampton might have exaggerated his close ties to Edward IV in order to maximise his own value, but the description suggests Brampton's involvement. It is possible that Brampton, realising that the boy he had protected demonstrated no trace of the skills he would need to make himself a king and having no martial ability at all as a soldier or a general, abandoned him to make his own way, freeing Brampton to find a passage back to the prestige he had enjoyed before whilst also ensuring he possessed valuable information. If Brampton warned Henry as early as 1489 that Richard, Duke of York was both alive and also incompetent as a threat, he may well also have been involved in the creation of a plausible backstory to give the pretender that would make him a believable imposter. Brampton had, as the constant references to Richard travelling with his wife demonstrate, trade connections in Tournai. If the Warbeck family, which did exist, held some offices around the town, such as the dean of the boatmen and keeper of the keys of Saint Paul's Gate, it is reasonable that Brampton had come into contact with them and could provide Henry with enough detail to flesh out a plausible story, particularly if the family had lost a son of a similar age to the long illness described in the confession, so that Richard could have the identity of that departed boy pressed on to him to better disguise his authenticity, or if Richard had lodged for a time with the family.

Whether Henry had this document already prepared and simply needed Richard to adopt it as his own true confession, or whether Richard really gave these details, perhaps knowing the Warbeck family himself from his time with Brampton or perhaps because, implausible as the whole thing sounds by the end, it was the truth, or at least a version of the truth he was willing to give Henry, is unclear. I strongly suspect that Henry travelled to the south-west with a prepared document and wanted the pretender alive to force him to sign it and declare himself a fraud. Richard was probably easy enough to convince that he should confess. He had already shown that he had no stomach for war. André describes how Henry's men had 'mockingly beaten him black and blue'. Henry had his wife, who Richard appears to have genuinely fallen head over heels in love with, as she probably had with him. It is also possible that Henry had Richard's child, or children, or that Catherine was pregnant when they landed in Cornwall. Any one of these elements might have been enough to make a man confess to a lie. In combination, they utterly undid Richard. He seemed to hope his life would be spared and must have been desperate to protect his family, whether only his wife or his wife and children, and physical violence had already been used against him by the time he repeated this confession. Few would not have capitulated under such physical and emotional tortures.

Henry went, with his captive finally under his control and the confession he needed, to Exeter, arriving on 7 September. It seems likely that Richard was drawn out of Beaulieu of his own free will by the promise, or the hope, of Henry's mercy, perhaps relying on the soft treatment Lambert Simnel had enjoyed only to fall foul of the same trap that Sir James Tyrell would later step into. André set about mauling the pretender's character, explaining his flight by the comment that 'The dissolute scoundrel despaired of his situation and saw that he could neither withstand the might of our king nor escape his clutches. Overcome with a feeble heart and womanish fear, and destitute of courage, he addressed his men.' The lack of courage would again be used to try and prove that he could not have been a true Plantagenet, but that argument does not improve by its repetition.

André goes on to relay the encounter between Henry, Catherine Gordon, retrieved from her haven at St Michael's Mount, and her husband Richard. This is where Richard 'was led in trembling, and after the royal servants themselves had mockingly beaten him black and blue and hissed at his laughable appearance, he was wondrously rebuked'. This was not to be the last report of Richard being beaten, particularly around the face, as though Henry felt an urgent need to alter his appearance before he could be taken to London. André recounts that Henry had received Catherine and assured her of his protection, sympathising that she has been 'cheated by such a worthless man' as she wept freely. Richard was then made to recite his confession to his wife, though 'he hesitated, partly for fear and partly for folly, but at last openly admitted that he was not who he had said he was and that he had followed bad advice.' Catherine gives a speech, according to André, berating her husband for tricking her and dragging her away from home, wishing there was some member of her father's family there to properly punish him.

The scene is meant to form part of Henry VII's triumph and the exposure of a fraud who has lied to Europe for years, securing a noble bride by his treachery. No doubt André meant the episode to be a glorious one for his patron, upon whom the blind poet was never slow to pour superlative exaltation. Read it again though. A man is lured from sanctuary by the promise of mercy, forced to sign a confession denouncing his own identity (or claimed identity, if he is still believed an imposter), beaten severely and dragged before his wife, a woman who, whatever other lies he may or may not have told, he appears to have genuinely loved, and forced to repeat his confession to her in order to maintain her, and possibly his children's, safety. It is not a glorious victory. It is the dirty deed of a man who knows what must happen if he is to protect his crown and his own family. If Henry was to survive, Richard must be an imposter, and the imposter must broadcast the fact himself. Henry could not kill a man who was, or might be suspected by some to have been, the legitimate son of Edward IV. He still relied too heavily on Yorkist support as the pillars of his regime. He needed Richard to be a lie and so he would make him one.

The first part of his work done with the securing of the confession, Henry returned to London, where he would need to be careful. Richard would have to be displayed, but the ground must be laid. Henry might be undone if he brought this young man, who had spent most of his early years in London, to the capital and he was recognised, or a similarity to Edward IV noted, and the seed of doubt was sown. Richard had toured the courts of Europe, wearing the armour of cultured, princely manners with a fine cloak of mystery and adventure to enhance his good looks and natural charm. Such a man could not be seen in London. Then, the king would have brought destruction to his own doorstep. Richard was left at Exeter for now. Within *Letters and Papers Illustrative of the Reign of Richard III and Henry VII, Vol. II* is a warrant 'To oure trusty and welbeloved servant Thomas Stokes' to transport 'Katerine daughter to therl of Huntlye from Bodman unto our derrest wife the Quene wheresoever she bee'. Catherine was sent to Queen Elizabeth's household, a fact which is immensely interesting. There is no record of Henry ever allowing his wife to see Richard after his capture, though it is not impossible in the months that followed that a glimpse might have been caught of the man who claimed to be her brother.

King Richard III, from a recently discovered Elizabethan panel portrait. (Courtesy of Mr J. Mulraine)

Middleham Castle, Yorkshire, the centre of Richard III's power as Duke of Gloucester, possible a safe place for the Princes in the Tower to have been kept. (Courtesy of Shutterstock)

Sherrif Hutton Castle, Yorkshire, the base of the household of the Council of the North during Richard III's reign and a potential location for one or more of the Princes in the Tower. (Courtesy of Shutterstock)

Above: A woodcut image of Edward V from John Rastell's The Pastymes of the People, 1529.

Right: A Victorian stained-glass image of Edward V from St Laurence's Church, Ludlow. (Author's collection)

Below: The Tower of London, where Edward V was placed to prepare for his coronation and joined by his younger brother Richard, Duke of York in 1483. Many believe they never left the Tower alive. (Author's collection)

The White Tower, the central fortress of the Tower of London, where the Princes are believed to have been moved to after an attempt to free them in the summer of 1483. The bones currently in Westminster Abbey purporting to be the remains of the Princes were found beneath a staircase near to the White Tower. (Author's collection)

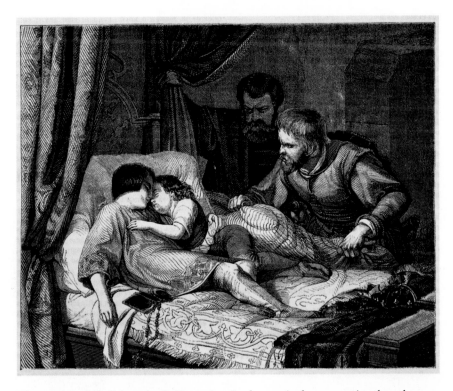

The murder of the Princes in the Tower, imagined centuries later, capturing the sadness and evil of the moment. (Courtesy of Shutterstock)

The removal of the bodies of
the Princes in the Tower, again
imagined centuries later to fit
Sir Thomas More's story, though
this was far from the only version
of their fate in circulation.
(Courtesy of Shutterstock)

St Botolph's, Colchester, the
town that harboured Lord Lovell
for many months after the Battle
of Bosworth and may have held
deeper secrets about the Princes
in the Tower. (Courtesy of
Shutterstock)

A pencil drawing of the boy crowned in Dublin being carried through the crowd by Great Darcy of Platten, a boy later remembered as Lambert Simnel, but who may have been Edward V.

The pencil sketch of Perkin Warbeck, who may in fact have been Richard, Duke of York, the younger of the Princes in the Tower, drawn during his time in Flanders at the court of Margaret of York, Dowager Duchess of Burgundy.

Drawing of Perkin Warbeck in the pillory after his capture, subjected to public display and ridicule after his face had been badly beaten.

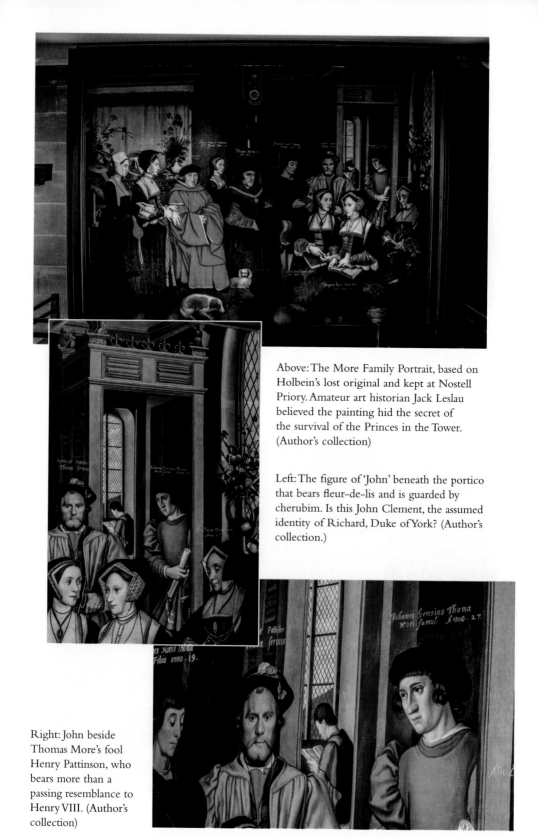

Above: The More Family Portrait, based on Holbein's lost original and kept at Nostell Priory. Amateur art historian Jack Leslau believed the painting hid the secret of the survival of the Princes in the Tower. (Author's collection)

Left: The figure of 'John' beneath the portico that bears fleur-de-lis and is guarded by cherubim. Is this John Clement, the assumed identity of Richard, Duke of York? (Author's collection.)

Right: John beside Thomas More's fool Henry Pattinson, who bears more than a passing resemblance to Henry VIII. (Author's collection)

Detail of John's hand, holding a scroll with two wax seals, his bent finger lightly touching the pommel of his sword and his warrior's buckler just visible beneath it. (Author's collection)

Detail of the book of *Oedipus* read by Margaret Roper, the visible passage extolling the benefits was taking a calm passage through life. (Author's collection)

Prince Arthur Tudor in the Victorian stained-glass window at St Laurence's Church, Ludlow. Arthur's planned marriage to Catherine of Aragon gave the Spanish monarchs a reason to support Henry VII against Richard of England. (Author's collection)

Prince Arthur's untimely death in 1502 heightened the nerves of the Tudor regime, left with only one male heir, and may have made the punishment of Sir James Tyrell harsh as a reaction. Prince Arthur's heart was buried at St Laurence's Church, Ludlow and his body at Worcester Cathedral. Tyrell's execution allowed him to become the fall guy for the murder of the Princes in the Tower, though there is no hard evidence that he ever confessed to the deed as Thomas More claimed he did. (Author's collection)

ARTHUR
PRINCE OF WALES
DIED AT LUDLOW CASTLE
2nd APRIL 1502
AGED 15 YEARS 7 MONTHS
His Heart was buried near this place

If Henry was so utterly convinced that Richard was a fraud, then surely his wife was the perfect person to dispel the myth that Richard, Duke of York was still alive once and for all by denouncing this imposter. The king had everything to gain by such a public statement, but everything to lose if she believed in Richard. Henry's reticence in trying to claim such a crucial prize as his wife's declaration that Richard was an imposter can only be because he wasn't sure enough himself. Or because he was entirely certain that Richard was genuine and could not risk that fact being made public.

Placing Catherine within Elizabeth's household may have served a dual purpose to a king always looking for his own advantage. If Catherine was pregnant, or at least if Henry feared she might be, a close eye would need to be kept on her in the coming months. In the company of the queen, there would be the opportunity for Elizabeth to question Catherine about her husband to try and find the truth of his identity without confronting the queen with the man who claimed to be her brother. Catherine would spend the next years in the queen's household and it is utterly impossible that the two women would not have discussed Richard, his story or who he really was. If Elizabeth had become satisfied that Richard was a fake that may have led to a meeting between them so that she could publicly denounce him. The continued silence on the part of the queen, a quiet that she took to the grave, is suggestive that she, like her mother, never became convinced that her brothers were dead. The black hole effect of the continued existence of at least one of the Princes in the Tower can still be seen exerting a gravitational pull on those close to them. If Richard was not the real Duke of York, then the silence of the queen makes no real sense. It protected an imposter and put at risk her own position and that of her children. It only becomes cohesive if Henry would not, or could not, force his wife to perjure herself by condemning Richard.

Whilst in Exeter, Richard was either given or was forced to write an odd letter to Perkin Warbeck's mother:

My Mother,
I recommend myself as humbly as I can to you, And may it please you to know that, by chance, under the pretext of an imposture, certain Englishmen made me take upon myself to be the son of King Edward of England, called his second son Richard Duke of York; I now find myself in such perplexity that if you are not in this hour my good mother, I will

be in great danger and inconvenience on account of the name which at their instance I took on myself and because of the enterprise which I have made. And so that you hear and recognise clearly that I am your son and none other, may it please you to remember that I parted from you to go to Antwerp with Berlo; you wept when you bade me goodbye, and my father brought me to the gate at Marvis. And also of the last letter which you wrote me in your hand, to Middelburgh, that you had given birth to a daughter and also that my grandfather and my sister Jehanne had died of the plague at the procession of Tournai, and how my father, you and myself went to live at Lannoy, outside the town, and you will remember the beautiful pig place [*Porquiere*].

The King of England has me in his hands, to whom I have declared the truth in the matter, and begged him very humbly to pardon the offence which I have done to him agreeing that I have never been his native subject, and that I pretended be such at the instigation and wish of his own subjects. But I have had no good response from him, nor expect any, and I am therefore in great dole. And however, my mother, I beg you and require you to have pity on me and purchase my deliverance. And I recommend myself humbly to my godfather Pierre Haes, to master John Stalin my uncle, to my friend Guillaume Rucq and to John Bourdeau. I hear that my father has departed this life, God rest his soul, which is heavy news for me. And God be with you, my mother.

Written at Exeter the 13th day of October, by the hand of your humble son, Pierrequin Warbecque.

'To Mademoiselle my mother, Catherine Warbecque, living at St. Jehan on the Scheldt.'

The letter was surely meant to provide further evidence of Richard's imposture, but proves little, other than that someone knew of the Warbeck family background, information that Henry may have already obtained from Brampton or another source. The alterations in names is odd, coming so hard on the heels of the confession. Katherine de Faro has become Catherine Warbecque, the family name of Osbeck now completely changed and the pretender's name has changed from Piers to Pierrequin, all in the space of a few days. From the research conducted by D.M. Kleyn into the Tournai records, the Warbeck family never lived at St Jehan, did not have a daughter at the time mentioned, did not have a daughter who

died as described and the family's father is described in the archives as
dying 'before December 1498', a note that at least suggests he was alive in
September 1497. Richard cannot have thought that he might be able to buy
his freedom with the money a middle-class widow might be able to send
him. The letter, much like the confession, has the air of convenient evidence
yet manages to be inconsistent in fact and spelling, even by the standards of
late medieval and early modern spelling.

Richard, now firmly branded as the imposter Perkin Warbeck, arrived in
London on 28 November 1497. An account recorded in *MS Vitellus, A. xvi f.
170* notes that he was 'conveyed about the city and Westminster with many
a curse and wondering enough', whilst Hall wrote several decades later that
people flocked to see him paraded 'as if he were a monster, because he being
an alien of no ability by his poor parents (although it was otherwise talked
and dissimulated), durst once invade so noble a realm'. Whoever Richard
was, he clearly did not possess 'no ability', having convinced people for years
that he was Richard, Duke of York. Amongst the *Calendar of State Papers of
Milan* is a note from Raimondo de Soncino, written to Ludovico Sforza,
explaining that 'Perkin has become a spectacle for the crowd: every day he is
led across London, so that all the world can judge his false past. To my mind,
he bears his lot courageously.' Clearly, he was still impressing people, and a
public displaying can hardly have hoped to achieve the aim of disproving his
identity when it was already widely reported that he resembled Edward IV.
Unless, of course, he still bore the disfiguring marks of a beating. Chastelain
records that Clarenceux, King of Arms did not consider this man handsome,
mainly because of a fault in his left eye that left it lacking lustre. Was this the
mark referred to previously, or had a heavy-handed attempt at obscuring
his Plantagenet looks damaged his left eye, perhaps blinding him in it? The
disfigurement in that area might have been deliberate if the mark near to
the left eye was one that would prove he really was the Duke of York.

The final weeks of 1497 seem to have seen Richard and Catherine
kept close to the king at court. Henry's accounts within *Excerpta Historica*
record numerous payments, such as £7 13s 4d to Robert Suthewell 'for
horses, sadells, and other necessarys bought for the conveying of my Lady
Kateryn Huntleye', £2 given directly to Catherine and £2 refunded to
Hugh Denes 'for Perkyns costs'. D.M. Kleyn has suggested that the fire
that gutted Sheen Palace on 21 December 1497 might have been started
deliberately on Henry's instruction to provide a cover for Richard to escape

as an excuse to deal with him once and for all. If it was, it failed in its aim, since Richard evacuated the palace but made no attempt to flee his custody. Such a move would have been rash in the extreme, with the king, queen and their children (with the exception of Arthur) in residence at the time, though the fire may have spread more quickly and more ferociously than planned. Certainly, if Richard's face had been badly beaten to obscure his features, there might be problems as the swelling reduced and his true features became more discernible. Richard's capture had been a watershed moment for Henry. He was no longer threatened by a game of international cat and mouse, but he was left with the task of finding out who this man really was, or who he could pass him off as.

On 9 June 1498, Richard did escape his imprisonment. He initially headed toward the coast but then wondered aimlessly for three days before seeking sanctuary from the Prior of Sheen Priory. The Prior immediately informed the king and Richard was swiftly apprehended. Henry feigned an utter disinterest which must spark a suspicion that he colluded in creating the opportunity and perhaps the intention as well for the escape. The day after Richard fled, Henry wrote to John de Vere, Earl of Oxford, whose lands extended eastward toward the coast, explaining that Richard had escaped due to 'the folly and simpleness of such as we put in trust to keep' him. Henry casually commented that 'it is no great force where he be come, yet to the intent he might be punished after his desert, we would gladly have him again.' A drastically reduced bounty of £100 was offered for any man finding Richard, his price falling with his fortunes, but it seems likely that he was never far beyond the eyes of Henry's men and that his escape was engineered as an excuse to deliver the punishment Henry needed to be able to inflict.

Richard was back in London as a prisoner on Friday 15 June. Edward Hall describes him being forced to stand on a scaffold at Westminster and being shut in the stocks for a 'good part of the forenoon'. On the following Monday, he was again displayed between 10 a.m. and 3 p.m. before being taken to the Tower. Stow adds the detail that 'Perken Werbecke endeavouring to steale secretly out of the land was taken again by his keepers and by the kings commandment cast into the Tower of London, and afterwards hee was showed in Westminster, and Cheape, stocked on scaffolds, to the great wonderment of many people: where he read his confession written with his own hand.' Bacon's assessment is probably accurate, that 'all the time of his flight [Henry] had him on a line: and that the King did this to pick a quarrel with him to put him to death and be rid of him at once.' There was not an immediate death sentence, but Richard was now shut in the Tower and no longer enjoyed the freedom he had previously had at court. Since his capture, Henry had been at lengths to keep Richard away from Catherine, traditionally understood to be a safety measure to prevent them enjoying a physical relationship that could leave Catherine pregnant (again?) which had the added benefit of emasculating the pretender. The true motive may have been to prevent him from coming too close to the queen or pleading with his wife to intercede with the woman he had claimed was his sister. Perhaps Henry even feared Elizabeth closely examining the young man and discovering that he was her brother. It might have been Elizabeth's influence that stayed Henry's hand from executing the man now.

A letter written by de Puebla to Ferdinand and Isabella in June 1498 and recorded in the *Calendar of State Papers of Spain* betrays a little of Henry's true concern over the pretender but also offers a glimpse of something important from Spain: a lack of a hard policy regarding him. De Puebla noted:

> I wrote a long while ago to your Highnesses, supplicating you to give your opinion and advice as to how the King of England ought to deal with Perkin. Your Highnesses have not to this day, no doubt for some just reason and impediments, sent a word in reply, or written any thing. I say this because the said Perkin fled a few days ago, without any reason. Your silence causes much pain to me, because I am sure the King of England would do what your Highnesses might advise. God be thanked! Perkin is already captured. The same hour that he was arrested the King of England sent one of his gentlemen of the bedchamber to bring me the news. I have not yet had time to ascertain what will become of Perkin, because I am writing these lines at the same hour that the King of England sent me the news. I think he will either be executed, or kept, with great vigilance, in prison.

Henry clearly deemed the matter of Richard's recapture so important that the Spanish ambassador was immediately informed. The king must have had one eye on the marriage treaty between his son Arthur and Catherine of Aragon and been keen to offer assurances not only that Richard was in custody but that he was being removed from court and from general view, suggesting that there may have been concern on the Spanish part at such a high-profile threat to Henry's crown being allowed the freedom to roam the corridors of Henry's palaces. Such concerns may have been behind Henry's scheme to facilitate Richard's escape as a premise to tighten his imprisonment. Certainly, there seemed no compulsion to jump to an execution on Henry's part that suggests he was reticent to deliver that ultimate sanction.

The second significant element of the letter is de Puebla's clear frustration or bewilderment at the lack of instruction from his masters of the course to be taken in the affair of the pretender. He implies that Henry would take their lead if only they would offer one, but perhaps the Spanish monarchs were waiting to see how Henry dealt with the threat himself. The English king seemed inexplicably lenient to a man who had tried to unseat him for over half a decade and the reason for such mercy might have been of concern. De Puebla was playing his own games, of course. He wanted offices and money from Henry for himself and his family and had used his involvement in the marriage negotiations to improve his own position, delaying the process when he was not getting what he wanted from Henry. De Puebla also wrote that when he saw Richard after his imprisonment in the Tower, his face was 'disfigurada', which Bergenroth translated in the *Calendar of State Papers of Spain* as 'changed' but which more accurately means 'disfigured', suggesting that Richard had been subjected to further beatings that might have been beginning to leave permanent traces on his face. The implication is that his face was still causing problems; he perhaps still looked too much like a Plantagenet, or was too recognisable as Richard, Duke of York and Henry's initial policy of clemency was backfiring. The episode took place when the Bishop of Cambrai visited London as an ambassador from Archduke Philip. Henry claimed that the bishop wished to see the pretender and that Richard was brought out to confirm that he had lied about who he was and that Margaret, Duchess of Burgundy had known all along. De Puebla was present at the meeting and wrote 'I saw how much altered "Perkin" was. He is so much changed [disfigurada] that I, and all other persons here, believe his life will be very short. He must pay for what he had done.' How could Richard fail to profess himself a liar under such brutal pressure?

Another Spanish ambassador, de Fuensalida, wrote to his king and queen in a completely different tone to de Puebla, advising 'Your Majesty ought to form a fleet in Biscay or elsewhere ... and forces should also be held in readiness in Flanders with the intention of attacking the King of England, to liberate the Duke of York Pierrequin and the Duke of Clarence who are prisoners.' He offered this counsel 'in spite of the marriage which Your Highnesses have arranged with England'. The *Calendar of State Papers of Venice* assert that 'the King arranged with some of Perkins attendants that they should suggest to Perkin to escape out of his Majesty's hands; and thus did this youth do: so the King had him put in prison, where he will end his days', suggesting that something had happened to harden Henry's attitude toward Richard. Either the lingering suspicion that he was genuine could not be dispelled or his imposture had been proven beyond doubt and he was no longer needed. There is no fresh news of proof of his identity, so the former might be implied from a lack of another satisfactory explanation.

Maximilian had still not abandoned Richard either. When news arrived of Richard's capture the emperor wrote in an almost frenzied hurry to Jean le Sauvage, president of the Council of Flanders ordering him to intervene and appeal for mercy for Richard. On 8 November 1497, he had followed this with a letter to his son Philip, over whose head he had gone to contact le Sauvage directly and Maximilian does not shy away from displaying strong emotion for Richard and his cause. He wrote from Metz:

Right dear and well-beloved son: We have heard that our very dear and well-beloved cousin the Duke of York has recently been taken prisoner and delivered into the hands of the King of England, his enemy, and we are very much afraid that, for the reasons you know well enough, he will put him to death. And because we hold our said cousin of York in very great love and affection because he is our kinsman and our ally, we are bitterly saddened by his evil fate and his misfortune and would be very much more saddened by his death; and we are held and obliged, for the quittance of our honour and the discharge of our conscience, to help and comfort him to all our power.

What was the reason that Philip knew? Was it that Richard could prove he was who he claimed to be? The emperor continued to ask his son to act as a mediator with Henry to secure Richard's safety. He pleaded with Philip to send le Sauvage to England to do all that he could 'for the welfare and salvation of our cousin of York'. Le Sauvage was to be given full permission

to plead for Richard's life on Maximilian's behalf and the emperor included
instructions that were to remain secret until needed, authorising him to:

> adjust these instructions to tell King Henry by way of remonstrance that
> in so far as he says and maintains that our said cousin of York is a coun-
> terfeit person and not the son of the late King Edward, nevertheless it is
> the common renown of the whole of Christianity that yes, he is, and he
> is held to be the son of the late King Edward, and because of this if he
> puts him to death he will be putting to death his own brother-in-law,
> which would be shame, dishonour and reproach to him for ever and to
> his people too, because he [York] will not be able to do him any more
> harm from henceforth, alive or dead.

It is clear the Holy Roman Emperor was still utterly convinced of Richard's
identity, or wanted Henry to believe he was, even though he had absolutely
nothing left to gain by adhering to the story from which he had not once
deviated. In permitting his representatives to come so close to begging
Henry, Maximilian was demeaning his own position to a man he had been
completely at odds with, and there can be no satisfactory explanation for
his willingness to do so except a genuine affection for Richard, which
might have been tarnished if Maximilian believed him a liar. There was
no political gain for Maximilian, only loss, in prostrating himself before
the King of England in such a way. The final note from Maximilian to
le Sauvage asked him to 'Do the best you can in this, for we have the matter
much at heart.' Shortly after sending these instructions, Maximilian wrote
to a papal legate to describe Richard's capture, ending his letter with the
miserable Latin phrase 'Sic transit Gloria mundi'; Thus passes the glory of
the world.

Maximilian was to be proven correct. Richard all but vanished within the
Tower for the remainder of 1498 and most of 1499. There is a brief mention within the *Calendar of State Papers of Venice*, in a note from Raimondo
de Soncini to Ludovic Sforza, Duke of Milan that in France a man named
John Taylor, 'who devised Perkin's expedition to Ireland when the latter first
declared himself the son of King Edward', had been arrested by the French
and handed over to the English. It seemed that Henry was in complete
control of the situation now. As 1499 chilled and winter moved in, the
scheduled date for Catherine of Aragon's arrival into England crept close

and it seems likely that this deadline marked a crisis point not only for Richard but for Edward, Earl of Warwick too.

Richard was around 26 now and the Earl of Warwick 24. The latter had been a prisoner for fourteen years with no signal that he would ever be rehabilitated. Whilst there is no direct evidence to support the assertion, it has long been believed that Henry was under pressure from Ferdinand and Isabella to ensure that his kingdom was entirely secure before their daughter would be sent. Unwilling to risk the unravelling of his prized Spanish alliance, Henry at least felt, if he was not expressly, under pressure to deal with the two most significant threats to his rule. It has been asserted that Henry's primary motive was to be rid of the Earl of Warwick and that the opportunity to deal with Richard once and for all was a fringe benefit. Warwick had been a prisoner for an unbroken fourteen years. He had no power base of his own and the only threat to Henry in his name had been twelve years earlier and may never really have been in Warwick's name, if the invader had actually claimed to be Edward V. There was no threat from this young man beyond the blood in his veins. The true threat remained Richard, or Perkin as he was now firmly branded. It seems more likely that Warwick's fate was a cover for what needed to happen to Richard.

At the beginning of 1499 there had been a brief and frequently over-looked episode that is instructive to the entire period of Yorkist revolt against Henry VII's reign. Polydore Vergil describes a plot instigated by an Augustinian friar named Patrick 'who, I suppose, for the purpose of making the earl unpopular' tried to convince a young man that he could win the crown by claiming to be Edward, Earl of Warwick escaped from the Tower. The young man's name was Ralph Wilford and the two conspirators tried their luck in Kent, but 'teacher and pupil were both enchained, the latter put to death, and the former consigned to eternal darkness of prison because he was a monk.' Vergil's version of the brief episode is interesting. Why would an Augustinian friar wish to make the Earl of Warwick unpopular? The only explanation that makes sense is that the desire to besmirch Warwick came from the king and that this was another of Henry's ploys to refocus attention on the plots he needed to appear to be about him to excuse what he knew he had to do. Vergil also asks 'For what man is there who fears the law or danger to the extent that he refuses to do or suffer anything in the world for the sake of gaining a crown?', a sentiment clearly squared at Richard, who was accused as an imposter just as Ralph was.

The second striking aspect of the episode is the swift and capital punishment delivered to the imposter, which is in stark contrast to the leniency shown to Lambert Simnel, whoever that boy was, and to Richard, whoever the government really thought he was. There are differences that may help to explain the firm response; Ralph was not a boy, as Lambert Simnel had been, though Richard was an adult by the time of his capture. It is possible that Henry had simply had enough of the threats, having only just brought to an end the longest and deepest one he had faced. Ralph was also perhaps a far more outlandish candidate than the others had been, more obviously an imposter, though that interpretation acknowledges the feasibility of Richard's pretension to be the Duke of York. What seems most likely is that Henry orchestrated the imposture, as Vergil intimated, to give him the excuse to deal with both Edward and Richard before the Spanish deadline came too close. If that was the plan, it seems not to have worked. It may not have generated the desired will for the deaths that Henry needed, because later in the year, another barely disguised plan had to be put in motion.

The *Plumpton Correspondence* record that on 16 November 1499 'was areyned in the Whyte Hall at Westmynster the forenamed Parkyn and iii other'. Hall added that the three were 'John Awater, sometyme Mayor of Cork in Ireland, one of hys founders and hys sonne', though the father and son were not named. The trial was held before Sir John Sely, the Knight Marshal, and Sir John Turbervile, Marshal of the Marshalsea. The accusation appears to have been an attempt to escape from the Tower, organised by several of the guards and to which Richard and Edward were convinced to consent. Before any escape could be made, the plot was miraculously uncovered and, to any who had even an inkling of what was happening, the fate of the two young men was sealed. The *Plumpton Correspondence* go on to recount that all four men were attainted:

> and judgment given that they shold be drawn on hirdills from the Tower, throwout London, to the Tyburne, and ther to be hanged, and cutt down quicke, and ther bowells to be taken out and burned: ther heads to be stricke of, and quartered, ther heads and quarters to be disposed at the Kyngs pleasure.

Eight other men were brought from the Tower for judgement, perhaps others involved in arranging the escape. Some confessed their guilt, others were arraigned for later trial, though 'as yet they be not juged'. The writer then notes that 'this present day', the Earl of Warwick was brought before the Earl of Oxford, the Duke of Buckingham, the earls of Northumberland, Kent, Surrey and Essex and several lords for trial by his peers, 'bycause he is a pere of the Realme'. Warwick might have been a little bemused by his first trip out of the Tower in years, and perhaps harboured little hope for the rest of his life even before this development, for 'Therle of Warweke confessed thenditments that were layd to his charge, and like Judgment was given of him, as is afore rehersed.' The distinction between the trials is telling, and perhaps much was made of it, since the writer felt compelled to note the reason Warwick received trial by his peers and Richard a separate proceeding. The government could not afford Richard any trappings of rank without admitting he held rank enough to warrant the treatment. Richard's execution was commuted by Henry from the traditional grue-some fate of a traitor to a simple hanging. Edward would be beheaded, as befitted his rank. It is hard to see why Henry felt the urge to provide Richard with this final clemency. He could not give him a beheading that might admit his nobility, but did save him from the torment of being hanged, drawn and quartered. Was this the only nod he was able to give to the true identity of this man? Perhaps the small mercy was the price of his wife's silence.

Hall records that 'on the three and twenty daye of the same month, Perkyn and John Awater were drawen to Tyborne, and there Perkyn stan-dyng on a lytle skaffolde, redde his Confession, whiche before you have heard, and toke it on hys death to be true, and so he and John Awater asked the king forgevenes, and dyed paciently.' The Milanese ambassador reported that Richard remained 'dignified, even in adversity', no mean feat given the beatings he seems to have endured. His co-operation on the gallows, re-reading his confession and confirming himself an imposter is less likely to have been genuine remorse than to have originated in the threat still hanging over his beloved wife, further reinforced if the couple had a child or children to ensure his compliance to the end. If that interpretation is correct, then this composure on the gallows displays a bravery and commit-ment to the protection of his family that is moving and admirable. Five days later, on 28 November 1499, Edward, Earl of Warwick was beheaded on Tower Hill, traditionally marking the extinction of the Plantagenet family in the direct male line.

Sir Francis Bacon summed up the threat of Richard by surmising 'it was one of the longest plays of that kind that hath been in memorie, and might perhaps have had another end, if hee had not met with a King both wise, stout, and fortunate.' On 2 October 1501, Catherine of Aragon would finally arrive in England for her marriage to Prince Arthur, aided by de Puebla's enthusiastic report to her parents, Ferdinand and Isabella, in January 1500 that:

> This Kingdom is at present so situated as has not been seen for the last five hundred years till now, as those say who know best, and as appears by the Chronicles; because there were always brambles and thorns of such a kind that the English had not occasion to remain peacefully in obedience to their King; there being divers heirs of the kingdom, and of such a quality that the matter could be disputed between the two sides. But now all has been thoroughly cleansed and purged, so that not a doubtful drop of royal blood remains in this kingdom except the true blood of the King and Queen, and above all that of the Lord Prince Arthur.

In the instant that Richard was gone, the Spanish monarchs broadcast their utter belief in his imposture from the outset. Richard had been believed by kings and rulers around Europe who had maintained that he was the true Richard, Duke of York even after his capture and confession. He had offered to show three marks that would prove he was who he claimed to be and his confession was extracted, or forced upon him, only when his wife and possibly their children were held as hostages for his co-operation.

Too much of Richard's story is compelling to dismiss him as a lie as easily as the first Tudor king hoped. It is as likely that Richard, Duke of York survived beyond 1483 as it is that he was murdered that year, and there is enough to support the idea that Richard of England could have been the boy grown into a man. The lack of consistency in the story of his life, his parentage and even his name cannot be explained easily. Moreover, Margaret, Maximilian and James IV never denounced him as a fraud, even when they had nothing left to gain by clinging to the idea that he was the son of Edward IV. Maximilian had remained steadfast against the pressure of the Pope and other members of the Holy League who desperately wanted Henry to join them. Indeed, the emperor was the only one to see clearly through Henry's manoeuvring, playing the League and the French off against each other whilst committing to neither. James IV may have looked for an excuse to go to war with England, but that does not mean he did not utterly believe in Richard.

It is possible to interpret the small amounts of evidence that survive to create a narrative in which the Princes in the Tower were not murdered by their uncle, but were in fact protected by him. They were reunited with their mother, who emerged from sanctuary and gave her daughters into Richard III's custody in relief at their survival, enjoying being able to see them at Gipping Hall and perhaps becoming involved in longer-term plans for their future. The boys were probably separated, one perhaps heading north with their sister Elizabeth and the other across the Channel to their aunt Margaret in Burgundy. Both would be safe and well educated but also prevented from threatening their uncle. The death of Richard's only legitimate son might have brought their futures back under discussion, with embassies to the Pope to enquire about the feasibility of relegitimising them. The Earl of Lincoln may have cared for Edward V, now Lord Edward, in the household of the Council of the North where Elizabeth and Edward, Earl of Warwick would also be raised. The younger Prince, Richard, was entrusted to Margaret and Sir James Tyrell acted as Richard III's go-between, providing money for the boy's care.

With the defeat and death of Richard III at Bosworth and the accession of Henry VII, these plans unravelled. Lincoln was required to deliver his Yorkist charges to the new king in London but may have been unsure what to do about Edward V. Lord Lovell's long stay at Colchester may have been the consequence of trying to resolve this problem. Lovell's trip to the north might have been an attempt to retrieve the boy and his flight to Flanders and the subsequent invasion from Ireland genuine efforts to restore Edward V to his throne, hidden by the Tudor government behind a younger boy, given the unusual name Lambert Simnel and the true aim disguised underneath a plot in favour of Edward, Earl of Warwick. The question that remains, if this is the truth, is what happened to Edward V; was he killed at the Battle of Stoke or captured alive?

In short order, Richard appeared in Ireland and travelled the courts of Europe garnering support and being recognised in almost every corner as the true Duke of York. His effort to unseat Henry VII spanned more than five years and three invasion attempts and his final failure allowed him to be painted a fraud, an imposter, a story he went along with to protect his loved ones. The tale of his life, travelling from Tournai to Portugal and then to Ireland may have contained elements of truth, particularly if Sir Edward Brampton had been involved in his protection until it provided him with no more gain. Perhaps the money ran out, or the collapse of the House of York forced Brampton to seek favour in Portugal and with the new Tudor regime. Whatever else can be claimed about Richard, or Perkin, he convinced many that he was the younger of the Princes in the Tower. Henry's prolonged fear of him demonstrates that he at least might have been who he said he was. The need to capture him alive and then to repeatedly beat him to obscure his features also strongly suggest he was recognisable as Richard, Duke of York. The silence maintained by Queen Elizabeth might also be construed as unwillingness on her part to condemn her brother.

Henry might have counted the Spanish as his most steadfast allies in denying Richard, but that is not quite the case. The dynastic interest of Ferdinand and Isabella in England's security must be borne in mind, though as with others, their true motives cannot be restricted by this one aspect. De Puebla slavishly promoted Henry VII's causes for his own aims but other advice to the monarchs urged them to support Richard. De Ayala would advise Ferdinand and Isabella when they sent Catherine to England to ensure that she was surrounded by suitably noble companions to impress the English, because the 'sentiments of the King towards a great number of Spaniards are not very friendly, partly on account of their dealings with King Richard, and partly on account of Perkin'. Of all the pieces of information that weigh in Richard's favour and against it, one stands out, even amid the continued support of rulers like Maximilian. Ambassadors' reports, diplomatic dispatches and public statements can always carry an ulterior motive that diminish their use. De Puebla wrote to his Spanish monarchs that Henry had aged twenty years in the space of a few weeks after the executions of Warwick and Richard, suggesting that something, or everything, about this episode weighed heavily upon him. It might have been his wife's disgust at her brother's execution if she had received assurances that he would be spared. The security of his dynasty and the love of his wife would then have been Henry's rock and hard place. An utterly private piece of evidence, meant never to see the light of day, would be the most instructive available. One exists, and it is an appropriate thought with which to close the episodes of pretenders painted as imposters to Henry VII's throne.

The translation of the *Calendar of State Papers of Spain* by G.A. Bergenroth contains within the introduction an explanation that much of the correspondence from de Puebla was encoded using a cipher. Bergenroth managed to crack the cipher, only to discover a copy of the code had turned up just after he completed his work, but the copy confirmed what he had decoded. One chapter of the codebook was headed 'The Pope, the Emperor, Kings and other persons of the Blood Royal' and contained an instruction that those who did not belong to royal families should be looked for elsewhere and that this section was strictly for royalty. The list contains the code to be used for each of these people. Between the code for Margaret, Duchess of Burgundy and King Alphonso of Naples is the code DCCCCVII, designated as belonging to Richard, Duke of York, second son of King Edward IV. This was the code used in discussions of the pretender who claimed Henry's throne. This is how Richard was referred to in the most secret and private correspondences between Spain and her ambassador in England. Not Perkin. Richard, Duke of York.

11

The Secret Princes

Ill-omened prophesies were rife. In secret, Henry ordered a Welsh priest to tell his fortune, but when that priest hinted that hidden dangers were still threatening, Henry ordered him to keep silent. The King became very devout, hearing a sermon every morning, and for a long period he continued his devotions during the day. By degrees he regained his mental health, but he never regained full physical fitness, suffering many illnesses of the body.

G.A. Bergenroth, *Translation of the Calendar of State Papers of Spain*

Henry VII's troubles did not end in 1499 with the deaths of Edward, Earl of Warwick and Richard of England. He might have seemed haunted, perhaps by a Welsh priest's prophesy that his problems were not over, perhaps by guilt at what necessity had compelled him to do. The warning of more trouble to come was soon to prove correct. In 1501, Edmund de la Pole, Earl of Suffolk fled England with his youngest brother Richard. When the Duke of Suffolk, brother-in-law to Edward IV and Richard III and father to the Earl of Lincoln, had died almost a decade earlier, Henry had downgraded the title from a dukedom to an earldom when passing it to Edmund, a fact that must have irritated the family for a decade. Edmund and Richard took ship to Calais and passed through Guisnes Castle on their way to the court of Maximilian. It is perhaps significant that no other Yorkist heir had made a bid for power whilst Richard of England had been in the frame, particularly if he was so widely known to be an imposter.

Edmund possessed the senior Yorkist claim now and began to style himself Duke of Suffolk, White Rose and rightful King of England. It should not be forgotten, too, that Maximilian had been appointed Richard's heir to his claim on England if he died without issue. The fact that Maximilian never sought to make capital from that fact suggests that there was a child, or children, blocking his right. The threat from Edmund would last for many years and his brother Richard was a constant menace to Henry's heir until he was killed at the Battle of Pavia in Italy in 1525. That heir, though, was not Henry's firstborn son.

Prince Arthur died at Ludlow on 2 April 1502, his heart buried at St Laurence's Church in Ludlow and his body interred in a magnificent chantry chapel at Worcester Cathedral, a monument to his parents' grief that is laden with Tudor, Beaufort and even Yorkist iconography. Henry's response betrays the natural panic at the loss of his heir that demanded attention above his personal heartache. He had another son, his namesake, Prince Henry, Duke of York, but this boy had not been trained for rule as Arthur had from his earliest years. When Edmund had been allowed to pass through Guisnes Castle, its governor was none other than Sir James Tyrell. Tyrell was arrested – in fact, tricked into leaving Guisnes so that he and his son could be apprehended – in the spring of 1501 and had since languished in prison. On 2 May, exactly a month after Arthur's death, Tyrell was suddenly put on trial at the Guildhall, found guilty of treason and beheaded on Tower Hill on 6 May.

Only some years after this sequence of events was Sir James Tyrell inextricably linked for eternity to the deaths of the Princes in the Tower, first by Sir Thomas More and in perpetuity by William Shakespeare. The link may, as we have seen, have been real, but the boys' protection became their murder. It has recently been suggested that Henry and his queen lodged at the Tower in order to attend Tyrell's trial there because of the accusation that he had murdered the queen's brothers, but this not only ignores the fact that the trial took place at the Guildhall, not the Tower, but also ignores the complete lack of contemporary evidence that Tyrell was ever even questioned about, let alone confessed in some long-lost document to, the murder of the Princes in the Tower. It also ignores decades more of different assertions about the fate of the boys that would surely have been negated by such a confession.

Sir Thomas More's part in this story, and his desire, or need, to bury the story of the Princes, literally at the foot of a staircase in the Tower (before they were moved elsewhere) may be significant. I have been utterly fascinated for a long time by a theory presented by Jack Leslau, an amateur art historian, who believed that he had decoded hidden evidence of the continued survival of the Princes in the Tower within the stunning paintings of Hans Holbein, the immensely talented artist born in Augsburg, in Maximilian's Holy Roman Empire, around 1497. Holbein worked initially in Basel before arriving in England in the mid-1520s in search of work as the Protestant Reformation swept across Europe destroying rather than commissioning the religious art that had been Holbein's early staple. One of his first major commissions was a family portrait for Sir Thomas More, a huge figure in London society and government by this point, and a close friend to Henry VIII who might be able to open doors for Holbein to the holy grail of royal commissions.

The Holbein original of the More family portrait was destroyed by fire in the eighteenth century, but what is asserted to be a direct copy by Rowland Lockey painted in 1594 is preserved in all its glory by the National Trust at Nostell Priory near to Wakefield and Sandal Castle, from whence Richard, Duke of York, grandfather to the Princes in the Tower, marched out to his death at the Battle of Wakefield on 30 December 1460. Two Lockey copies exist, the second being held at the National Portrait Gallery and showing the family in late Elizabethan attire with many of the figures from the Nostell Priory version omitted. Mr Leslau has also suggested that the signature 'Rowlandas Locky 1530' (or 1532) may have been added later to cover up an anti-Catholic slogan, since Lockey cannot have painted this picture around 1530. The suggestion is that the portrait at Nostell Priory is an original Holbein masquerading as a copy by Rowland Lockey.

The crux of Leslau's Theory is that Richard, Duke of York, the younger of the Princes in the Tower, can be found, hidden in plain view amongst the members of the More family portrait as John Clement, the figure at the right-hand end of the back row of the portrait. There are two connected but separate elements to be considered in assessing this possibility. First, John Clement is a reasonably well-documented figure, at least from early adulthood, whose life may be able to shed some light on the notion that he was a royal figure living incognito. The second is the evidence provided by the painting for a connection between John Clement, the portrait and an heir to the throne of England. Examination of the potential viability of this theory, like much of the rest of this book, requires acceptance of at least the possibility that the Princes in the Tower survived beyond 1483, but this strand of their possible histories also requires the acknowledgement of the possibility that the Tudor government knew of their existence and preserved at least this person. The idea is not as ridiculous as many may think. All that is required is an acceptance that Richard III was not monstrous enough to murder his nephews before they reached their teens, that Henry VII was no murderous villain either and might have been in love with his wife enough to be convinced to spare her brothers' lives if they would remain secrets and that Henry VIII was brash and confident in the extreme when he first came to the throne. None of these are impossible to imagine.

Details of John Clement's birth are almost completely lacking. The place of his birth and his parentage are utterly unknown, though there has been speculation that he originated from Yorkshire, which might be an interesting link. A John Clement appears amongst the list of pupils in *Gardiner's Register of St Paul's School*, London, studying under William Lily, and he seems then to have been educated at Oxford. The year of his birth is usually estimated around the turn of the century, though there are reasons to believe he was some, perhaps even many, years older. In 1519, John Clement was appointed rhetoric reader by Cardinal Wolsey at Corpus Christi College, Oxford, a foundation of Bishop Richard Foxe dedicated to humanist studies, soon afterwards becoming Greek master there too. At some point, Clement made a connection with Sir Thomas More. He appears to have gained an impressive reputation as Greek master at Oxford and was employed by More to tutor his children.

Amongst those children was Margaret Giggs, a girl who may have been a distant relation to More but who was certainly brought up in his household alongside his own children as, perhaps, an adopted daughter. Margaret was probably born around 1505–08 and was undoubtedly a gifted academic, thriving in More's humanist household. She became well versed in Greek and Maths, particularly algebra, and remained deeply attached to Sir Thomas, retrieving the shirt in which he was executed as a relic. She features in the More family portrait, as will be discussed later. At some time around 1526, but possibly as late as 1530, Margaret Giggs married John Clement, who by this time had focused his studies on to medicine. A letter from Thomas More in the early 1520s to one of his contacts contains the claim that More himself had succeeded in convincing Clement to devote himself to medicine.

Clement left Oxford in the early 1520s, as More wrote, to travel to Italy and study medicine. It is known that Clement went via Louvain and Basel, where he met Erasmus and delivered to him a copy of More's book *Utopia*. It is interesting to note that Basel was also Holbein's home at this time and that a separate theory suggests Erasmus may have been Edward V. Clement had completed his medical studies by March 1525, when he received his MD in Siena. When he subsequently returned to England, Clement helped his successor at Oxford University complete a translation from the Greek of the Aldine Edition of Galen. Later that same year he appears in the royal accounts as a Sewer (Server) of the Chamber in the Royal Household, performing the same role again in 1526. On 1 February in either 1527 or 1528, Dr Clement was admitted to the Royal College of Physicians and in 1529 was sent, along with two other physicians and under the management of Dr Butts, to treat Cardinal Wolsey as he ailed following his fall from the king's grace. In 1535, Dr Clement again appears, treating Bishop Fisher for a liver problem during the bishop's imprisonment in the Tower. He was granted a semi-annual income of £10 from the Royal Household in 1538, though this appears to have been cancelled in 1539. John Clement reached the pinnacle of his career in 1544 with his appointment as President of the Royal College of Physicians.

Clement's career was impressive but perhaps unremarkable in the detail easily accessed, but Jack Leslau, in digging deeper, uncovered some odd and fascinating facts about Dr John Clement that suggest there was more to him than a simple man rising high in his chosen profession. The date of John Clement's birth is not known. It has traditionally been placed around 1500. Clement is identified by More as the 'puer meus' – my boy – from his allegorical tract on the perfect society, *Utopia*, demonstrating a closeness to and perhaps even paternal affection for Dr Clement. However, John Clement's age becomes less clear when Jack Leslau's discovery of an entry in the register of enrolment at Louvain University is considered. The entry is dated 13 January 1489 in the name of 'Johannes Clement' and is marked 'non juravit' – 'not sworn' – to show that the person enrolling had not sworn the traditional oath to the university.

Leslau found a second entry, dated January 1551, that read 'Joannes Clemens, medicine doctor, anglis, noblis (non juravit ex rationabili quandom et occulta sed tamen promisit se servaturum consueta)', which might be translated as 'The Lord John Clement, doctor of medicine, English, of noble birth (has not sworn the oath for a reasonable hidden cause, but has nevertheless promised to keep the customary oaths)'. These entries are sixty-two years apart so it must be questioned whether they relate to the same person. If they do, or if the earlier reference is to the John Clement of Leslau's Theory, then his date of birth must be significantly earlier than 1500, since he would most likely have been around sixteen or seventeen at the time of enrolment in 1489, placing his date of birth around 1472–73. Significantly for Leslau's research, Richard, Duke of York was born in 1473. Also of interest is Louvain's position on the northern coast of Europe, within Burgundian controlled territory.

The second entry significantly describes Clement as 'Lord' and 'of noble birth', though there was no noble Clement family in England. The entry is either wildly inaccurate or was made to account for the fact that John Clement was the assumed name of a nobleman from England. The brack-eted note is also interesting, since it states that John Clement had not sworn the customary oath, as he had not in 1489. In the second entry, a reason is offered for excusing the swearing of the oath, stating that there is 'a reason-able hidden cause'. Jack Leslau discovered that this entry is utterly unique amongst the 49,246 entries in the university register between 31 August 1485 and February 1569. If John Clement was an assumed identity, then swearing the university's oath in a false name would have been perjury. Such a crime would leave the university open to prosecution and might explain their willingness to excuse the swearing of the oath. If this was the case, it also implies that the university were aware of the false name that John Clement was using and accepted the reason that he used it.

Further weight can be added to the suggestion that John Clement was older than a date of birth around the year 1500 would allow by a document in *Letters and Papers of Henry VIII, 1, Part 2*. A note within the papers refers to a set of challenges and answers for a feat of arms planned to take place on Wednesday 1 June 1510, just over a year after Henry VIII's accession when the athletic young king was nearly nineteen. The list runs:

King – Lord Howard
King – John Clement
Knyvet – Earl of Essex
Knevet – Wm Courtenay

Howard – Sir John Audeley
Howard – Arthur Plantagenet
Brandon – Ralph Eggerton
Brandon – Chr Garneys

The lists contain eleven names, including the king. Five of them – Lord Howard, Thomas Knyvet, Henry Bourchier, Earl of Essex, William Courtenay, Earl of Devon and Arthur Plantagenet – were close relatives of the king by either blood or marriage. Thomas Howard had been married to Anne of York, a daughter of Edward IV and therefore an aunt of Henry VIII. Thomas Knyvet was one of Henry's favourite jousting partners and became Master of the Horse in 1510. He was married to Muriel Howard, a daughter of Thomas Howard, 2nd Duke of Norfolk and an aunt to the Lord Howard listed above. Henry Bourchier, Earl of Essex was a nephew of Elizabeth Woodville, the king's maternal grandmother and could trace his lineage back to Thomas of Woodstock, Duke of Gloucester, the youngest son of Edward III. William Courtenay, Earl of Devon had defended Exeter from Richard of England and was married to another sister of the queen, Catherine. Arthur Plantagenet was Henry's uncle, an acknowledged illegitimate son of Edward IV. Another of those listed, Charles Brandon, was Henry's closest friend who would later become his brother-in-law. Ralph Eggerton was Henry VIII's standard-bearer from 1513 and Christopher Garneys was a gentleman usher of the Chamber and therefore close to the king.

The question is, how does John Clement fit into this glittering array of friends and family of the new king? His appearance here would at least place his date of birth further back than 1500, since he cannot have ridden in the lists aged 10, but it does raise the fascinating prospect that John Clement deserved a place amongst such elite company, that his was indeed an assumed identity and that Henry VIII knew very well who he really was. It is important to remember that when Henry VIII came to the throne on his father's death on 21 April 1509, he was an 17-year-old athlete, possessing the tall, broad, muscular body inherited from his Yorkist grandfather Edward IV and filled with youthful confidence that exploded into exuberance when he was able to come out from under his father's close watch. The final years of Henry VII's life had been spent jealously guarding his last living male heir, trying to cram a lifetime's teaching into whatever time he had left to prepare Henry for government and keeping the teenager a virtual prisoner in his chamber for much of the time. Suddenly free, the Henry of his early years was not the paranoid, troubled man of years later. Would he have allowed one of Plantagenet blood so close to him? Yes. He did. Arthur Plantagenet may have been illegitimate, but he was a son of Edward IV nevertheless and Henry loved him, at least until his fear swallowed his capacity to do so freely.

Leslau's theory is that Dr John Clement was, in fact, Richard, Duke of York, who survived under an assumed identity that must have been known at least to Henry VIII and may have been something of an open secret at court, kept quiet by the threat of Henry's outrage if it was ever made an issue. Empson and Dudley had provided an early marker of Henry's ability to ruthlessly kill if it suited him. Both men were executed ostensibly for doing as his father had instructed them and only because Henry found it made him popular to do it. The impact of this moment on the story is not only as a warning, because Jack Leslau also believed he had found evidence to suggest that Edward V lived on under the assumed name of Sir Edward Guildford. The evidence for John Clement in fact being the younger of the Princes in the Tower is drawn from Hans Holbein's portrait of the More family, hidden in a series of artist's tricks that, when understood, lead to the revelation that Dr John Clement was a Yorkist prince.

The people within the portrait, from left to right, are identified by the inscriptions above their heads as: Margaret Clement (née Giggs, More's adopted daughter, married to John Clement), Elizabeth Dauncey (née More, Sir Thomas' second daughter, married to Sir William Dauncey), Sir John More (Sir Thomas' father), Anne Cresacre (fiancée to Sir Thomas' son), Sir Thomas More, John More (Sir Thomas' son), Henry Patenson (More's fool), in front of Pattison is Cecily Heron (née More, Sir Thomas' youngest daughter, married to Giles Heron), Margaret Roper (née More, Sir Thomas' oldest daughter), Lady Alice More (Sir Thomas' second wife), beside Pattison is an unmarked man in the background reading a book and the final figure in the upper right is traditionally understood to be John Harris, More's secretary. It is this figure that caught Jack Leslau's attention.

The inscription above this figure is unusual when compared to the others. The inscription reads 'Johanes heresius Thomae Mori famul: Anno 27'. The surname 'heresius', unlike every other surname on the painting, does not have a capital letter. In Latin, the word heresies can be translated as heres – heir – and ius – rightful – so that 'Johanes heresies' becomes 'John, the rightful heir'. Combined with the fact that the top of this figure's hat, confirmed by Jack Leslau using infrared photography, is the highest of any figure in the painting, traditionally denoting the most important or most socially senior person in a group painting, the figure becomes more interesting. The figure wears old-fashioned Italian clothing, which could be a reference to Dr Clement's training in Italy. Every other member of the group is dressed in contemporary English attire.

The figure of John wears at his hip, almost out of the picture, a sword and buckler. It would be odd for More's secretary to appear in an informal family portrait armed and the figure's bent middle finger lightly touches the pommel of the sword, suggesting that it holds some significance he cannot openly display or that he is perhaps trying to stop it rattling, keeping it quiet. The buckler has a polished outer rim and spokes heading into the obscured centre and Jack Leslau began to apply the courtly French language of the period to create a series of homophones that add to the intriguing theory. In French, the spoke of a wheel is *rai* and the rim a *jante*, creating the split homophone rai-jante, equivalent to *régente*, the French word meaning regent. John also carries a scroll which has two seals hanging from it, a feature of his paintings pointed out by P. Ganz in *The Paintings of Hans Holbein the Younger*, who noted that 'Holbein sometimes resorted to riddles and painted in the background of the portrait a slip of paper, covered with writing and closed with sealing-wax' and there are other examples of two pieces of wax being applied to such pieces of paper. Leslau interpreted this feature as another homophone, from the French *deux cires tiennent le parchemin*, meaning 'two waxes hold the parchment' to *deux sires tiennent le parchemin*, which can mean 'two lords hold the right and title of nobility'.

John stands in a portico, oddly placed in the room and looking out into another room where a figure is reading a book, apparently oblivious to the portrait being captured behind him. John is emerging into the room, but it looks as though his is coming through a solid wall, suggesting that there must be a hidden doorway there, so perhaps that he is or has been, to some extent, hidden or hiding something from the world but is now emerging into the open. John is the only figure in the painting that appears to be in motion, as though he has walked into the room during the sitting and frozen, realising he should not really be there. The top of this portico is also interesting. On the front are a series of unfurling scrolls that appear blank, as though there is some secret they might tell, but they remain obscured and maintain their silence. Perhaps the most striking feature of the portico is the row of fleur-de-lis, the symbol of French royalty, laid out over John's head. On the three top corners that can be seen are small cherubim-like figures, each holding a blank shield against an unseen threat, and the one at the front left corner of the portico appearing to look down on John. The purpose of cherubim and seraphim in Christianity is to attend upon the throne of God and worship him. Cherubim hold the second highest position in the Christian hierarchy of angels, second only to seraphim and directly above the thrones, a set of divine beings who symbolise the justice and authority of God, much as a medieval king would claim to do, and who have a throne as one of their symbols and are usually represented by older men receiving the word of God and passing on the prayers of men, perhaps making the scroll held by John appear more significant. The cherubim, then, appear to be defending Richard's corner beneath them from any threat, suggesting that he represents the Thrones. The false door through which John enters is, in French, a *porte-à-faux*, and *en porte-à-faux* can, Leslau discovered, mean 'in an unstable condition', pointing to the precarious nature of John's existence if he was, in fact, Richard, Duke of York. Above the portico, the ceiling beams appear to be out of perspective, creating a line fault – a *faute de ligne* – which could refer to the error in royal lineage that was present if Richard, Duke of York was still surviving.

Mr Leslau believed that Sir Thomas More's date of birth was 6 or 7 February 1477, though it is believed by historians to have been 1478. The fact that Sir Thomas More is shown, by the inscription above his head, to be 50 years old places the portrait's setting as 1528. Until August of that year – and the blooming flowers suggest it is spring – Richard, Duke of York would have been 54 years of age and Jack Leslau noted that John is marked as being 27, significantly half the age of the Duke of York. The clock in the middle of the portrait above Sir Thomas here becomes significant. The glass front of the clock is open, indicating to the viewer that time has been altered in some way. The painting was most likely completed some time after 1528, but meant to refer to the family members at that time, perhaps when Holbein made his initial sketches during his first visit to England. The next significant aspect of the clock is that it is missing a pendulum, indicating that time has been frozen near to the eleventh hour. The application of hindsight might see 1528 as something of an eleventh hour, since Wolsey

would fall the following year, More would become Chancellor, a position
that would make his failure to recognise the Royal Supremacy all the more
embarrassing to Henry VIII, and the king's Great Matter, his divorce from
Catherine of Aragon and marriage to Anne Boleyn, had not yet reached
crisis point, at least as More would see it, not least by opening the door to
Protestantism in England.

The clock face displays a radiant *sun in splendour*, the personal badge of
King Edward IV, with the hand – a literal hand – pointing ominously toward
the approaching eleventh hour. Above the clock face is a lunar phase display
which shows a half moon, offering an intriguing hint at the division in half
of the age of Richard, Duke of York to arrive at John's 27 years. Beneath the
clock face stands another fleur-de-lis and the ornate arrangement at the top
is not unlike a crown. Each of the small elements of Leslau's Theory might
seem insignificant or could be written off as coincidence, or even as looking for a hidden meaning that is not there, but it is the continued weight of
the number of these scraps of evidence that make the theory increasingly
compelling. The figure of John, the portico and the clock are not the only
indicators that something else is going on within the painting.

The figure of Sir Thomas More himself is unshaven, a traditional sign of
mourning, and only three fingers of his left hand are visible beneath his
red velvet sleeves. Leslau suggests that this is a reference to More's work
on Richard III and supports this notion with several observations relating
to the chain that More wears around his neck, which is positioned in the
very centre of the painting, traditionally an area of importance. The chain
displays a series of 'S' links and a large Tudor rose hanging from it. The links
on the left-hand side are reversed, but on the other side they are the correct
way around. Leslau opined that this central feature was a reference to the
secret that was hidden within the painting and which More's own writing
on Richard III had been designed to help conceal. Returning to the use of
the French language, the left side is wrong. *Gauche*, the French word for left,
also means clumsy or maladroit, whereas the right-hand side – *à droit* – was
correct, adroit, clever. Holbein may have been asking whether the decision
to preserve the Princes in the Tower, hidden behind assumed identities in a
plot layered by More's own writing that condemned Richard III in order to
create the belief that they were dead, was clumsy, or clever. Either way, the
fate of the Tudor rose hung from the decision. The little dog sat at More's
feet with his ear cocked suggests that there was a secret to be heard within

the More household, and to be found within the painting if the viewer knew what they were looking for.

The other figures within the portrait offer clues that there is something more going on than a simple family portrait. The figure on the far left is identified as Margaret Clement and Leslau suggests that her unflattering portrait is evidence that Holbein did not like her. Her cap is of plain white rabbit skin, whereas the other ladies all wear expensive headdresses. Perhaps this singles her out as one from outside the immediate family, but Leslau notes that she has a sullen, unfriendly face. Margaret holds a book, but the pages are blank and her finger is pressed into the spine of the open book, *le doigt dans l'éspine*, which Leslau asserts can also mean 'she keeps on at him'. The lute behind Margaret, which points at her, might represent a homophone also, since the French *lutte* means to fight. The flower arrangement behind Margaret is untidy, in contrast to the other two on display, and may represent an untidy arrangement in her marriage to the doctor. Within the vase is a purple peony, which is significant. Peonies are associated with medicine, taking their name from Paeon, a physician to the Greek gods, and purple is a royal colour, creating a reference to a royal doctor, or rather a doctor who is royal, who can only be Dr John Clement, since Margaret is clearly described as his wife. The implication is that their relationship was not as happy as it could have been and perhaps even that Margaret did not know John Clement's secret, as shown by the blank pages of the book she is reading.

The lady beside Margaret is Elizabeth Dauncey, More's second daughter, painted, as Margaret is, in profile, which is somewhat unusual outside of royal portraits for this period. Behind her, a viol extends from the flower display with the purple peony but the line of the viol is broken by Margaret Clement's head and is clearly out of line on either side of her. The viol also has a strange cut just above where it rests on the lute which resemble upside down bull's horns. The bull horns are an ancient insult referring to a cuckold and Leslau suggests that Elizabeth, who is clearly heavily pregnant, might be carrying the baby of the purple peony, the royal doctor, John Clement. Elizabeth holds a book marked as *Epistolae*, Seneca's collection of letters of advice, suggesting that More had been forced to give his daughter plenty of counsel. Many of the letters that make up *Epistolae* are openly concerned with death and the political use of forced suicide that might have hung over Seneca as his own position deteriorated. Such a death might await those who opposed the emperor's authority and Elizabeth, in bearing a child with Plantagenet royal blood, might have been wandering precariously close to a similar fate. Elizabeth is in the process of putting on one glove but doesn't seem to have the other. The French *le pair lui manqué* – the pair is missing – is a homophone for *le père lui manqué* – the father is missing. Portraits of Elizabeth I, such as the Ditchley portrait, show the queen holding one glove that might be a derogatory reference to the marital status of her father and mother. Was Elizabeth Dauncey carrying the illegitimate son of John Clement, the royal doctor, having cuckolded her husband?

The figures of Sir John More, Anne Cresacre and John More do not add to this aspect of any messages hidden within the portrait, though it may be significant to other messages that the inscription above John More, Sir Thomas' son, had *filius* – son – misspelt as *filuis*. Sir Thomas' son was rumoured to have been far less intelligent than his sisters, though, through persistence, had written one letter in Latin to Erasmus. The error is perhaps an unkind reference to his poor Latin and his struggles with education. The next figure with a potential impact on this interpretation of the More family portrait is Henry Patenson. The most striking thing about this figure is his strong resemblance to King Henry VIII, particularly as later painted by Holbein himself; a broad, ruddy face, wide stance standing square on and looking directly at the viewer. Patenson's hat bears a white rose and a red rose badge, separate rather than combined as a Tudor rose, and it may be significant that Henry VIII was, on his accession, held up as the personification of the joining of the houses of Lancaster and York, as the son of Henry Tudor and Elizabeth of York. The other two badges, just to the right, are a jewel with a pearl hanging from it and a shield bearing the cross of St George, patron saint of England and of the Order of the Garter. Patenson is the only other figure wearing a sword in the portrait, gripping the scabbard just below the hand guard, tipping the point of the sword toward the figure of John, who emerges into the room behind Henry with a concerned look, a complexion that is pale and waxy compared to Henry's and his own hand tentatively reaching out to touch the pommel of his own sword, suggesting some kind of tension or suspicion between the two men. If Henry Patenson is meant to represent Henry VIII as a foil to John, who stands above Henry in the line of heads in the portrait, suggesting seniority, it was a dangerously bold move. The resemblance to Henry VIII is not hard to see.

The two ladies seated in front of Henry Patenson are Cecily Heron on the left, More's youngest daughter, and Margaret Roper, his oldest daughter, on the right. Margaret Roper is widely considered to have been one of the best educated women of her era and the relationship between More and his Dearest Meg would remain incredibly close throughout his life and imprisonment, and when Margaret died in 1544, she had her father's skull buried beside her in the Roper family vault. Cecily and Margaret each have sleeves to their dresses that match the colour and material of the other's bodice, red and cloth of gold. Cecily has a closed book on her lap, but Margaret's is open and the words on the page can clearly be read. The titles at the top of each page show that she is reading Seneca's *Oedipus*, and clearly pointing to the word Oedipus at the top of the page on her right. The Latin text 'Fata, si liceat mihi fingere arbitrio meo …' that can be read is part of a speech by the Chorus.

Oedipus was a mythical King of Thebes, the son of King Laius and Queen Jocasta. Jocasta was a member of the Spartoi, believed to have sprung from dragon's teeth to become Theban royalty, and Laius had become King of Thebes as a minor. His throne was usurped but he eventually regained it, offering parallels that fit both Elizabeth Woodville and the mystical descent from the water goddess Melusine claimed by her mother Jacquetta's family in Luxembourg and Edward IV's period as king, his deposition and subsequent regaining of his throne. Laius received a prophesy from an oracle of Delph that if he had a son, the boy would kill his father King Laius and marry his mother Jocasta. When the queen bore a son, Laius tried to frustrate the prophesy by abandoning the baby to die on a hillside. Found by shepherds, that baby was raised by the neighbouring King Polybus and Queen Merope as their own son. When the oracle tells Oedipus that he is prophesied to kill his father and marry his mother, he flees from his adopted parents to avoid harming them, still believing them his true parents. Travelling to Thebes, Oedipus meets, argues with and ends up killing a stranger before arriving to find King Laius of Thebes is recently dead and the city is in thrall to a Sphinx. Oedipus answers the monster's riddle, freeing the city, becoming the new king and marrying the widowed queen as his prize. When Thebes is afflicted by a plague, Oedipus is tasked with finding the old king's murderer to lift it, only to discover that the stranger he killed was Laius, his father, and his wife was his mother, thus fulfilling the prophesy. When Jocasta discovers that she has married her son and the murderer of her husband, she hangs herself and Oedipus takes two pins from her dress and drives them into his eyes to blind himself. This may refer to Elizabeth Woodville's political suicide in becoming involved in the 1487 revolt and her two sons turning a blind eye to their claim to the throne.

As Margaret reads, Cecily counts on her fingers. Her book is closed, suggesting that Margaret's is the far more interesting and important story and she may be counting tragedies on the scale of Oedipus, or counting kings. The speech that can be read on the page is translated 'Were it mine to shape fate at my will, I would trim my sails to gentle winds, lest my yards tremble, bent 'neath a heavy blast. May soft breezes, gently blowing, unvarying, carry my untroubled barque along; may life bear me on safely, running in middle course.' The passage may refer to advice that Margaret was trying to give her father regarding his refusal to swear the Oath of Supremacy that would ultimately cost him his life, but it could also refer to the path chosen by Richard, Duke of York. If they had survived after 1483, it is feasible that either Edward V or Richard, Duke of York, or indeed both, might have been induced to live out a quiet life and refrain from pursuing the crown. There is a tendency to believe that if either were still breathing, they would continue to fight, but that need not be so. One or both may have tried and failed, accepting anonymity as the only way to stay alive. It could even have had a strong appeal after so many of their family's lives had been destroyed by the constant struggle. The speech is a plea to seek out calm waters, avoid trouble and live out a life of peace that would have offered the sons of Edward IV security and saved their necks.

Oedipus has become a name synonymous not only with Freud's complex relating to men and their mothers but also as a nickname for those who are good at solving riddles and puzzles. Oedipus, in solving the Sphinx's riddle, displayed an astounding ability to solve such a conundrum and the reference suggests to the viewer that there are mysteries to be found within the painting too, if the viewer is able to solve them as Oedipus might have been. Cecily's counting offers the tantalising imprecision of there being more than one secret or meaning, without telling us how many to look for. The final lady seated on the right is Lady Alice More, Sir Thomas' second wife, who reads her own book with her pet monkey at her feet, but looks out at the viewer with a knowing gaze and the hint of a cheeky smile as John enters the painting just over her right shoulder. In Holbein's original sketch, made between 1526 and 1528 and now part of the Royal Collection at Windsor, the figure of John is absent altogether and Lady Alice is looking down at her book, the glance at the viewer and the knowing smile clearly added later, when John arrived.

At the left-hand side of the painting, a sideboard is covered by a carpet, hinting at a secret that is covered up, but a door in the sideboard is open to reveal several items inside, suggesting that the concealed information within the painting is a partially open secret, known to others. Jack Leslau also believed that the painting was not silent on the fate of Richard, Duke of York's older brother, Edward V, either. The top of John's head is level with the bottom of the lower weight on the clock, their suspension offering a true line in the painting without reference to the ceiling beams that are out of perspective or the edge of the portrait. The weight hangs directly above the 'M' of Thomas More's surname and above his head. The higher weight is in a vertical line with the Tudor rose on More's chain, suggesting a person of higher status than John who, whilst John occupies Thomas' mind, is of more consequence to the Tudor dynasty and out of More's direct influence. At a right angle to the left of this weight is the top of the flower arrangement behind Sir John More. The flowers at the top of this display are purple and gold flag irises, colours that do not appear naturally but which again denote royalty, and the flowers are marked by the lines of the higher and lower weights as being above, and therefore senior to, John if they represent a person. Iris was the Greek goddess of sea and sky but was also a messenger of the gods, particularly Hera. Leslau believed that the flag iris was an allegorical reference to the Standard Bearer of King Henry VIII, who by this point was Sir Edward Guildford, the identity Leslau believed was a cover for the continued existence of King Edward V.

Sir Edward Guildford was a close friend of Henry VIII from the outset of his reign, just as John Clement appeared to be. He is traditionally recorded as the oldest son of Sir Richard Guildford and had a half-brother from Sir Richard's second marriage, Sir Henry Guildford, who also enjoyed a successful career. Sir Edward held several offices including Master of the Armoury, Constable of Dover Castle, Lord Warden of the Cinque Ports and Marshal of Calais. In 1513, the *Letters and State Papers of Henry VIII* record a warrant given to John Daunce for the payment to Sir Edward of £125 10s 4d toward 'the costs he has sustained in making the tilts and jousting places, scaffolds and other necessaries, and providing stuff, spears, etc' for a tournament and in 1515 Wolsey received a letter explaining some issues in France, adding that 'Sir Edward Guildford on his return to England will report the various matters he has heard'. In his capacity as Master of the Armoury, Sir Edward was heavily involved in the preparations and securing of lodgings for Henry's retinue at the Field of the Cloth of Gold. By 1521, there is a demonstrable connection to Sir Thomas More. On 11 September, the King's Book of Payments records money 'Received from Thos. More, Sir Edward Guilford, Sir Nic. Vaux, lord Fitzwater, &c., for money lent to Sir E. Guildford', demonstrating that More was helping Sir Edward repay a debt that he owed to the king.

After 1525, when he was able to take up the post of Warden of the Cinque Ports, Sir Edward remained in England and can be found mentioned throughout state papers sitting on commissions and writing to Wolsey about local issues in Kent. A few years earlier, Sir Edward had brought charges against Lord Bergavenny for illegally retaining men in Kent following the attainder of Bergavenny's father-in-law, Edward Stafford, Duke of Buckingham, a man Edward V would have harboured no affection for. The case brought into contrast the differences between Bergavenny and Sir Edward's positions. Bergavenny was a great landholder and Guildford held powerful offices, the two balancing each other in the region. The significance of Guildford's position was that he had no personal powerbase, his offices, income and authority relying entirely on the king; a fitting position for one who might pose a very real threat.

One of the most striking connections of Sir Edward Guildford was John Dudley, who later became Duke of Northumberland under Henry VIII's son Edward VI. Richard Empson and Edmund Dudley were two of the strong arms of Henry VII's unpopular fiscal policy. The moment he succeeded his father, Henry VIII had them arrested and on 17 August 1510, both men were executed in a shallow bid for popularity. Sir Edward Guildford was given four of Dudley's manors and custody of his son John, who was aged about 6. In 1512, Guildford petitioned Parliament for Edmund Dudley's attainder to be reversed and to have marriage rights over young John. His requests were granted and by 1526, John Dudley was married to Sir Edward's daughter Jane.

Sir Edward Guildford is recorded on 4 June 1534 as having died in a detailed letter sent to the Duke of Norfolk and recorded in the *Letters and Papers of the Reign of Henry VIII*. Written by John Gage, the letter recounts that he found Sir Edward ill at Leeds Castle on Trinity Sunday and advised him to make a will, which must not have been a welcome suggestion, though Sir Edward said that he would do it. Shortly afterwards, news reached Gage that Sir Edward was dead without having made a will, though he had made his desires known to several men, including Gage, who also wrote that 'Sir Edward's burial is postponed till the King's pleasure be known' and informed the duke that he had asked Baron de la Ware to come to Leeds 'to be a stay between Sir John Dudley and John Guildford'. Such a barrier was needed because it seems that Sir Edward had made his wishes known and that they would be disputed. Sir Edward's only son, Richard, had predeceased him and so he had left his manor at Haldon and other property to his daughter Jane. John Guildford, Sir Edward's nephew, was his closest male heir and would have expected to inherit, but if Sir Edward Guildford was an assumed identity of Edward V, then he would have harboured a strong desire to keep what little he had within his own bloodline, since Sir Edward's half-brothers would actually have been no relation to Edward V. The absence of a will is also potentially interesting. Sir Edward was wealthy and had been ill for some time. To fail to provide for his impending death seems incredibly lax, particularly if what he wanted to do was contentious, unless making a legal will was all but impossible for a man living under an assumed identity who would struggle to see such a document legally enforced. Part of the deal for remaining quiescent may have been that a verbal will would be properly executed.

In 1534, there is also an interesting joining of the two strands of the possible survival of the Princes in the Tower. When Sir Thomas More was imprisoned for failing to accept Henry VIII's supremacy over the Church, John Clement was also incarcerated in Fleet Prison. This may be no surprise, as a member of More's family who shared his Catholic devotion, but might also have reflected the devastating threat John Clement could pose if he became disaffected. On 11 October, John Dudley, who, it will become clear, must have known his father-in-law's secret, wrote to Thomas Cromwell about Clement:

Farthermore as towchyng maistr Clements mattr I beseche your maistership not to gyve to much credens to some great men who peraventure wyll be intercessours of the matter and to make the best of it for Mr Clement by cause peraventure they theym selves be the greatest berers of it as by that tyme I have shewed you how whotly the sendying of Mr Clement to the flete was taken, by some that may chawnce you thinke to be your frende you wyll not a little marvayle.

Dudley is clearly interceding on John Clement's behalf for no obvious reason. He asserts that 'some great men' will seek to intervene but that Cromwell should resist their pressure and seek to protect John Clement. He suggests that there has been something of a backlash at Clement's imprisonment, and if this relates to his true identity, it again demonstrates that it was, to some degree, an open secret in England. Cromwell must have been aware, some of the senior nobility too, of the great men Dudley is worried about, and Henry VIII must have known of both identities. The intercession suggests an interest in Clement on Dudley's part that is hard to fathom, particularly since the Dudley family were attached to the evangelical cause rather than the Old Religion, unless he was assuming the responsibilities his father-in-law left him with.

John Clement was released and survived Sir Thomas More's execution. In 1544 he was appointed President of the Royal College of Physicians and Jack Leslau discovered that he is the only President in the College's entire history whose signature has never been recorded, an odd fact that might have been affected again by the knowledge that his identity was assumed and that perjury might become a side effect of trying to create legal documents. As Edward VI's Protestant government settled in, Clement and his wife quit England with their children and John was exempted from Edward's general pardon after his coronation. The family moved to Louvain, a town in Burgundian territory where Clement had been enrolled in the university, and it is interesting that they found safety there. When Queen Mary came to the throne and England became Catholic again, Clement and his family returned to their home at Marshfoot, though John was unable to regain his 180-book library, lost when he had fled England.

The Public Record Office in Chancery Lane holds an inventory of the Marshfoot house, listing property seized by Sir Anthony Wingfield on the instruction of Sir William Cecil, the future Lord Burghley who would become the stalwart minister of Elizabeth I's rule. A collection of Catholic items was found in the Chapel, including 'an awlter, a picture of our Lady, a picture of the V woundes'. The five wounds had been the badge of the

Catholic Pilgrimage of Grace revolt against Henry VIII's reformation and symbolised Catholic resistance. The inventory is a result of the Clement family's second flight from England in 1558 on the accession of Queen Elizabeth, when they returned to Louvain. During this time, John Clement appears in the Louvain register in March 1462 as 'Dominus Joannes Clemens, nobilis, Anglus' – 'Lord John Clement, of noble birth, English'. There is a final entry in 1568 showing 'Dominus Joannes Clement in theologia' – 'Lord John Clement in theology'. In total, the entries referring to a nobleman named John Clement from England who had an acceptable reason to be excused swearing the university's oath span an incredible seventy-nine years.

Dr John Clement died on 1 July 1572, just two years after Margaret, his wife of over forty years. In a final act of significance, John was buried near to the high altar of St Rombold's Cathedral in Mechelen, the city in which Margaret of York had spent much of her time as she desperately tried to unseat Henry VII. The place is significant as it was usually reserved for members of the House of Burgundy, Margaret's family by marriage which had become extinct in the male line and been subsumed by the Hapsburgs. If Dr John Clement was Richard, Duke of York, he had lived to the ripe, improbable yet not quite impossible age of 98. Such a lifespan would surely demonstrate the benefits of not sitting on the throne.

John Clement's family all but disappear from the record with his death. He and Margaret had children but they would slip into anonymity. If Leslau was correct in his belief that Edward V had survived and lived as Sir Edward Guildford, then his descendants' impact on English history was far from over. Sir Edward's death without a will is of interest, as is his determination to provide for his daughter in preference to a nephew, defying the traditional laws of inheritance. Despite the lack of a will, Sir Edward's wishes were carried out. John Dudley's intervention with Thomas Cromwell on behalf of John Clement demonstrates that Dudley would have been aware not only of who his father-in-law was but who John Clement was, or at least that his father-in-law had wanted Dudley to keep a watchful eye on the man. John Dudley was in good favour at court, though not long before the king's death a French ambassador reported that Dudley was expelled from court for three months after responding to some abuse from Stephen Gardiner, Bishop of Winchester during a Council meeting by punching the bishop squarely in the face. Despite this, Dudley survived changes in

Henry's will to remain one of the executors of the king's will. After the death of Henry VIII in 1547, John Dudley was created Earl of Warwick and became an ally in the Protestant cause to Edward Seymour. Dudley would later be created, or perhaps take for himself, the second highest rank in the land as Duke of Northumberland, catapulting him to the summit of English nobility. The rise was not exactly from nowhere, since the Dudley family had baronial links and John's mother, Elizabeth Grey, had left him the title Viscount Lisle and could trace her own descent from the famous warriors of the Hundred Years' War Richard Beauchamp, Earl of Warwick and John Talbot, Earl of Shrewsbury, who had been known as Old Talbot. Dudley's climb to the summit, though, was extraordinary.

His downfall would be even more spectacular. When Edward VI was dying, he drafted his will, including his Device for the Succession. The section dealing with who should follow the young king was revised, originally allowing only for male heirs of his Grey cousins, but as the end drew near and none of these ladies had a male heir, he settled the succession on Lady Jane Grey, a maternal granddaughter of Henry VIII's sister Mary and Charles Brandon, Duke of Suffolk and therefore a great-granddaughter of Henry VII. Jane's father was Henry Grey, Duke of Suffolk, a title he had acquired by marrying Frances Brandon, the daughter of Mary Tudor and Charles Brandon. Henry Grey was the grandson of Thomas Grey, Marquis of Dorset, son of Elizabeth Woodville from her first marriage, making Jane the great great granddaughter of the former Yorkist queen Elizabeth Woodville. John Dudley is frequently asserted to have been behind much of Edward's will, not least because it skipped Jane's mother Frances, Duchess of Suffolk, and made Jane heir. This is significant because Lady Jane had, in the spring of 1553, become engaged to marry Guildford Dudley, John's fourth son. The couple married on 25 May 1553 and King Edward VI succumbed to his illness on 6 July 1553.

A significant element of the difficult days that followed, which saw Lady Jane Grey proclaimed as Queen Jane and in power for just nine days before Edward VI's older half-sister Mary thundered into London to claim an inheritance she asserted was rightfully hers, is the position of Jane's husband. In his *History of Events in England*, Girolamo Raviglio Rosso recorded that Lady Jane had recounted:

I was with my husband, and of that I discussed with him much, that I reduced him to consent, that, if he must be made King, it should be done by me, and by way of the Parliament. Afterwards I commanded to be called the Earl of Arundel, and the Earl of Pembroke, and I told them, that, when the crown came to me, it was resolved by me not to wish to make my husband King, nor ever to consent to it: but that it contented me to make him a Duke. The which being related to his mother, she angered herself with me in every way, and persuaded her son, that he should not sleep with me anymore: the which he obeyed, declaring to me that he did not desire to be a Duke, but King.

If we accept that Sir Edward Guildford was, in fact, Edward V and that his daughter Jane Dudley was therefore an heir of the House of York, then Guildford Dudley was a viable Yorkist heir. The insistence of John Dudley, and particularly his wife Jane, that Guildford should be made a king in his own right, not a consort or the duke that Jane intended, is hugely important. It would mark an attempt in 1553 to restore the Yorkist line through marriage to an otherwise somewhat obscure Tudor heiress. Jane's instruction that her son should refuse to sleep with his wife until she agrees to make him a king becomes a desperate and frustrated reaction to a final thwarting of plans so carefully laid by her and her husband. The intention would have been to use a female Tudor heir, appointed by Edward VI, but then to play upon the fact that a female monarch was still anathema in England to see Guildford, a Yorkist heir, take the real power and authority for himself.

The nine days of Queen Jane's reign were to end in tragedy. Mary had the popular support and rode that wave into London, sweeping Jane away to a confinement with the victory of her claim, laid down by Parliament, over Jane's, created by Edward VI's will. John Dudley was tried for treason on 18 August 1553 at Westminster Hall and condemned to death. His execution, scheduled for the morning of 21 August, was cancelled at the last moment and instead he was taken to St Peter ad Vincula in the Tower precinct and took Catholic communion before confessing his sins in following the Protestant faith. The following day, Dudley recited his confession before a crowd estimated at around 10,000 people on the scaffold before being beheaded.

Wyatt's Rebellion in January 1554 against the planned marriage between Mary and Philip II of Spain forced the queen to deal with Jane, who the rebellion had sought to free and restore. On 12 February, Guildford Dudley was taken from his room to Tower Hill and beheaded, his body drawn back on an open cart past the window of Jane's apartment. She reportedly watched it pass, shouting 'Oh, Guildford, Guildford' from her window. Jane was then also taken down to Tower Hill and beheaded. Guildford's four brothers, John, Ambrose, Robert and Henry, were also imprisoned through-out this period, kept in the Beauchamp Tower where they scratched graffiti on the walls that can still be seen today, though their mother's efforts to court the new Spanish nobility arriving in England secured their release in October 1554.

The oldest of John's sons, his namesake John, 2nd Earl of Warwick died on 21 October within days of his release. Ambrose became 3rd Earl of Warwick and lived until 1590. Henry, apparently aware that the Dudley brothers were only suffered at Mary's court on her husband's account, joined the Spanish king's forces in his war against France and was killed at the Battle of St Quentin on 10 August 1557, just over the French border from the Low Countries. The career of Robert Dudley, later Earl of Leicester, is without doubt the most fascinating and remarkable. His lifelong courtship of Elizabeth I is one of history's greatest unrequited loves. Both seemed to ache to be together but were never able to be. If Robert Dudley was the grandson of Edward V, this prolonged episode takes on a far more sig-nificant and slightly darker edge. The love may have been genuine, but if Elizabeth was a Tudor and Dudley a York heir, then their love was doomed to be denied. If the identity of Sir Edward Guildford was a well-known secret amongst the Tudor monarchs and their closest advisors, and if John Dudley knew who his father-in-law was and planned to place one of his sons on the throne as heir to the House of York, then the decades of fruit-less and frustrated wooing between Elizabeth and Robert takes on the air of Shakespeare's Romeo and Juliet. Could the bard have known, from his Catholic allies amongst the nobility?

There is a final tantalising hint about the Guildford family that cannot be ignored any more than it can be explained, except by Leslau's theory. The final burial place of Sir Edward is not well recorded, though one entry in the State Papers records that he was buried at one o'clock in the morning somewhere near Leeds Castle. An odd funeral for such a notable man with a family. There is a myth that cannot be confirmed that Sir Edward was in fact buried in the More Chapel, purchased by Sir Thomas, within Old Chelsea

Church. Certainly, an engraving of Sir Edward's coat of arms was made within the chapel, surrounded by the motto of the Order of the Garter: *honi soi qui mal y pense* – 'shame on he who thinks badly of it', a motto created by Edward III during the Hundred Years' War and believed to refer to his claim to be the rightful King of France. In this situation, it is poignant that it was chosen to mark the coat of arms of Sir Edward Guildford.

When Lady Jane Dudley, Duchess of Northumberland, who had been so determined, according to Rosso, to see her son made a king, died in 1555, she was buried in the More Chapel at Old Chelsea Church, perhaps joining her father. In her will, Jane left money to London's prisons and asked for a quiet funeral, favouring the payment of her debts over any pomp. She also pleaded that her body should not be examined after her death, writing that she wished 'nor in no wise to let me be opened after I am ded: I have not loved to be very bold afore women moche more I wold be lothe to com into thandes of any lyving man be he phisicion or surgeon'. No reason is given for such an apparent unwillingness to be seen unclothed in front of women whilst alive and examined by men once dead, leaving the lingering possibility that she bore some sign of Plantagenet descent that cannot now be proved, beyond DNA testing that would defy her last wishes, but the inscription that marks her resting place is worthy of further note:

> Here lyeth ye Right Noble and Exellent Prynces Lady Jane Guyldeford, late Duches of Northuberland, daughter and sole heyre unto the right honorable Sir Edward Guyldeford, Knight, Lord Warden of ye Fyve Portes, ye which Sir Edward was sonne to ye right honorable Sir Richard Guyldeford, sometimes Knight and Companion of ye Most Noble Order of ye Gartor, and the said Duches was wife to the Right High and Mighty Prince John Dudley late Duke of Northumberland, by whom she had XIII children, that is to wete VIII sonnes and V dawghters, and after she had lyved yeres XLVI, she departed this transitory world at her maner of Chelse ye XXII daye of January in ye second yere of ye reigne of owr sovereyne lady Quene Mary the First and in anno MDLV, on whose soule Iesu have mercy.

How and why is Lady Jane described as a 'High and Mighty Princess', when her descent from humble Guildford knights is then described? John Dudley is further described as a 'High and Mighty Prince', suggesting that she may have attained the rank from him, though he was also not a prince by any measure. Their daughter-in-law had briefly occupied the throne, but this would not entitle them to adopt such royal titles, and doing so two years into Mary's reign would seem utter folly when she had living children to consider. It is significant that the 'Noble and Exellent Prynces' is referred to by her maiden name of Guildford, suggesting that this was more important than her later, married name of Dudley and that her husband became a prince through marriage to her rather than the other way around. It is an incredible claim to find written down, though, and perhaps demonstrates an unwillingness to leave no trace on earth of her heritage after her failed attempt at power in 1553. In this light, the location, within the More family's chapel, also becomes significant. As John Clement found rest at the place Margaret of Burgundy may have provided for his protection after her death, so Jane Guildford and her father may have found it in a place kept safe for them by Sir Thomas More after his own execution.

Jack Leslau's theory continues to utterly fascinate me. I am sure that many will dismiss it as improbable and unprovable, both of which accusations are true. There is as much evidence for this theory as there is for the murder of the Princes in the Tower in 1483 by their uncle, King Richard III. If it is true, at some point during the reign of Henry VII, a decision was made and an agreement reached that the sons of Edward IV should be allowed to live on in peace as long as they did not threaten the Tudor monarchy. Richard, Duke of York assumed the identity of Dr John Clement, a noted physician who was, on more than one occasion, excused from swearing oaths for a reason deemed acceptable but not recorded, which might be to protect him and the university in Louvain from charges of perjury. Dr Clement ended his days a Catholic in exile and was buried in a place of honour reserved for Burgundian royalty in the city Margaret, Duchess of Burgundy had based her court in.

Sir Edward Guildford was the identity adopted by Edward V, becoming successful and close to King Henry VIII, but never allowed to hold too much land. Predeceased by his son, Sir Edward subverted the normal laws of inheritance, despite leaving no will, to bequeath his assets to his daughter Jane, who was by then married to John Dudley, a man whose restoration and promotion Sir Edward actively championed. Jane and John's children were to have a huge impact on later Tudor history. Their son Guildford was married to Jane Grey shortly before she became queen and there is some evidence that Jane Guildford in particular insisted that her son should be king, not just a consort or a duke. Robert Dudley would go on to spend a lifetime desperately wooing the last Tudor queen, who appeared so many times to want to reciprocate, only to be prevented by unseen barriers easily explained if both knew he was an heir of the House of York who might assert the superiority of his claim over hers. The significance of this family also stretches further, to encompass Jane's grandson Sir Philip Sidney, one of the most prominent figures of the Elizabethan age as a poet and courtier. There is even a story of an Arthur Dudley, captured in a boat heading to France by a Spanish ship, who claimed that he was the illegitimate son of Elizabeth I and Robert Dudley. Arthur claimed he had been raised by Robert Southern, a servant of Elizabeth's friend Kat Ashley who he had believed was his father. On his deathbed, Southern had confessed that he was not Arthur's father but refused to tell him more, so the young man investigated and uncovered a tale from a man named Smyth who was a schoolmaster that Southern had been summoned to Hampton Court, handed a baby and told only that his name was Arthur and that Southern was to raise him as his own.

Smyth revealed that when Arthur had once tried to run away in his teens, letters from Elizabeth I had been sent to ensure that he was brought back and placed in the custody of John Ashley, Kat's husband, leading everyone to understand that he was an important child in some way. Smyth told Arthur he was the son of Elizabeth and Robert, and the young man recalled having been taken before Robert Dudley on one occasion by two men, Blount and Fludd, who were recorded, real people. Robert Dudley had, Arthur claimed, told him 'You are like a ship under full sail at sea, pretty to look upon but dangerous to deal with' before arranging his removal from the country with the help of Sir Francis Walsingham, Elizabeth's spy master. Walsingham so frightened Arthur that he escaped and began a series of travels around Europe. The letter detailing Arthur's story received by William Cecil in 1588 describes Arthur as being 27 years old, placing his date of birth around 1461. The queen's movements for this period are poorly recorded, though a Spanish ambassador described Elizabeth in the summer of 1461 as 'swelling extraordinarily' and 'dropsical' as though she had just emerged from childbed. The question of whether Queen Elizabeth concealed one or more pregnancies has long been asked but never definitively answered. Like much of this theory, it remains possible but cannot be proven.

12

To The Victor, The History

Treason doth never prosper: what's the reason?
For if it prosper, none dare call it treason.

Sir John Harrington

In a final twist on the story of the possible survival of the Princes in the Tower, an entry can be found in the records of Eastwell Church in Kent of a death on 22 December 1550 for a man named as Richard Plantagenet. The entry relates to a story that was told by the Earl of Winchelsea in 1720 to a Dr Thomas Brett. In 1733, Dr Brett retold the story in a letter to his friend William Warren, the President of Trinity Hall, Cambridge:

When Sir Thomas Moyle built that house (that is Eastwell Place) he observed his chief bricklayer, whenever he left off work, retired with a book. Sir Thomas had a curiosity to know, what book the man read; but it was some time before he could discover it: he still putting the book up if any one came toward him. However, at last, Sir Thomas surprized he snatched the book from him; & looking into it, found it to be in Latin. Hereupon he examined him, & finding he pretty well understood that language, he enquired, how he came by his learning? Hereupon the man told him, as he had been a master to him, he would venture to trust him with that he had never before revealed to any one.

He then informed him that he was boarded with a Latin schoolmaster, without knowing who his parents were, 'till he was fifteen or sixteen years old; only a gentleman (who took occasion to acquaint him he was no relation to him) came once a quarter, & paid for his board, and took care to see that he wanted nothing. And one day, this gentleman took him & carried him to a fine, great house, where he passed through several stately rooms, in one of which he left him, bidding him stay there. Then a man finely drest, with a star and garter, came to him; asked him some questions; talked kindly to him; & gave him some money. Then the 'forementioned gentleman returned, and conducted him back to his school.

Some time after the same gentleman came to him again, with a horse & proper accoutrements, & told him, he must make a journey with him into the country. They went into Leicestershire, & came to Bosworth Field; & he was carried to K. Richard Ill. tent. The King embraced him, & told him he was his son. But, child, says he, tomorrow I must fight for my crown. And, assure your self, if I lose that, I will lose my life too: but I hope to preserve both. Do you stand in such a place (directing him to a particular place) where you may see the battle, out of danger. And, when I have gained the victory, come to me; I will then own you to be mine, & take care of you. But, if I should be so unfortunate to lose the battel, then shift as well as you can, & take care to let nobody know that I am your father; for no mercy will be shewed to any one so [nearly] related to me. Then the king gave him a purse of gold, & dismissed him.

He followed the king's directions. And, when he saw the battel was lost & the king killed, he hasted to London; sold his horse, & his fine cloaths; &, the better to conceal himself from all suspicion of being son to a king, & that he might have means to live by his honest labour, he put himself apprentice to a bricklayer. But, having a competent skill in the Latin tongue, he was unwilling to lose it; and having an inclination also to reading, & no delight in the conversation of those he was obliged to work with, he generally spent all the time he had to spare in reading by himself.

Sir Thomas said, you are now old, and almost past your labour; I will give you the running of my kitchen as long as you live. He answered, Sir, you have a numerous family; I have been used to live retired; give me leave to build a house of one room for myself in such a field, & there, with your good leave, I will live & die: and, if you have any work I can do for you, I shall be ready to serve you. Sir Thomas granted his request, he built his house, and there continued to his death.

The tale was astounding, but Sir Thomas Moyle, who had employed the man as a bricklayer, was captivated. Enticed by the sight of this older man sitting apart from his colleagues and reading, Sir Thomas had finally caught him engrossed in a Latin book, which he was able to demonstrate that he understood, and extracted his story from him. This Richard went on to live in a cottage he was permitted to build on Moyle's land and became a cause célèbre at Moyle's dinner parties. The truth of what he said is hard to get to. Richard III had two illegitimate children, John and Catherine, who he acknowledged and provided for. Why would a third be kept secret? It cannot have been for the sake of his mother's reputation, since the mother(s) of Richard's two acknowledged illegitimate children are not known.

Perhaps this was Richard, Duke of York, hidden in Colchester after the problems of 1485 and taught a trade. Raised in obscurity, was he the Richard Grey given a pardon in the early years of Henry VIII's reign? Did he claim to be a bastard son of Richard III because it would allow him to remain more obscure than acknowledging himself an heir of Edward IV? Did he twist his words to give the impression that Richard III was his father when what he really meant was that Richard III had made him illegitimate? Was he simply a confidence trickster who saw a comfortable retirement opportunity?

The truth of the fate of Edward V and Richard, Duke of York remains as obscured to us now as it was to the people of England and Europe in the years after 1483. The identity of their murderer has long been questioned and most remain satisfied that their uncle, Richard III, ordered their deaths in the summer or autumn of 1483 either as part of a prolonged plot to snatch the throne or as a panicked response to the events of the spring and summer of that year. If Richard III ordered the deed done, it can only have been to remove them as a potential source of rebellion, but this could not be achieved unless their deaths were publicised. However suspicious people may have been, they would have to know the boys were dead for any threat they might pose to be removed. Without this crucial element, the murders were for naught. In October, Richard had the perfect opportunity, if he was uncertain how to break the news, to blame the Duke of Buckingham, who had risen in revolt in favour of Henry Tudor and who, according to the *Crowland Chronicle*, had started the rumour that the boys were dead. If Richard needed to publicise the deaths whilst avoiding blame, he had a golden opportunity, but conspicuously passed it up.

There are snippets of information that refer to Lord Edward after he was declared illegitimate and suggest he might have been expected at his uncle's coronation. The provisions for the household of the Council of the North are also tantalising, but might refer to children due to arrive later. The emergence of Elizabeth Woodville and her daughters from sanctuary only makes sense if she believed her sons were still alive and cannot be reconciled to a belief that Richard III had ordered their deaths. The attachment of Sir James Tyrell to their story becomes interesting in the light of a family story that Elizabeth and her sons were entertained together in Tyrell's home at Gipping Hall during Richard III's reign under the trusted watch of Sir James. The flurry of messages between Richard and Margaret, so secret that the messengers were granted exemption from any search, might signify plans to send one or both of them to their aunt in Flanders and that possibility is supported by Tyrell's positioning in Calais and the vast sums of money sent to him for a secret purpose.

If the Princes in the Tower survived until 22 August 1485, and there is as much evidence that they did as that they did not, then the nature of the provision for their future and any plans the heirless Richard III might have investigated in Rome for their relegitimisation were lost with the king's life on the field at Bosworth. It is obvious that Henry Tudor did not know clearly what had happened to them and that must offer evidence that he did not find them in the Tower on his triumphal arrival in London and have them done away with. If he had, pretenders would never have worried him as much as they did. This leaves two questions: What might have happened to the Princes in the Tower after 1485, and why do we think we know they were murdered in 1483 by their uncle?

The second question is the easiest to answer. Winston Churchill famously said that 'History is written by the victors' and this was never more true than in the case of the Tudor dynasty. Richard III needed to be a villain so that Henry VII could be the hero who rid England of him. The Princes in the Tower needed to be dead so that Henry could relegitimise and marry their sister Elizabeth in order to preserve the Yorkist support that had won him the crown and formed the core of his governmental machinery. The dearth of conclusive evidence about the fate of the Princes is to be expected. It is well known that Henry VII went to immense lengths to destroy *Titulus Regius*, expunging it from the Parliament Rolls unread and demanding the return of every copy on pain of imprisonment. It only survives because one copy remained unreturned in the records of Crowland Abbey. It is perhaps no coincidence that the period of the Wars of the Roses and Richard III's reign was penned by the unknown but well-informed continuator at Crowland Abbey during early 1486 and that this is where the only stray copy of *Titulus Regius* was found. It seems likely that if there had been evidence, provided by Bishop Stillington, to satisfy those gathered in London in June 1483 of the pre-contract and Edward V's illegitimacy, then this would have been sought out and destroyed along with any reference to the continued survival of the Princes, who Henry desperately needed everyone to believe were dead. It is even possible to see how this might have been done. John Morton, who would become Archbishop of Canterbury and Chancellor to Henry VII, had a nephew named Robert, who had been Master of the Rolls between 1479 and 1483. Robert was restored to this key archival position in 1485 and a year later was made Bishop of Worcester. Was this his reward for purging the records of any mention of the sons of Edward IV after the summer of 1483? If so, are the fragments we have, like the Crowland copy of *Titulus Regius*, small pieces that slipped through Robert Morton's net?

Answering the first question is more difficult because almost all official records seek to deny the continued existence of the Princes in the Tower, an expedient to preserve Tudor security that might be expected. However, applying the theory of a gravitational effect of the unseen continued survival of the Princes, events that cannot otherwise satisfactorily be explained begin to make complete sense. Francis, Lord Lovell was allowed to remain in Colchester for far longer than the right of sanctuary would usually permit. He was unmolested there and appears to have been courted by the new Tudor government, or at least, Henry VII was unwilling to believe ill of him. Lovell's survival of the Battle of Bosworth seems inexplicable if he was there, since every other close friend of Richard III died at his side. Sir William Catesby, executed three days after the battle in Leicester, seemed to believe Lovell would come to terms with Henry VII, perhaps to protect the Princes. If that was the intention, Lovell seems to have decided not to entrust the boys to Henry. He may have made for Colchester, close to the coast, on a direct line to Burgundy, but also not far from the de la Pole heartland in Suffolk and Tyrell's Gipping Hall home, to await the sons of Edward IV, as instructed by Richard III. It seems likely that Edward V had been lodged with the Council of the North and Richard, Duke of York with Margaret in Burgundy, though he may have been in England visiting his mother at Gipping when the battle took place, perhaps the Continent, where John Morton had been prowling, becoming, for the moment, too dangerous. If one of the boys failed to arrive, Lovell's recorded attempt to seize Henry VII in Yorkshire might have been a cover story for the far more serious race between Lovell and the king to recover Edward V, his location perhaps let slip by Lincoln or his father, the ever-careful Duke of Suffolk. Lovell's flight to Burgundy may have marked his success, or his failure, to recover the Prince.

In 1487, the first Yorkist attempt on Henry VII's throne took place in the form of an invasion, led by John de la Pole, Earl of Lincoln and Francis, Lord Lovell. It has been remembered as the Lambert Simnel Affair, in which a boy was made to impersonate Edward, Earl of Warwick as a figurehead for the rebellion. The plot and the odd name of its leader-come-victim are comical, and are probably meant to be. Warwick was a prisoner, barred by his father's attainder still and had no natural support to become king. Why would these men use an imposter when Lincoln was perfectly able to make a claim on the throne himself, or at least state his intention to liberate Edward, Earl of Warwick when he was successful? It is striking that contemporary sources are so muddled about the affair, and most striking that André, a witness to the events, wrote that the boy was held up to be a son of Edward IV named Edward and that heralds and messengers sent to Ireland could not deny his identity. The invasion is believed to have favoured the Earl of Warwick because that suited the Tudor regime. It made the boy a demonstrable imposter and the plan an odd joke that no one would follow. The manipulation is incredibly clever, particularly if the real boy at the head of the army was a 16-year-old Edward V, having undergone the coronation in Ireland he had lacked in London and coming, as Vergil wrote, to *reclaim* his kingdom.

Only this explanation makes sense of suddenly stripping Elizabeth Woodville of all her lands and income and her confinement to Bermondsey Abbey, as well as the arrest of her son Thomas Grey, Edward V's half-brother, for suspected involvement in the plot. The Woodville faction had nothing at all to gain and everything to lose by removing Elizabeth of York from the throne and replacing her husband with Warwick, whose father many believed had been killed at Elizabeth Woodville's behest. The only reference to a regnal number, that of Edward VI, comes from the *York Books*, which might have been entered, or doctored, after the uprising had failed and when the official story of a rebellion in favour of the Earl of Warwick had taken hold. What would be the use of defiance then? This leaves the possibilities that Edward V was killed during the Battle of Stoke Field, or immediately after, that he escaped or that he was captured. The *Herald's Memoir* records the capture of a boy called John who seems to have gone on to become Lambert Simnel, and who was offered a comfortable life in royal service to keep up his pretence. Certainly, the Irish lords who had crowned a King Edward in Dublin in 1487 did not recognise the boy who served them wine two years later so that they had to be told he was the same boy.

A few years later, a mysterious young man of inescapably Plantagenet appearance stepped off a boat in Ireland to again ignite that tinderbox of Yorkist sympathy. Whether his arrival was part of a drifting around Europe or a timed plan is unclear, but his later confession that he was a boy from Tournai forced to pretend to be Richard, Duke of York and taught English against his will is so improbable that its position as accepted history is hard to fathom. Richard would spend many years tormenting Henry VII, though the king would always bluster at his own indifference when his more secret actions betray a mounting panic. If nothing else, this clearly demonstrates that Henry did not know for certain that he was rid of the threat of the Princes in the Tower, at least of the younger one. The fact that Richard was recognised and accepted in France, Burgundy, the Holy Roman Empire, Scotland and Denmark is traditionally written off as the power politics and games of rulers with their own agendas. Whilst that aspect cannot and should not be ignored, it should neither entirely obliterate their opinions and actions. Maximilian never denied that Richard was the real Duke of York, even after his cause was lost and Maximilian had nothing left to gain and even against the desire of other members of the Holy League to admit England. Charles VIII in France only promised not to aid Richard after a flash invasion by Henry, whilst Charles' attention was on Italy, forced him to find peace terms. James IV in Scotland, who undoubtedly ached for an excuse to make war with England, gave Richard a noble Scottish lady, whose father would not have taken kindly to his daughter being made to marry a commoner as part of a game, and, like Maximilian, never repudiated his belief that Richard was genuine.

Lacking any military ability, Richard's cause was doomed and he was consigned to history as Perkin Warbeck, another unusually named imposter with an improbable backstory. There is some evidence that Richard had at least one child, if not more than one, with Catherine Gordon. She would remain a focus of Henry VII's interest, traditionally believed to be because he hoped to marry her after his wife's death. She would eventually settle in southern Wales, where her children might have been sent to grow up in obscurity. Richard was forced to sign his outlandish confession and write an odd letter to his supposed mother as soon as he was caught, but there is also testimony from André that he was severely beaten at the same time and from the Spanish ambassador de Puebla that he continued to be beaten beyond recognition once he reached London. The obscuring of his undoubted Plantagenet features was surely deliberate, but did it also allow him to be switched for another personage when he arrived in London? Once the swelling went down, who would know if this was a different man? The man remembered as Perkin Warbeck was executed for treason, which only a subject of the king, an Englishman, should have been capable of committing, along with Edward, Earl of Warwick in 1499. Henry VII reportedly aged twenty years in the weeks that followed. Was this due to the execution of the innocent Warwick, or of the final relief from Richard, Duke of York's threat? Perhaps it was even because he now had two heirs of the House of York to keep secret.

No medieval king can tolerate a threat to his crown. More accurately, no medieval king can be seen to tolerate a threat to his crown. There is a strong theory that Edward II survived his deposition and lived out his days in Italy in the full knowledge of his son Edward III, who even visited his father. The key was the belief that Edward II was dead. If Henry VII ever gained possession of one or both of the Princes in the Tower, he was faced with a real dilemma. Killing them was the only way to end their threat and increase his own dynastic security. However, they were also the brothers of his wife, a woman he seems to have genuinely loved and cared for and upon whose family support he relied heavily. Elizabeth would surely have been keen to protect her brothers if she could and their disappearance into anonymity, just like Edward II's, might have provided an answer.

This situation would make it possible that Edward V was placed into the household of Sir Richard Guildford after the 1487 plot, taking the identity known to history as Sir Edward Guildford. Edward lived out a successful life, never threatening the Tudor kings but never being allowed to accumulate too much land and power. Sir Edward took up the cause of the minor baron John Dudley after the boy's father was executed, perhaps believing it would be easy to work him against the Tudor monarchs. When

Henry VIII died, John Dudley rocketed to power and prominence so that as Edward VI died, he saw to it that his son's wife was made heir to the throne and tried to have Guildford made a king in his own right, completing a Yorkist restoration of his wife's line. The plan failed, costing John, Guildford and Jane Grey their lives. Lady Jane Guildford would be buried in Sir Thomas More's family chapel with an inscription that describes her as a 'Noble and Exellent Prynces' with no explanation for such a wild claim. Her son Robert would go on to play a critical part in Elizabethan politics, his relationship with Elizabeth I perhaps providing more of a parallel with Shakespeare's Romeo and Juliet than is well known. Star-crossed lovers they certainly were, but were they also from two families so long at war? What too of Arthur Dudley's story? The truth lies beyond reach at the moment, but the weight of these small pieces of evidence begins to sway the scales against the traditional history.

If Richard, Duke of York really took part in the rebellion known now as the Perkin Warbeck Affair, then might he have been spared at his sister's pleading, switched after arriving in London for some other similarly beaten man who, when the swelling subsided, would not have the Plantagenet looks of a son of Edward IV? He had initially been well treated by Henry despite his attempts on the throne, betraying a lack of a will to kill him. This would have been to Henry VII's advantage in disproving the claimed identity of the man who had opposed him too. Could the real Duke of York have been secreted in Sir Thomas More's household, a protégé of Archbishop Morton's who had been vouched for, and married to his adopted daughter Margaret Giggs? John Clement seems to have come to his medical training late, his date of birth traditionally recorded as around 1500 but probably earlier, given that he took part in a tournament with King Henry VIII in 1510. The earlier references in the Louvain register might hint a planned future for the younger Duke of York, before he tried to take the throne of England, which was then resurrected and used by the Tudor government to screen his continued existence. This would explain his interesting burial in a spot reserved for Burgundian royalty and makes the fate of the couple's several children intriguing but hard to pin down. If Richard was Perkin, then there is also the issue of his marriage to Catherine Gordon and the evidence of at least one child that the couple had. By the jousts of 1510, Perkin's son would have been about 14 years old. Might he have been another candidate for the true identity of John Clement?

The possible assumption of the identity of Dr John Clement by Richard, Duke of York adds a twist to the entire story of the Princes in the Tower. Most people believe that they know the grisly and sad fate of the murdered little boys from Shakespeare's version, which repeats precisely the version written down, but never published, by Sir Thomas More. The story recorded by More and only published after his death by his nephew would then have been a smokescreen, designed to blame Richard III for the murder of his nephews in order to disguise their continued existence into the reign of Henry VIII, who was, in his early years, confident enough to have felt himself impervious to such a threat from old uncles. If More became disillusioned with his own story, perhaps the inherent dishonesty hinted at by his opening error in the age of Edward IV at his death rankling with the lawyer's pious devotion to truth, he might have abandoned it in favour of another method of concealing the secret. As the 1520s wore on, when Hans Holbein first visited England, Henry was becoming dangerously obsessed with Anne Boleyn and would soon tear the country apart in his quest for a divorce and a son. Thomas More may have seen this coming and realised the threat to both John Clement and Edward Guildford. In order to at least preserve the secret, he commissioned Hans Holbein to paint a family portrait in which the greatest secret in Tudor England was preserved for all time, visible to those able to decipher the clues. The connections between More and Clement are clear to see, but there is also the interest taken by John Dudley in Dr Clement's incarceration and the burial of Jane Guildford, and perhaps her father Sir Edward, in the More family chapel at Old Chelsea Church that appear to make little sense if their families were not joined in a dangerous secret.

It is possible to suggest several theories for the fate of the Princes in the Tower beyond their murder by their uncle in 1483. One or both of them may have attempted to unseat Henry VII and failed. In that failure, one or both of them might have been killed, or they may have survived. Whether or not they were embroiled in these uprisings, one or both of them may have lived in peace and virtual anonymity well into the next century of the Tudor dynasty. This potential alternative history requires the acceptance that several key Tudor figures knew of their survival. Henry VII must have learned of it. His wife Elizabeth of York must have known. Archbishop Morton was probably a key figure in constructing the safeguards around them and Sir Thomas More knew the secret. Henry VIII was aware of their continued existence, as were John Dudley and his sons. Thomas Cromwell probably knew, as Thomas Wolsey surely had before him. It becomes possible to see this conspiracy right at the very heart of Tudor government. Did More rise so high because of what he had learned from Morton? Did Cromwell spring to his lofty position on information given him by Wolsey? Henry VII and then Henry VIII would have needed men who knew the secret to ensure that it was kept, but how might Henry VIII have felt about German painter Hans Holbein learning it? How far was it allowed to spread? Why did no one ever reveal it? The answer to the last question is simple: there must have always been wider considerations to any attempt to unveil the secret. If John Dudley had sprung it, he would have endangered his sons and John Clement. Clement, likewise, had a family and his brother's children and grandchildren to consider. Perhaps the best way to keep both men's secret under control was to give both plenty to lose.

If Hans Holbein knew the secret he was required to hide, then it is possible that he left other clues in other works. Leslau's theory can be extended and applied to the most famous of Holbein's paintings, The Ambassadors. The men standing at either side of the central table have been identified as Jean de Dinteville, Seigneur of Polisy and Georges de Selve, Bishop of Lavaur, but this identification was only made as late as 1900 by Mary Hervey based largely on the marking on the globe of de Dinteville's home town of Polisy. Until 1900, the identities of the two men were widely contested. The Ambassadors shares a green background with the More family portrait that may be a reference to 'la langue vert', the Green Language or the Language of the Birds, used as a secret language and favoured by French troubadours, giving a further link to French courtly language in deciphering the paintings. The table in between the two men has on the top an array of scientific equipment that represents the Heavens. A celestial globe shows that the date of the painting is 11 April 1533, after the date of Henry VIII's marriage to Anne Boleyn but before his marriage to Catherine of Aragon was officially annulled, marking it as a dangerous time of upheaval. The date was also Good Friday, making the image of Christ on the cross visible behind the pulled back curtain in the top left corner important. The cylindrical sundial shows the time as either 8.15 a.m. or 3.45 p.m. and the latitude is set for North Africa, suggesting that time and location are out of order. One of the most important lines of the painting passes through the star Cygnus on the celestial globe. The line runs from the position to the right of the portrait at which the famous anamorphic skull can be seen properly when looking down, from which point a line to the cross in the top left runs through several items on the top of the table, the globe at the star of Cygnus and Jean de Dinteville's left eye. Cygnus, the Swan, was a badge used by Princes of Wales, as Edward V had been. The globe also shows Lyra, the falling eagle, which might refer to a lost imperial position.

The lower part of the table contains items relating to the earthly plane and the arts. A lute with a broken string is a well-used symbol of discord and disharmony. The anamorphic skull, which is warped when seen from the front but becomes perfectly formed when the painting is viewed looking down from the right-hand side, represents death, which seems to linger, obscured but always conspicuously present, between the two men. The floor they stand upon, and which the skull partially covers, is a copy of the Cosmati pavement, which stands before the altar in Westminster Abbey, the birthplace of Edward V and the location of coronations. The suggestion may be that this path leads to the men's deaths. The table is covered by a carpet, as the sideboard in the back left of the More family portrait is, a symbol of a secret, a matter covered up. A door in the More sideboard that is ajar suggests that the secret might be out.

The date of Good Friday 1533 and the inclusion of Christ on the cross allows for some numerical trickery too. Christ was widely held to have been crucified at the age of 33. Subtracting this from the year 1533 leaves us in 1500. Dinteville's dagger gives his age as 29, which would have been Edward V's age in 1500. De Selve's book shows his age, but not clearly. The last number is obscured and could show his age as 23, 25 or 26, though looking most like 25. Richard, Duke of York, born on 17 August 1473, would have been 26 on 11 April 1500, though as previously mentioned, he may have been unclear about his own date of birth. The area showing his age is obscured by a sealed clasp on his book, hinting again at a hidden secret that must be kept safe. The identification of the two men in the painting relied heavily on the appearance of the town of Polisy on the globe on the left of the table's lower level, but the name in fact reads Policy and has a river running through the word, which no other place name has. Was the town of Polisy simply used to show this as a matter of policy, obscured and kept secret by the Tudor government? As English politics became more fraught and dangerous and Henry VIII grew more paranoid and intolerant, that might have spelt danger for Edward V and Richard, Duke of York, even if they had posed no threat to their nephew. The timing of the painting, coming in the midst of such political upheaval, just a year before Sir Edward's Guildford's death and two years before Clement fled England after More's execution, may be highly significant.

Tradition recounts that King Richard III ordered his nephews' murders and that Sir James Tyrell carried out the deed. This version of events has become enshrined by Shakespeare's genius and can be clearly traced to Sir Thomas More. It does not, however, stand up to rational investigation. Richard III gained nothing from the deaths of his nephews whilst it remained a secret and there is evidence to suggest that they lived to see the end of his reign and that plans were made for their futures. Sir James Tyrell may well have been involved in watching the boys as they met with their mother, who would surely only have emerged from sanctuary on being convinced that Edward IV's sons were not, in fact, dead. From the kernel of truth of Sir James' involvement in their protection came the believable slander of his part in their murder. Sir Thomas More wrote that Tyrell and Dighton, one of the men who carried out the murders, confessed in 1502, yet no other writer at the time or over the decades that followed knew of the confession or repeated the story of it, neither has any document, surely precious beyond measure to Tudor security, ever been found or recorded. The confession exists only in More's story and other writers both before and after offered varying stories of the fate of the Princes, with just as many positing their survival as their murder at the hands of Richard III, the Duke of Buckingham or some other.

The reason that we think we know the Princes in the Tower died in 1483 is an allegorical drama written by More, made fiction by Shakespeare and absorbed as fact by the popular consciousness. So much more of the story of the early Tudor years make far more sense if the continued existence of the Princes in the Tower is accepted. The Lambert Simnel Affair and the Perkin Warbeck threat may well have been real uprisings in favour of the sons of Edward IV. It is notable that other Yorkist heirs only began to press their claims in 1501, when Perkin appeared to be gone. It is easier to believe that Richard III did not publicise the deaths of his nephews because they were alive and well and being provided for. It is equally likely that Henry VII, whilst feeling their threat, did not wish to execute a 15-year-old Edward V or even a 26-year-old Richard, Duke of York if he truly loved his wife, their sister, and agreed to keep them alive as long as they promised not to threaten his throne or his dynasty. Neither is it impossible that in his early flushes of freedom and confidence Henry VIII invited his two incognito uncles to tournaments to celebrate his accession, allowing him the opportunity to measure them for himself. He certainly invited his uncle Arthur, Edward IV's illegitimate son. Sir Thomas More may have abandoned his own attempt to throw up a smokescreen to protect Edward and Richard as either unsatisfactory, clumsy or an uncomfortable lie, choosing instead to hide their continued survival in art and relying on a network of key Tudor statesmen to keep them safe and keep them in check.

For many, this explanation will defy belief, but the alternative is to cling to a conviction that Richard III, in defiance of a lifetime of evidence of his personality, murdered his nephews when they were 12 and 9 for no real gain, since he kept it a secret. Elizabeth Woodville and Thomas Grey were punished for unknown crimes, coincidently at the time of a completely unrelated invasion in the name of a boy named Edward who had been crowned King of England in Dublin. Henry VII then had no idea what had happened to his wife's brothers and she could throw no light on the subject so that Perkin Warbeck was successfully able to impersonate a murdered boy for most of the 1490s, fooling European heads of state and even appearing in the Spanish State Papers' codex of encryption as a royal personage who was the Duke of York. The Spanish denial of Richard's identity had political reasons just as those who supported him might, since Ferdinand and Isabella hoped for an alliance with England. Sir Thomas More then wrote a version of events based on a confession that he alone knew about yet which has, for centuries, been accepted as accurate and factual. There is more that does not add up about this version of events than an alternative when the identity of a murderer in 1483 is no longer the focus of attention. The Tudors cleverly crafted the thirty-year civil war that we call the Wars of the Roses to present themselves as a force for stability and unity. We have believed in that construct for centuries. We have perhaps believed in another Tudor construct designed to protect their dynasty and missed the truth: the survival of the Princes in the Tower.

Bibliography, Resources and Further Reading

Websites

British History Online: www.british-history.ac.uk
Jack Leslau's Theory: www.holbeinartworks.org
The Ambassadors by Hans Holbein:
https://commons.wikimedia.org/wiki/File:Hans_Holbein_the_
　Younger_-_The_Ambassadors_-_Google_Art_Project.jpg

Selected Bibliography

Bacon's History of the Reign of King Henry VII, Rev J. Lawson Mumby,
　1885
Calendar of State Papers of Spain, G. A. Bergenroth, 1862
Calendar of State Papers of Venice, Rawdon Brown, 1862
Desiderata Curiosa Hibernica, 1772
Documents Relating to Perkin Warbeck, with Remarks on His History, Frederic
　Madden, 1837
*Extracts from the Municipal Records of the City of York During the Reigns of
　Edward IV, Edward V and Richard III*, Robert Davies, 1843
Hall's Chronicle, 1558 and 1550 Editions, J. Johnson, 1809
Harleian MSS 433, Vol. I, II, III & IV, P. W. Hammond and R. Horrox,
　Alan Sutton, 1979

Henry VII, S.B. Chrimes, London, 1972

Henry the Seventh, James Gairdner, 1909

Historic Doubts on the Life and Reign of King Richard the Third, Horace Walpole, 1768

Historie of the Pitifull Life and Unfortunate Death of Edward the Fifth, Sir Thomas More, 1641

History of King Richard III, Sir Thomas More, 1543

History of Prince Maurice, Prince of Orange, Sir Aubrey de Maurier, 1682

History of Scotland including the Lord High Treasurer's Accounts, P.F. Tytler, 1831

Holinshed's Chronicles of England, Scotland and Ireland, Raphael Holinshed, 1577

Lady Jane Grey and Her Times, George Howard, 1822

Letters and Papers Illustrative of the Reigns of Richard III and Henry VII, Vol. I & II, James Gairdner, 1861

Letters and Papers of the Reign of Henry VIII, www.british-history.ac.uk

Letters, Despatches and State Papers Relating to Negotiations Between England and Spain, G.A. Bergenroth, 1868

L'Imposture de Perkin Warbeck, Jean-Didier Chastelain, 1952

Materials for a History of the Reign of Henry VII Vol. I & II, Rev. William Campbell, 1873

Original Letters Illustrative of English History, Vol. I, Henry Ellis, 1824

Parliament Rolls of Medieval England, www.british-history.ac.uk

Polydore Vergil's English History, Sir Henry Ellis, 1844

Rymer's Foedera, Sir Thomas Duffus Hardy, 1873

State Papers of King Henry VIII, 1830

The Annals of England, John Stow, 1601

The Crowland Chronicle, Henry T. Riley, 1908

The History of the Life and Reigne of Richard the Third, Sir George Buck, 1619

The King is Dead: The Last Will and Testment of Henry VIII, Suzannah Lipscomb, Head of Zeus, 2015

The Life and Letters of Sir Thomas More, Agnes M. Stewart, 1876

The Life and Reign of Richard III and The Story of Perkin Warbeck, James Gairdner, 1898

The Life of Henry VII, Bernard André, translated by Daniel Hobbins, Italica Press, 2011

The Life of Lady Jane Grey and of Her Husband Lord Guildford Dudley, Edward Baldwin, 1824

The Parallel: or a Collection of Extraordinary Cases Relating to Concealed Births and Disputed Successions, 1744

The Pastymes of the People, John Rastell, 1529

The Plumpton Correspondence, edited by Thomas Stapleton, 1839

The Proclamations of the Tudor Kings, R.W. Heinze, Cambridge University Press, 1976

The Roll of the Royal College of Physicians, William Munk, 1861

The Usurpation of Richard III, Dominic Mancini, translated by C.A.J. Armstrong, 1969

Further Reading

Lambert Simnel and the Battle of Stoke, Michael Bennet, Alan Sutton Press, 1987

Perkin: A Story of Deception, Ann Wroe, Jonathan Cape Press, 2003

Richard III & the Princes in the Tower, Alison Weir, Vintage, 1992

Richard III and the Princes in the Tower, A. J. Pollard, Bramley Books, 1997

Richard of England, D. M. Kleyn, The Kensal Press, 1990

Royal Blood, Bertram Fields, Sutton Publishing, 2006

Stoke Field: The Last Battle of the Wars of the Roses, David Baldwin, Pen & Sword, 2006

The Dublin King, John Ashdown-Hill, The History Press, 2015

The Last White Rose, Desmond Seward, Constable, 2010

The Lost Prince, David Baldwin, Sutton Publishing, 2007

The Mystery of the Princes in the Tower, Audrey Williamson, Alan Sutton Press, 1978

Index